EAST IS WEST

Freya Stark was born in Paris in 1893, and made her first journey, to the Middle East, in 1928. Once described as 'a traveller of genius' she has opened up the world of an adventurer to her many readers by her vivid accounts of travel in Persia, Arabia and the Near East. *East is West* concerns her war-time experiences in Egypt, Palestine and Syria, and is written with the freedom of the independent and intrepid traveller, with the authority of an official of the Diplomatic Corps.

Now over ninety years old, Dame Freya Stark lives in Asolo, Italy, where she was brought up.

'Freya Stark possesses the gift of style. She has written the best travel books of her generation and her name will survive as an artist in prose' *Observer*

'Ms Stark . . . is a perpetual source of interest, entertainment and lasting pleasure' *Daily Telegraph*

'That she so triumphantly holds our attention to make us long for more is due to her sensibility, her courage, her honesty and, above all, to her gift that must leave all other travellers and writers desperate with envy' *Listener*

'I do not see how her books can avoid their obvious destiny – inclusion at last in the aristocracy of letters' *Evening Standard*

D0814100

EAST IS WEST

Freya Stark

Century
London Melbourne Auckland Johannesburg

First published by John Murray
(Reprinted 1945, 1946, 1947)

This edition first published in 1986 by Century,
an imprint of Century Hutchinson Ltd,
Brookmount House, 62–65 Chandos Place, London, WC2N 4NW

Century Hutchinson Publishing Group (Australia) Pty Ltd
PO Box 496, 16–22 Church Street, Hawthorn, Melbourne, Victoria 3122

Century Hutchinson Group (NZ) Ltd
PO Box 40–086, 32–34 View Road, Glenfield, Auckland 10

Century Hutchinson Group (SA) Pty Ltd
PO Box 337, Berglvei 2012, South Africa

ISBN 0 7126 1280 7

Printed in Great Britain by
Richard Clay (The Chaucer Press) Ltd
Bungay, Suffolk

To my friends the Young Effendis,
this book is dedicated
wishing them well

Contents

PART III

PALESTINE   SYRIA   TRANSJORDAN

PART IV

IRAQ

Foreword

IT is customary, at the beginning of a book, to write a word of thanks to those who have been helpful in its making. Such a word is here due in the first place to Sir Sydney Cockerell, who has laboriously read my typescript from end to end, to Elizabeth Monroe who encouraged me to begin, and to Professor G. R. Driver, Professor H. A. R. Gibb, Mr. R. Davies, Sir Walter Smart, K.C.M.G., and Mr. John Hamilton, M.C., who have kindly looked through various portions of it.

There are other people whom I like to thank—old friends or new acquaintances who, all over the Middle East in these four years, have offered their generous and kindly hospitality. They are too numerous to mention and yet every one of their names is linked with some pleasant memory. Colonel Gardiner and his wife in Damascus: Mr. Pirrie Gordon on his terrace—with Safed in the moonlight beyond it; days with the Footes in Transjordan and with the Springfields in Port Sudan. Dora Altounian and the Teagues in Jerusalem, and a renewal of old acquaintance; or pleasant weeks in Cairo, in the Cawthorn and Empson households, which never seem too busy for their friends. There was the hospitality of Lady Spears, of Joan Ali Khan in Beirut: of the I.P.C. in Haifa with the kindness of the Herridge and the Hedgcock families; of lifelong friends like Michael and Esther Wright and Mrs. Marriott and her mother, or of places where one came for a night or two nights and vanished again, and yet was treated as if expected, and welcomed, from the Arabian West, and the Moneypennys in Tunis, to India and Baluchistan, Persia, and Cyprus—all outside the scope of this book, but not forgotten. Particularly I would thank the political officers scattered in Iraq whose quiet work, sympathetic and efficient, cannot be praised too highly and whose kindness to me in all my travelling has been so great; and with these, Robert Mason and Mr. Tett in Mosul, and Mr. and Mrs. Knight, Cecil Savidge, and the Macphersons in Basra, and Judge Pritchard's long hospitality in Baghdad.

It would be pleasant to write in detail of the time spent among them, and of the time spent among Arab friends equally numerous and equally remembered : but a book, like a picture, requires the sacrifice of much if it is to say what it means to say. This one deals with the young effendi and the influences that mould him in the history in which we live to-day : the small-ness of space allows me only a few strokes to represent a vast and multitudinous background which in truth is largely built by the lives of these whom I have mentioned and many others, in their repeated kindness, their quiet labours, their infinite variety.

November 1944.

Introduction

THIS book is not a text-book. It has been written with a minimum of figures and with perhaps a haphazard series of facts. And yet, unlike books I enjoy reading myself, it has not been written merely for pleasure.

When I left the Middle East after four years of friendly contact with its people, and travelled first to England and then to the United States, I found that the Mediterranean had moved too fast for the Atlantic; the popular idea of the Arab world in both countries was out-of-date except among small, travelled societies of experts. Already the symptom of historic tragedy was there—for the To-day of those who talk about Arabia is Yesterday to the Arabs themselves. And because so many historic tragedies have begun in this manner and with such misunderstanding, Dr. Brandt, as we discussed it in the pleasant quiet of Chicago Oriental Institute, suggested the usefulness of writing a book of this kind, which makes no ambitious claim, but presents such things as I have myself seen, and hopes to give an impression, as true as so complex a matter can be given in simple form, of the Arab world as it is *to-day*. It is written, not for the specialist, but as an armchair journey for the average reader.

Various causes make it natural that the actual features of this world should be so little known. The old Arab society is picturesque, and the modern is becoming less so every hour; artists in words or colours find the shaikh in his draperies easier to deal with than the effendi in his cosmopolitan sameness; and another cause of ignorance is the speed with which the changes have been and are yet coming. A less general reason is that much has been written lately about Palestine, which affects the Arab position, and is either deliberately or unconsciously misleading. And it is also a fact that the desert, with all its enchantment, no longer gives the essential picture of Arabian life.

Even in its conception of the *past*, popular imagination gives to the desert and its nomads far too great a part. What the Arabs represent in history is *the greatest commercial empire of the West between the fall of Rome and the rise of Britain*. In their rich and varied sheaf they gathered, at one time or another, South Spain and North India and all that lay between, and penetrated into Europe, so that Malta still remembers them in her language, and Italy in the weaving of her brocades, and the whole of Europe in the traditions of chivalry and the forms of literature that were first imported by the courts of Sicily or Provence.

In 875 A.D. Salerno, Naples, Amalfi and Gaeta join the Arabs in an attack on Rome.[1] A treaty between Naples and Benevento restrains the former from selling Lombard subjects to the Saracens. In the 13th century, Vincent of Beauvais devotes thirty pages in his *Speculum Historiale* to Muhammad. The Crusades brought the Arab world vividly near to Southern Europe and the great Frankish lords who were settled in Antioch, Tripoli or Palestine, opened new doors to the West. The origins of the novel have been traced from Asia by Arabian ways through Provence and Spain; and Monte Cassino studied the medicine of Avicenna, whose grave—rarely visited—still has a library held dustily and drowsily in his honour, in Persian Hamadan.

But the wall of the Arabian world, against which the Crusades threw themselves, was not the wall of the desert. It was the line of trading cities which stretched, and still stretches, from Mosul, Baghdad, and Basra in the East, through Antioch and Alexandretta (now Turkish), Aleppo, Homs, Hama, Damascus, Jerusalem, and Cairo. The truce of the Crusades was broken and their fate was sealed when René de Chatillon, from his castle at Kerak in Transjordan, interfered with the caravans of Palestine and Syria, and therefore with the commercial life of Arabia. By the time of the Crusades, the *desert* Arabs were only what they had been for centuries before the Christian era, links in the great chain of Eastern commerce, where the waterless emptiness divides one city from the next, and the beduin alone can live among its rocks and sands. They were also what they still are, a constant reserve of tough human beings, drifting imperceptibly to revitalize the towns.

This is in no way to minimize that seventh and eighth century irruption which altered the history of the world. The invasion from the desert, and the Muhammadan faith which it carried, acted as a solvent so powerful as to alter the identity of nations for ever, leaving them with the language or religion of their conquerors, or both. It is as if the countries which Hitler seized

[1] Heyd: *Commerce du Levant, I,* 42.

and lost, were to continue to speak German, or to believe in his Valhalla, in perpetuity. The Muslim faith in India, in Afghanistan, in Persia, in Egypt, North Africa, Syria, Palestine and Iraq, came to stay; it remained in Turkey, and in parts of the Balkans, brought, not by Arabs, but—at a remove—by their later invaders. The Arab language filled Persian and Turkish with new words and was one of the ingredients of Urdu, but survived as a spoken tongue only in North Africa (including Egypt), and in what their own people call "the island of the Arabs," the lands bordered by Persia, Turkey, and the sea. This narrower region, which has remained preponderantly Arab in religion and language, I refer to in this book as the "Arab World."

In speaking of it, it is important to remember that its unity is one of language, largely of religion,[1] and of the civilization they have produced; it is *not* a unity of race. The chief peoples of the north of their "island," who call themselves Arabs to-day —the people of Iraq, Syria, Palestine, Egypt—if they came from the desert at all, came from it in milleniums before the Muslim invasion; the wave of the eighth century was the last wave, and left only a small sprinkling of human beings compared to the solid mass of population built up through the ages. That so small a contingent was able to impress its faith and its speech on so many various regions remains one of the miracles of history; the future unifying of the Arab nations seems child's play in comparison.

Some of the ancient cleavages remain. They are represented by a great variety of religious "enclaves," many Christian, some Jewish, some—such as the Yezidi Devil-worshippers of Iraq, or the Mandeans of the Euphrates, or the Ansayri of north Syria— representatives of a yet older order in the history of those lands. Schisms also in the Muslim faith show ancient difference of races, the most important being that between Sunni and Shi'a, brought, roughly, by Persian influences into Islam.

The spirit of nationalism, growing intensely during the years of this century, has also brought out the ancient and underlying variety, very much as the rise of nationalism in Europe broke the surface unity of the Christian church. It seemed, twenty years or so ago, as if this centrifugal process would eventually disrupt such Arabian unity as yet remained; but a new, and not a separatist tendency is abroad in the world to-day; and the

[1] Not entirely, since the Christian and most of the other minorities would consider themselves 'Arab' in the area referred to.

blending of these two strands—towards individual nationalism and commonwealth amalgamation—will provide much of the interest of Arabian history in the coming time.

All this lay, unhappy, restless yet immobile in the Ottoman embrace, from 1517, when Sultan Selim I conquered Egypt, for almost exactly four hundred years, until the entry of Lord Allenby into Jerusalem and of General Maude into Baghdad. The Arab liberation, already in the hearts of the Arabs since the middle of the 19th century, was actually accomplished by the first World War.

I am here interested in what belongs to a later day, to our own day, and in drawing attention chiefly to what, I think, is the most important factor in the modern Arab world: this is the ascension of the middle class. It has been born, has become adolescent, and is almost grown up; and this book is, or tries to be, the picture of the young effendi who represents it and of the background against which he moves.

Who is he?

He has had a school and usually a college education, and is trained to a profession in the Western way; he belongs indeed to the West, and it is the West that, for good or bad, will mould him, and with him the future history of his world. His origin may be very varied; he may come from the tents of the desert, from the villages and their settled farmers, from the craftsmen of the towns, or from the old-fashioned governing community symbolized by the Pashas, with whom he must not be confounded, for they were more of a bureaucracy than a middle class, with roots not in the middle of anything, but floating with longer or shorter tendrils round the distant centre of Stambul. They were not all by any means Turkish Pashas, but the Turkish Pasha was their prototype, and the distinction between him and the young effendi should be remembered, since the change over from one to the other is as much of a revolution as many that are taking place in other lands.

It may be asked why, in all these centuries of Oriental sleep, the young effendi should only now awaken, like a mass-produced version of the Sleeping Beauty? Who has kissed him? Like a modern beauty who is rarely content to be awakened by one Prince only, I should say that the effendi has responded to at least three: the internal combustion engine, the (mostly) American educator, and the British Government.

If it is plausible to say that the continuance of the American federation was secured by the invention of railways, and that of the British Commonwealth by the invention of aeroplanes, it is equally probable that the aeroplane and the motor-car together may secure the future cohesion of Arabia. The existence of its governments, from the days of Asshur and Sheba to our own, has always depended on security of transport for the long and fragile lines of caravans; and civilizations such as that of Palmyra have vanished like the smoke of a nomad's fire, when some internal tumult or foreign inroad—which would be temporary in lands of a different geography—have snapped the policing and control of the camel tracks, even for a week. Now with mechanical transport neutralizing the desert and linking securely the great oases that form the Arab nations, the young man with a good education becomes more important than a chieftain of the tribes.

Before this happened, American and other teachers were at work.[1]

The first educational impulse of a genuinely Arab character after the long twilight of Turkish dominion, came, strangely enough, through Albanian strangers, Muhammad Ali and Irbahim his son, in the early years of the 19th century; and the reason was that the modernizing of their armies required a nucleus of educated men. The missionaries—the earlier Catholics, the later and more dynamic Americans (with a small proportion of British and others), sowed the ground that Ibrahim and his father had prepared.

In 1847 the first Society for Arts and Sciences in any Arab country was started with a Syrian, American and English membership in Beirut; it was a direct result of American interest, and the names of Cornelius van Dyck and Eli Smith are in the vanguard of any record of modern Arabian history. In the opening of his book, George Antonius says: "The story of the Arab national movement opens in Syria in 1847, with the foundation in Beirut of a modest literary society under American patronage."

I cannot in this introduction give an account of the educational achievement of the following decades. In 1834 Eli Smith and his wife had founded the first separate school for girls, and

---

[1] This account is largely taken from *The Arab Awakening*, by George Antonius, where the whole subject can be studied in more detail.

their example soon came to be followed. By 1860 the Americans had established 33 schools, with about 1000 pupils, nearly one-fifth of whom were girls. In 1866 the University of Beirut was founded, whose friendly and disinterested light still continues to shine upon the westernizing of the Arab nations. "Its influence on the Arab revival, at any rate in its earlier stages," says George Antonius, "was greater than that of any other institution." It has had the rare merit of changing with the needs of the changing generations, and now serves the young and self-confident intellectuals of the Arab world with the same devotion with which it first led them towards their national destinies; nor is there anyone wiser, I believe, in the thoughts and needs of the Arabs, than Professor Bayard Dodge, in Beirut.

Many other foreign institutions followed, and fed the demand for education, insatiably growing. The high standard was maintained, by the American university in Cairo, by the British Gordon and Victoria colleges in Khartoum and Alexandria, by the Society of Friends in Syria, by smaller schools, such as those of Dr. Van Ess, of Dr. Stout, of the Jesuit Fathers in Iraq. In the period after the World War, they merged with the growing stream of national Arab enterprise in education; they created the first teachers, but the teachers themselves have now built up and are building schools, universities, and educational departments of their own in their own countries. The quality of the effendis who govern will depend on the standards they set; and these standards came in their origin, and are still immensely affected by the labours and devotion of the American and other pioneers.

The third awakener of the young effendi is—I have ventured to say—the British Government.

At the end of the first World War Britain, who had the Protectorate of Egypt, was given three out of the four mandates for the Middle East (America having refused to accept one). The French had the mandate for Syria, thus separating it from Palestine and putting asunder what geography and history had joined. The French had difficulties inherent in the combination of a genuinely mandatory policy in Syria with the practice of a centralizing policy in North Africa; I hope to touch on this question later, and here only deal with the result, which was to take away the political lead of the Arab renaissance, which might easily have belonged to Syria, and which in fact fell to Egypt and Iraq.

The effect of the British years of administration was that they provided as it were an umbrella of comparative security—a security which was used to allow the renascent Arab peoples the elbow room they needed. The mandates and protectorates were interpreted with integrity and have to their credit, after this short period of twenty-five years, the establishment of two sovereign nations, Iraq and Egypt. Transjordan is on its way; and Palestine would be self-governing already if the Zionist question had not brought into that unhappy country its ancient tangle, renewing in modern form the old wars of Israel, Philistia, Edom and Moab, and the Hittites of the north. One may note in passing that it took the Children of Israel 476 years[1] to conquer Palestine without, except for a very short time, its Philistine or Phœnician coasts; it seems unreasonable to expect the Colonial Office to do for them in a generation what they themselves accomplished only in a very temporary manner after nearly half a millennium of war.

This is by the way: the important point to notice is that—to a British view—the Arab world is a region of transit; apart from oil, which the Arab people are at present content to see handled by others on a royalty basis, there is no British interest in Arabia as such; but it is a vital region from the fact that it lies between Asia and the Mediterranean, right across the highways of the Commonwealth.

Safe transit, and not "imperialism" is, therefore, the motive in the Arab world. I think this is one of the most important points for an understanding of the Middle East and I wrote[2] in 1940 in *The Times* to explain how, for centuries, Britain has seen in the "island of the Arabs" the gateway of her trade. India, Australia, China, Burma, Ceylon, lie on the farther side. The sons of Joktan, the merchants of ancient Middle East emporiums, have held the keys ever since the days when the Levant Company first played cricket in Aleppo, or the master of the Tiger wandered in its streets. For a time the Cape of Good Hope deviated traffic; the Suez Canal and aeroplanes have restored it; sea and air have ousted the camel caravan; but the direction of the trade of Asia is the same. There is an important difference. When the Romans, and later the Crusaders, tried to acquire Asiatic trade they were snatching the livelihood of

[1] See I Kings 6. 1. to the end of King David's reign.
[2] *The Times*, March 1940.

people whose markets they captured; their aim was to hold the termini of traffic for themselves. The Romans went farther, and substituted a Red Sea route, with harbours of their own, for the ancient overland Arabian way, and the riches of the trade, gathered in Antioch, Edom and Egypt, went into patrician coffers. The British position in the Middle East has been different from the very beginning, owing to the fact that their interest was in transit and not in capture. Already established in far Western markets to which Rome never had direct access, their only preoccupation was to get the merchandise safely to Europe across all intervening lands. To capture the depots, as Rome had done, was not in the programme, since they already had their interest in the goods at the point of departure.

This vital difference is at the root of Britain's position in the Arab lands. It has made it her business to strengthen and not to weaken the communities through which her commerce passes; her true role is one of mutual advantage with all trading countries that lie between the Mediterranean and the far Asiatic lands. By this guiding thread a simple policy is discernible in a constant fight against anarchy, the threat to safe and easy travel. The days of financial chaos and social misery in Egypt, when the *corvée* and the pasha between them sucked the land; the desolate condition of north Arabia, restive under the wiles of Abdul Hamid; the chaos of Iraq split into tribal factions under a nominal and distant rule; all these were disintegrating factors disastrous to the peaceful roads of commerce that ran across the Muslim world. It is—let us be honest—this matter of interest which is the centre of British dealings, but it happens to coincide with the interests of Arabia also; and this double bond builds a friendship which may well stand the wear and tear of time.

A natural affinity between Arab and English need not be forgotten. When great questions come, as now, into the arena, the human values are found to be the same. Even the clothes of the Arab, so dignified in their easy flowing lines, are the only exotic garment an Englishman will don with pleasure. The love of personal independence, the equal human status under God, have a peculiar likeness to those things which an Englishman in his heart is most ready to fight for. But we need not deceive ourselves; such sentimental grounds alone do not move armaments or alliances to-day. The Arab shares with England

xvi

another quality, a fine sense of political realism, and it is this which tells him that where others wish to divide and spoil, the necessary British policy is to unify and strengthen.

In spite of every partial failure, the result of this policy has been very great in the "island" of Arabia. Egypt is independent, prosperous and friendly. Under a great king, Saudi Arabia is at peace. Iraq in the north-east is unique in being a kingdom imagined, fashioned, and established without restriction by an alien race. The whole of the eastern coast, the whole of the south, is prosperous and warm in friendship, and even in Palestine, tossed and troubled for several thousand years, few Arabs would think themselves as unhappy now as they were a century or two ago.

Not all this has been done by Britain; but all has been made possible by the mere fact that Britain is interested in the integrity of Arabia. Like a great rock in a thirsty land, she has not grown the herbage in her shadow, but her shadow—by being there—has permitted the herbage to grow. If anyone doubts this, let him but look at the map of Europe and think how different the fate of many small nations might have been if the paths of commerce had made it vitally necessary for Britain from the very beginning to keep their frontiers safe.

This is a creditable record, and I think few realists would regret that the "great rock" rests on a solid basis of interest as well as of sentiment. It explains at any rate how Britain has every reason to encourage the young effendi in the care of his own country's affairs. While he has been learning, the umbrella of safety has been held above his head, and this security, more than any other single factor, has made possible the general and rapid progress of the last twenty-five years in all the north Arabian lands. Other factors have come in (the remarkable Zionist achievements in Palestine in particular should not be forgotten); but the progress has been general over a number of different countries, and security has been the general cause behind it.

Since her entry into the war, America's interest has greatly increased in the Arabian world. It is a business interest, centred on oil, and not—like the British—a geographic interest also affected by vital communications. But like the British, this interest coincides with the unity and strength of the Arab nations and there is every reason to hope that the great area of the Middle East may become a centre of co-operation and

xvii

not of short-sighted rivalry. The Middle East Supply Centre, which is a joint American and British venture, has already had a valuable influence in promoting the economic unity of the Arabian world.

To help in such a task, a real understanding is necessary of the forces that are moving there. American enterprise, now chiefly concentrated in the feudal lands of King Ibn Saud, comes little into contact with ideas stirring in the regions of the north. Neither in Saudi Arabia, nor in North Africa (which is the Doughboy's Arabia), has the reign of the young effendi yet begun. For this reason, the picture given in this book may be of use.

During my four years of war out there, American and Arabian contacts were slight in the countries in which I happened to be: and as my life was almost entirely among the Arabs, I scarcely saw our allies except in friendly fleeting moments or which, in those busy years, there were too few. Visitors came; General Maxwell, General (then Colonel) Donovan, made pleasant interludes in Cairo; I remember a remark made by the latter at a dance as he watched the moving uniforms (officers still wore mess kit in 1940) and the billowy gowns that were soon to disappear; "There is no doubt," said Colonel Donovan with his Irish twinkle, "that in war-time man should be disciplined and woman acquiescent." A Wellington remark, pleasant in the Napoleonic atmosphere of that strange world.

In Baghdad, there were Sunday bathes and rides and breakfasts with the young men of the Legation, and above all there was the staunch help and friendship of Mr. Knabenshue, who rescued H.H. the Regent through the sentries of a rebellious army, hidden under the rug of his car, and whom everyone, British or American, in Iraq in the spring of 1941, remembers with gratitude and regret.

There were the educational people, and the experts—the small orientalist society that comes naturally together in the friendship of a common bond. They have mostly learned to love the Arab for his own sake and so to understand him, realizing that in friendship as in matrimony the basis of all durable kindness is a liking for people's faults as well as for their virtues—and that what the young effendi needs is the help not so much of a governess as of a brother.

How thoroughly one agrees with him!

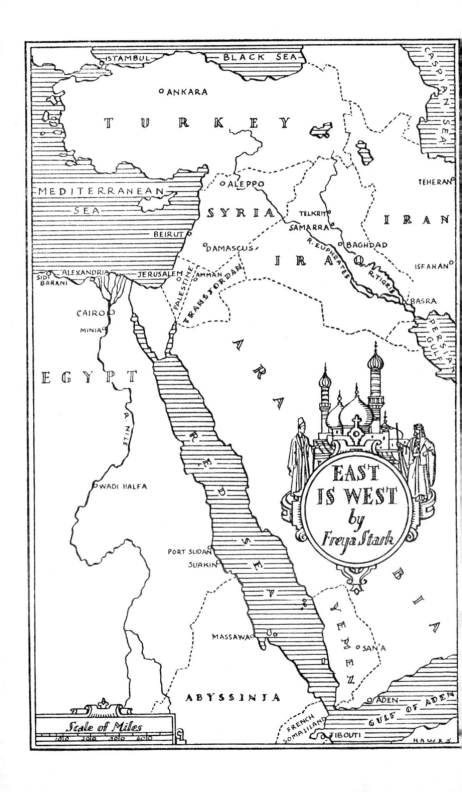

ISTAMBUL BLACK SEA CASPIAN SEA

ANKARA

T U R K E Y

MEDITERRANEAN SEA

BEIRUT

ALEPPO

S Y R I A

TELKRIT
SAMARRA

TEHERAN

I R A N

DAMASCUS

ISFAHAN

R. EUPHRATES

BAGHDAD

R. TIGRIS

I R A Q

SIDI BARANI
ALEXANDRIA

JERUSALEM AMMAN

BASRA

PALESTINE

TRANSJORDAN

PERSIAN GULF

CAIRO

MINIA

E G Y P T

A R A B I A

R. NILE

WADI HALFA

R E D S E A

PORT SUDAN
SUAKIN

EAST IS WEST
by
Freya Stark

MASSAWA

YEMEN

SAN'A

ABYSSINIA

ADEN

GULF OF ADEN

FRENCH SOMALILAND

JIBOUTI

HAWES

Scale of Miles
100 200 300 400

PART I

ADEN

CHAPTER I

JOURNEY TO ADEN

Be'old a cloud upon the beam,
An' 'umped above the sea appears
Old Aden, like a barrick stove
That no one's lit for years and years.
(R. KIPLING.)

ALL spring and summer in 1939 the thunderclouds were
gathering. At the end of August I left my home near Venice
and came to offer whatever service I could give in London, and
was taken, because of my knowledge of Arabic, as an expert
by the Ministry of Information. We began to function inside
the Foreign Office, in temporary quarters, on September 4th,
the second day of the war.

That September month in London was singularly beautiful.
It hung like a golden apple on a bough, soon to be detached.
The sun, through windless days, shone on the cherubic aluminium
roundness of the tethered barrage balloons. They floated
benevolently passive, silver at noon, rosy like air-islanded Alps
in dawn or sunset. Beneath them was a clearness and a stillness
—not the silence that lies in the midst of the havoc of war, the
silence found for instance last year in deserted North African
vineyards—but a waiting stillness, the majestic pause and
gathering together of all that is about to be destroyed. So
London waited, sunning itself in the gold of falling leaves, a
city of the young and the useful, for the old and the children
had then mostly gone away. The hospitals were empty, ready
for 30,000 casualties in the first expected air-raids; the parks,
round their slit trenches, were dotted with small groups in
khaki learning the handlings of signals and rifles and guns.
People walked with their gas masks slung like cameras over
one shoulder, pleasantly in the daylight or with difficulty in
the darkness of the first black-out. The searchlights lay like

swords above the silhouetted battlements of chimneys. When the moon shone, the parks with their billowing trees, now open to the public, took on an eighteenth-century loveliness of ballet; but at midday, in all the neighbourhoods of Whitehall, they were filled with open-air lunchers, clustered in ever-growing swarms round those hives of Government.

Flowers in wide borders still showed their lavish discipline of peace. Dahlias overflowed in saffron and crimson; and in one quiet place beneath the trees I came upon a multitude of autumn crocus clothing a little knoll; they grew leafless from the dappled leaf-strewn ground, and held their white chalices erect; so delicate, so unstained, so confident, their spirit of beauty bore them in our disorders; and I remember standing for many minutes, looking at them with tenderness, as if those cups of petals held in their yellow centres the very heart of England.

I used to walk during that month from Wilton Street through St. James's Park to the Foreign Office. A policeman let one in by a little back door to where in frescoed splendour the Locarno room offered hospitality to plain chairs and tables of our Mid-Eastern Division of the Ministry of Information, which bivouacked here in a corner under the gilt and decorated arches, rather like Beduin among the ruins of some lost civilization. We were indeed accused of making the Foreign Office look like a Bazaar, for we discussed our problems in common over cups of tea at one of those long tables, reducing seven separate memoranda to one for the benefit of Prof. Rushbrook Williams, our chief, whom we liked, and who dealt with his oriental experts rather like a hen with a brood of ducklings, affectionately anxious lest they swim out too far.

We were a small group, and all of us friends. Sir Kinahan Cornwallis, who comes back into this story in Baghdad eighteen months later in difficult times, shared a table with me; his long legs stretched right across beneath it and emerged on my side in the place where one would expect a waste-paper basket. His huge size, the rugged irregular face like some old portrait, the slow and husky voice, were made more noticeable by very pale blue eyes, searching and honest. Among us he held quiet authority which no one dreamt of gainsaying, made up of wisdom and kindness and courage. We had little to do in those early days. Our new-created ministry was carefully sheltered in its Locarno Paradise by the archangels of Admiralty and War,

2

who prevented any intercourse, however innocuous, with the tree of knowledge. (It was the time when a cartoon showed a fenced-off wilderness with the notice: "This war is between Hitler and the Admiralty; British public please keep out.") So we amused ourselves by putting up plans for the building of a Muslim centre in London. At the end of a few weeks Stewart Perowne telegraphed to ask if I would be his Assistant Information Officer in Aden, and I left on my overland journey to the East.

The Simplon Orient express still started from Paris at the usual time.

The glass dome of the station was painted midnight blue, and under it, in tunnels of echoing darkness, the train and its passengers united. Pinpoint blue lights showed to each traveller the hollow faces, unnaturally shadowed, of his neighbours; none travelled for pleasure. I groped to my compartment, and found the *chef de train* ejecting seven suitcases on which I counted to live through a five-year war; inside them, among other things, were some government newsreels, the first procurable. I told the *chef* about them, describing the nine frontiers that lay before me—each with a danger of confiscation—and dwelt particularly on the necessity of getting by the Italians next morning. They would be less likely to look if the things were with me in my sleeper. "If it is to annoy the Italians, allez-y, Mademoiselle."

The seven suitcases were reinstated; the *chef* gave me a friendly tap on the shoulder. "It is not the first time I help the English Intelligence," he said (overestimating me); he stepped back and was swallowed in the night. There were no good-byes upon the platform, no gay holiday waving; a few whispering groups remained with harassed faces. Like shadows among shadows, the bumpers knocked, the carriages shuddered; the most romantic of trains slid from its darkness into the outer dark.

There had been dim lights in Paris streets, but they could not dispel a blackness deeper than that of London, a cold anger, a gloom of the spirit. This bleak feeling hung all over the continent of Europe. The sunlit southern slopes of the Alps could not dispel it, garlanded in vines. In Venice, on the 13th of October, small desolate groups beside empty canals were reading Mr. Chamberlain's refusal of a German peace. They

3

read it in silence; it came to them as a surprise. I think they saw for the first time where the grim road was leading. I left with a heavy heart, for my home was near by in those green and pleasant hills, and I travelled on through Bulgaria, shunted in stations while innumerable troop trains passed. We were made aware of the discomfort of war by the fact that the restaurant car ran out of food as our delays lengthened, until we came to Stambul and saw that scimitar-shaped city brilliantly lighted for Ramadhan, its streets and mosques and minarets shining like a sanctuary against the wild background of Europe.

There we stepped into what seemed a fairly rooted world, for General Weygand and his army in Syria held the defences of the Middle East; the southern buttress of our civilization seemed secure.

In Ankara I spent a day, and went to visit our Ambassador and his wife. Turning from their most noble view, which stretches beyond the Hittite citadel to open, far hills of Anatolia, I met in their drawing-room an officer with many ribbons, active, not tall, with grizzled hair and a steadfastness as of friendly granite all about him; and, in his general expression, a look of gaiety and youth. He carried with simplicity a rare atmosphere of greatness. He had just arrived from Egypt to visit the Turks, and the matter of his dress was under discussion by the A.D.Cs.: was it to be with or without a sword? While this point was being settled for him, he listened with amusement but with pleasure, such as any good game deserves, and caught my eye and smiled. He was General Wavell, commander of the few British forces we had in the Middle East; and the impression he made on me was so distinct that his achievements when they came seemed inevitable, and their fortitude, integrity and imagination the natural expression of himself.

The train winds for two days across the uplands of Asia Minor, a citadel between two worlds. Walking there along his natural battlements, the Turk looks down and sees in the south the awakening of Asia, the clamour of Europe in the north. In the last five years the contrast has grown, for the European war and its ruin has never quite overflowed the Arabian lands, and the restrained flood has come to quicken and not to destroy the renascence of nations there.

One rushes down into Arabia with the torrents, through the

Cilician Gates. The train loops itself round precipices, under pines, from winter to spring, from Europe to Asia, in reckless spirals, with giddy steepness, from the ravines of Taurus to the Ægean Sea.

In the late afternoon, in the golden light, we reached the Syrian border and the cities of the dead were about us, and the strange beauty of Asia who makes her ornament of the secrets of her past. A beauty that relies, like a Paris gown, on subtle line with a single knot or ribbon, a trifle of decoration, a broken column in the barren cup of hills, a lad with black goats browsing, a lonely tree, to give the desired note and waken the spirit. Style, I suppose it is, both in the French costume and the Syrian landscape—to renounce all but the essential, so that the essential may speak.

I saw it in the night of Aleppo whose darkness seemed remote from the rigid black-out of Europe. The old city wrapped herself in it as in a veil, lifting from swathes of shadows the sloping stones of her glacis and Saladin towers to the moon. The blank walls of the well-built Syrian houses, the tunnelled archways of the suqs, were as they had been through all the ages before progress touched them with electric light—obscure, full of questions: the daytime's contours had melted into some uncatalogued infinity of night. The dim blue lights seemed right here, for they showed what had always been shown—a stretch of wall, a pool of arch, some head-enveloped figure walking on sandalled feet; it was only when one reached the trams and the modern side of Arabia that a black-out in the interior of Syria seemed foolish at that time.

From Aleppo I had to rely on the odds and ends of transport that led to Egypt. After many long but pleasant hours in a little train that browsed its dilatory way to Damascus, I was rescued by John Teague, a friend from years ago in Baghdad, who had a car and was going to Jerusalem: we were back in that happy East which is like a club, for everybody knows you, and the unexpected happens so punctually that you are saved from the bondage of plans. As we scooted along the good asphalt in morning light, French Africans were manœuvring among the hills of Anti-Lebanon, horses and figures scattered on the rocky background like some small vivid painting by Meissonier. I did not realize that I was seeing cavalry with horses for the last time in this war.

Mechanization in the shape of an armoured car appeared at the Palestine frontier and kept a hundred yards or two ahead to protect us through the reeds and lowlands south of Ras Nakura where ambushes had been frequent during the last few years. Precautions were still taken everywhere; when my train steamed into Lydda station I noticed an open truck before the engine; in it were seated, comfortably but silent, a small and gloomy group of village elders. If their fellow parishioners, through whose districts our engine was going to pull us, happened to leave a bomb upon the track, these men would be the first to meet it. When I returned to Palestine a year later all such traces had vanished, for the Arabs there, with a sporting instinct which endears them to their adversaries, spontaneously promised to give no trouble while the British had a greater war upon their hands. Palestine and its guerillas had been, since 1936, the training ground for British arms, and the Arab truce allowed our yeomanry regiments, toughened in those hills, to be sent at once to Egypt; they formed the hard substance round which the 8th Army eventually was built. These regiments perhaps tilted the balance in our favour, for our numbers in 1940 were very small. It is pleasant to think that old-fashioned chivalry, a Crusading tradition, may have saved the Middle East, and even the mechanized world, in the clash of its mechanized armies.

All this came in 1940, when Italy entered the war. But in November '39 the Mediterranean was open, the ribbon of Egypt was prosperous and busy, and Cairo, that ever-changing, never-changing city, followed its social life with a preoccupied air, with dinner parties extremely late because men in offices were working, with scented jasmine wreathed round ladies' wrists, with gatherings on houseboats, on roofs, at Mena, under the blue lamps that made conversation lingering and easy and seemed an opera version of the Parisian reality.

My nine frontiers were crossed and my newsreels were still with me intact. In November I was sailing down the Red Sea, the only passenger on a very small steamer coasting to Aden. I have now made many such journeys in and out of the roadsteads of Arabia, but it takes a war to get the full flavour of this travelling, to surround it with the suddenness and danger that makes the unity of its history, tying it to the tale of Ulysses and all the seafaring chronicles of man. Nothing really has

6

changed, and the same gossip floats with the lapping sunset wavelets about the quiet and forgotten harbours. In the following year I translated some navigation instructions for submarines: I came into an enchanted world whose very language was different from ours, with an ageless tang of sea; it led one (in silhouette, for one never landed), among the coasts and reefs and sucking currents and tiny nameless islands, their landmarks untroubled by men, a strip of whiter beach, a rock, two trees together—things drawn in the pirate maps of one's childhood. In the prosaic typescript of the captured instructions the words were magic, a casement opening on the foam. And the skippers and engineers (mostly Scotch), and mates of the coasting steamers belong to this world. You will find them ashore, stocky and self-reliant, spending their money freely and wearing, with a quaint dignity, the shore clothes to which they are not accustomed; but on their decks they are at home, or in their cabins, where reigns the framed photograph of a woman, mother or wife or sweetheart, or perhaps children grown up during their absences at sea. There will be a pet, a canary in a cage, or dog or cat, and a modest cache of spirits under the skipper's hand; and every one of these men will be able to make up his mind at a second's warning, on any problem that concerns his craft.

It is pleasant to be with people who make up their minds. Now as we travelled, with the North Star dipping and the Southern Cross gaining upon us, I would climb to the bridge in the darkness and watch the chart of the heavens under the skipper's lamp, carefully shaded, and watch the heavens themselves reel with the swinging bulwarks in the night. On our port side the house-lights of Arabia twinkled in far-spaced clusters, while we moved in the unlit sea-trough and listened to the Admiralty in London, ticking to us in morse. From square to square of the plotted oceans it moved the ships, great and small, and held their ranks as regular as any rank of battle; this was wide war, flung about the oceans, wrestling for giant highways, joined in by the elements, trade winds and storms. The cockle-shell we rode in, the skipper with the light on his hands and his face in shadow, even the silent Lascar at the wheel, were there rejoicing, for war is in the history of shipping in all its ages, even in times of peace.

We swung round Perim whose light still shone upon the

narrow channel, and ploughed along the beaconless coast of South Arabia, wrapped in medieval night. No lighthouse swept from British shores across the Indian ocean; only the morse ticked incessantly. In the early morning of the eleventh day, when the minesweepers had opened a lane through the mine-fields of Aden, we landed near the statue of Queen Victoria, sitting there among the long-limbed black Somalis who stroll about the quay.

CHAPTER II

THE SONNETS OF WORDSWORTH

*"And We are left, or shall be left alone;
The last that dare to struggle with the Foe."*

MR. FRAMROSE, an ample, loose-fleshed, elderly man, billowing in many folds of white with black biretta on the summit of it all, was patriarch of the Parsee firm of ship-owners and merchants who came with the British troops to Aden in 1839. They were the first contractors to the army.

The harbour, seen as a coaling station on the route to India before the Suez Canal was thought of, was then a place of solitary lavas. From high jagged cliffs of their crater peninsula they poured and hardened in the warm sea. On that crater, first bought and then conquered, the Victorian soldiers in hot red uniforms settled, and still their tiny cemeteries, naked under the cliffs, where the average age of the dead is less than thirty years, tell eloquently enough the story of their days. So do the walls interspersed with blank gates, built in a Victorian, utilitarian, undecorative way, festooned over steep miles of lava against marauding tribes. The Governor of Aden of 1940 had still received, as a younger man, a small sum paid by Bombay to compensate her servant for living in the dangerous zone of Government House in Aden.

The Arab town lay some five miles away, like St. Laurence on his gridiron, in the heart of the crater, baking in the sun. But on the outer spokes of the dead volcano, along glistering bays, the paraphernalia of one of the world's harbours grew rapidly, and the fortunes of the Parsee family with it. They bought ships and began to capture the coasting trade; and theirs were among the foremost shops that, with shallow porticoes and dark interiors, began to appear in crescents where the new quays were rising. There is a sharpness in Eastern commerce, its dangers not all in ledgers, but vividly connected with deserts and seas; in Crater town, whence Monsieur Besse with ships and dhows rules from Zanzibar to Oman, he and his

9

office staff can see with their own eyes the skins and frank-
incense and coffees gathered and distributed from Somaliland,
Abyssinia, Yemen or Mukalla.

Mr. Framrose and his family had not quite so princely a
range; but their door also was busy with "the merchants of
Sheba and Raamah", with slender ebony-coloured Somalis from
Berbera and Jibouti whose narrow loins are wrapped in coloured
ginghams and their skull-caps embroidered with red and yellow
aeroplanes and ships. Passengers would be hanging about there
for or from every harbour or open roadstead of the neighbouring
coasts—Parsee merchants or relatives from Bombay, or Hindu
dealers; or tribesmen with but a few hundred sea miles between
them and their home; or pursers from big liners collecting
stores; or pilgrims; or their own skippers, mates and engineers,
in from their journeys. There was always a crowd seething
into activity where some clerk, submerged and smooth as the
centre of a maelstrom, wrote at an invisible table and handed
papers to the waving arms.

Above all this clamour, up steep wooden stairs, our office
of information opened to a panorama of the harbour.

Mr. Framrose presented it as a free war-gift to the British
Government, under whose shield along that pirate coast the
family fortunes had been made. As assistant information officer
I benefited by acquiring two rooms at the back to live in, stacked
with intricate Indian and massive Victorian furniture, hung
with pictures of every royal family that had passed through
Aden in the last hundred years, and with a neglected canary
who, in the presence of one live commoner among so many
dead tiaras, began to chirp and sing.

Lying through hot nights on a mahogany four-poster bed
on which whole families of Parsees must have lived and died,
the first distant muezzin call to prayer would wake me in the
dark; I would then lie listening to sounds of breakfast and
prayer mingled in the courts of the Parsee staff below. They
gathered at about 5 a.m. for a chant, a sort of organ voice to
greet the dawn. Then came a scent of incense, carried in
braziers to every desk before the day began and at its end. I
soon asked for our office to be included in this pleasant benediction.

Our own office was an immense room where maps and
pictures from the Ministry of Information soon began to

vie with the kings and emperors in which Mr. Framrose delighted.

Stewart Perowne, my chief, swooped in and out here, long-necked and bald-headed like a young vulture, but with none of that pompous slowness which gives vultures their official look and comes—in both cases perhaps—from so much contemplation of things which are dead. Stewart, in spite of his beaked profile, had a butterfly gaiety about him and sipped honey even from Government telegrams, embellishing them with scriptural quotations. He hovered with outspread wings at the centre desk, pounced on the strange language of Whitehall, disembowelled the files with an epigram at incredible speed, and was out again, followed by the adoring gaze of Ali the office boy, who would always contrive to stand, covered in purple ink, a pace or two behind him. Unkind people called Ali mentally deficient; Stewart looked upon him as a fancy buttonhole to be worn for fun, and his constant kindness to someone so exasperating and so useless endeared him more than his many more conventional qualities to our Arabians, who like the non-utilitarian charities.

"I wish Mr. Perowne would get rid of that frightful boy," said Dyllis the secretary at her desk in the corner, regularly every day.

But Muhammad at the opposite desk would murmur: "It is the goodness of his heart"; and Ali, bungling and devoted, continued with us. So did the sparrows who lived in the beams above the typewriter (I cut lengths of string for them to build their nests with and used to open the glass doors for them every morning); so did our broadcaster who interpreted newsreels in the cinema before Arabic sound tracks were made, and spent his wages in undesirable ways. But the centre and mainstay of our office was Ali Muhammad the translator.

Ali Muhammad was twenty-three years old. He was very slight, dressed in a white drill suit with gay, rich ties. He had sensitive hands, like many Arabs, very fine and slender, instruments made to carry nerves and tendons and the thoughts that move them, with no superfluous flesh. He was darker than his white clothes, but there was nothing swarthy about him; rather, one felt him as one felt his land—tempered by so many ages of the sun; Europeans who roam outside the shelter of their colonial lives acquire the same resistant, dusky quality.

11

Muhammad moved quietly. When he came in, after bicycling the five miles from his home in Crater, he waited till one's eye fell upon him to say good morning, and then it was the smile rather that the words that one noticed. I was interested in him because there, in his young person, one could see the future of Arabia; when he stood up in his discreet way, like some ambassadorial secretary acting for his chief, and with an imperceptible condescension shook the hands of independent Beduin who came swaggering in to see us from the outer edges of our land—it was like two periods of history meeting, Viking and Wall Street, united perhaps by a tradition, but with all the circumstance of time and place to separate. In that meeting was embodied the fundamental problem of all Arab government—the immense gamut of civilization which it has to cover.

Other governments, in fact all governments, have this problem. Town and country, business and leisure, learning, art, and everyday utilities have to be included in one comprehensive set of regulations, and the beliefs and loyalties of all these facets do go back to different times and sources in the general history. But in lands where nomad and town exist together this difference is pushed to an extreme; it is almost impossible to arrange a way of life comfortable for both. In days of poverty, strife, and broken threads of traffic the nomad—needing so little— grows in power at the town's expense; with the coming of the combustion engine in Asia, the influence of the town has come to stay. It is this general factor, the elimination of the desert and its distances, and not one or other political arrangement, which has altered the quality and tempo of Arab life. And its result is the progress of the young effendis, the professional middle class.

In themselves they are not so new. The scribes and merchants of the Arabian Nights, the Sinbads of Basra, and even the most exalted names, the Prophet himself and his Companions, grew in the professional, commercial atmosphere of a great society based on traffic; this has given its democratic foundation to Arab thought; in their outlook and upbringing they were the young effendis of their day. The difference now is that circumstances are playing into their hands; from being only one part of a community where dangers and difficulties kept the feudal chieftain and his tribes also in power, they are becoming paramount; their ledgers and invoices can be written, their bales and cargoes sent, without help or hindrance from the desert; what is taught and believed in the universities of Beirut and Cairo matters more than all the words spoken in the tents of the tribes; Fords and Chevrolets are becoming as common in the sands of Arabia as they are in New Mexico or Arizona. It was this new background of his that interested me so much in young Muhammad.

He made it a labour of love to build Arabic prose out of the daily news which I picked from the air and wrote over my breakfast on the terrace. Destroyers and the Red Sea sloops, battleships and neutral ships and transports from New Zealand or Australia moved in and out below, beyond the ample bronze petticoats of Queen Victoria. In the clean sunshine and a breeze that fluttered the table-cloth edges, Muhammad would come out to discuss English meanings and Arabian cadences, building sentences that were to counter Italian propaganda and give to the people of Aden their only real news of the war. They would listen in the evening, clustered under the starlight of their square in Crater, hearing through a loud-speaker the sweet intoning voice of a Reader from their Mosque. No other Press as yet existed; Muhammad's father, a well-to-do lawyer, was planning what is now the only newspaper of South Arabia, and Stewart was trying to collect paper and machinery to help him, on the understanding—which the lawyer bargained for staunchly at every interview—that the ideas expressed should be his own.

Muhammad no doubt inherited this innate Arabian wish for freedom.

I do not know if he would have put so much of his heart into the work if the news we distributed had been intended to deceive. I think, because of his trust in us, he would have *tried* to accept such a standard of propaganda and, in doing so, lost that feeling for the responsibility and honour of Knowledge, which the Arabian as well as the Western world carried into this age from medieval darkness, like a torch whose shining is not so very visible in our daylight. Anyway, Muhammad's faith was put to no such test. If one has a cause, and believes in it, one need not model oneself on Dr. Goebbels; the twelve apostles were more inspiring and more successful; and why should one's voice waver merely from telling the truth? So Muhammad and I wrote our bulletins believing in our news; and as it got worse and worse from April 1940 onward, we stressed the celestial city in the distance and pointed out with stronger emphasis the temporary nature of those swamps and thickets that lay in the immediate path. Luckily the celestial city is as real as any swamp. In the Red Sea lands, in that disastrous year, I never met a British man or woman who thought the war was lost.

But the faith of Muhammad, and of the young effendis, was built on much more fragile, and indeed invisible, foundations. Every Englishman knows, or can know, that there is no defeat unless it is the acceptance of defeat. The Arabian world has frequently made this discovery in religion, but not in political life.

As the bastions of Europe fell away from us, as the Red Sea gates were closed, as the Indians, and many of the Parsees, and most of the European women were shipped to safer places and the smallness of Aden became apparent with the new Italian empire looming huge against it—Muhammad's punctual serenity every morning at his desk became more and more remarkable. It came from no unconsciousness of danger. No one could walk through the half-empty streets, by the barricaded beaches or the bullet-pierced ships from Norway, and not feel that we were a threatened outpost very much alone. When the wireless spoke in the morning, defeat upon defeat, Muhammad at his desk, his head a little raised, shared the silence in which we all faced our dwindling prospects; he made no comment.

We got together three bands of young Arabs to do volunteer work, guarding streets and houses in air raids; no one gave us much help, the harassed army and civil authorities looked upon us as just one more straw if not the last one. But we felt it was good even for amateurs to have a share in their own defences, and a sudden light in Muhammad's eyes as we planned drill, and arm-bands, told us we were right. The same light came on the morning when a ship took away a number of our women and Muhammad found that I was staying. He was an A.R.P. warden, and would run out from his desk when the raid warnings came, pleased to have a mission, and shyly proud of its insignia; and on his way he would cheer Mr. Framrose, shivering but obstinate, in an armchair on his roof, strangely convinced that the blue sky was the safest canopy from shrapnel.

I found out gradually what lay behind Muhammad's confidence. He *believed* in what we were fighting for. The words of the innumerable pamphlets whose meaning we took for granted were living words to him. The Arab has not yet had time to think of words from an advertisement angle; he still vaguely connects them with the presence of God. Englishmen, being inarticulate, avoid the snares of advertisement by suspecting *all* words; they reach the things that lie behind them in silent ways of their own; but when in 1940 we came down to fundamental matters, we found the Arabian sentences and our own silences to be much the same at heart.

Muhammad's feelings about it all were shown to me in June. The tired lines of infantry were still on the beaches of Dunkerque. I was reading the sonnets in which Wordsworth in the years between 1801 and 1806 faced the invasion of England. Pamphlets, posters, everything with which London Information had hitherto supplied us was either becoming uselessly inappropriate or unattainable by the closure of the Red Sea. I wondered if the sonnets of Wordsworth would appeal to the Arabs of Aden in a time of danger, and gave them to Muhammad to take home. He came to the office next morning with the same bright light in his eyes and two sonnets already translated into Arabic verse. "This," he said to me with a sort of vehemence, "this is for the Arabs. It is *brave.*"

We thought that through Aden and the small coast towns, where readers are few, we might sell 500 copies, printed in tiny volumes. Muhammad worked at them, and Stewart printed 2000: every copy was sold and more were asked for. Muhammad was right; the poet's words carried Dunkerque straight to the Arab heart.

CHAPTER III

ANCIENT ARABIA

" To what purpose cometh there to me incense from Sheba and the sweet cane from a far country?"

(Jeremiah.)

IF you look at Aden in Time instead of Space, it is the most varied sort of island. Leave its quays, its signal stations, hospitals, heaps of coal, the tangle of masts and funnels, the lines rectangular like modern painting, the harbour boom against submarines, the fuel tanks so alluring to Italian airmen; leave the childish architecture of cantonments, and the asphalt which chokes in sand beyond the village of Shaikh Othman—and in a matter of hours you can visit any age you like, between that of the Queen of Sheba and Muhammad Ali.

Even in the modern town the Past has a way of jostling you off the pavement in the shape of some blue-painted bedu, naked-torsoed, ballet-skirted, his hair matted under a fillet and waist broad-belted and jewelled with a dagger—who leads his camel by a rope in the space reserved for walking and looks at the ousted passengers as if they were a column of ants in the dust.

I have often wondered what gives the nomad Arab that superb and arrogant poise which he loses as soon as he enters our modern world as a townsman or a tiller of the soil. It is, I believe, his feeling of Equality.

Not American equality, which depends on equal justice, equal opportunity, equal motor-cars, frigidaires, permanent waves, equal comforts and movies. Your bedu, if he could bring himself to envisage it at all, would call this Captivity. What he feels is something independent of possessions or even of rights; it is the innate equality of human beings, implicit in their subservience to God. If he wants a radio set, or a gun, or an education, he wants them for themselves, but not with the idea of being somebody else's equal: that he is already, by the inalienable right of his manhood. This gives him his

16

unselfconsciousness, his dignity, his easy courtesy and careless walk, whatever his contrast of rags may be with others' kingly garments. This feeling lies at the bottom of Arab democracy and naturally finds no difficulty in combining with feudal forms of government, since its essence lies far below such surface shows. It lies very deeply embedded in Arabian learning. And I am sure that the West is doing the East no service by destroying it in the mind of the Young Effendi; an Equality which inspires you to meet your neighbour without envy and your death without fear is not to be despised.

However this may be, the Past was welcome in our office, and knew it. The door would open and there, as in a dark frame, with orange loin-cloth amply pleated from waist to knee, with a striped shawl on one shoulder and a green turban in loose calico-folds slipping down the back of his head, would be the chieftain of Beihan in the far north-west, with his travelling companions behind him.

Stewart would give one despairing look at the mountain of files, doomed for the morning; little cups of coffee went to the terrace; the chieftains, folding their petticoats neatly about their knees, sat on wicker armchairs like Biblical figures astray, with the modern harbour beyond them. They brought presents of millet in small bags to send our fighting armies, or offered men for the war. They took it as their war; photographs of tanks and ships, of the King and Queen, would travel back in camel saddles, a ten days' journey across hills where scarce a Westerner has ever ridden. They brought the news of the Yemen where Fascists were busy, and the gossip and feuds of the valleys, and heard in return the prospects of Europe. Thousands of years ago they were accustomed to listen to the tales of foreign places, Indian tales when the Spice road ran through their lands, merchant stories later from Basra and Hormuz and Muscat through centuries of the medieval world when striped cloths of Yemen were sold in the East; behind the three-hundred-year darkness of the Turkish rule there is always this unifying factor of the Arabs' commercial past, a factor which, I believe, has no small part in the unifying of the Arab world to-morrow.

We too went to visit the Past, beyond the end of the asphalt, across dunes where the car at any moment was liable to stick in sand. We had our portable cinema projector and a handful of films, and would put up our screen in the starlight, on flat ground where the camels were couched to be unloaded, below village huts.

The villages run where sand and stone meet, and water from the plateau slips to silt itself up and disappear in the shore-land "Tihama." Tribesmen gather here to grow their date palms and supplement the dwindling revenue of looted caravans. This method of making a living, now strenuously discouraged, we spoke of only in the past tense; but we could talk about shipping in Liverpool and Cardiff and many Asiatic harbours, for strangely enough many of these inland Arabs are sailors. Five hundred men were at sea from one valley alone, solitary and sunburned and surrounded by the desert. They are mostly stokers; the engine rooms of ships are probably not unpleasant to anyone born to the climate of South Arabia.

Where the low dunes and the versatility of motors ended, camels would take one on, and men slipped barefoot on blue-painted feet to guide us to the chief's square tower, built of loose stones. Here, tucked by some headwater, tiny plantations rise, terraced one behind the other, to the very utmost range of moisture, under the rampart of the plateau which sailors far on the Indian ocean see and call Arabia.

To one of the poorest clans which we now and then visited, a few hours' drive from Aden, Stewart was a sort of Agricultural Demi-god, having safeguarded their water rights against more powerful neighbours higher up the stream. That was in days when Stewart was a political officer. But it was remembered, and the whole male village, a hundred men or so, would turn out with banners and keep us standing in the sun while their procession, small and nearly naked but disarmingly gay, went round and round their open threshing ground, singing a chant of welcome. As the leaders and elders reached us, they shook hands in passing, with a smack on the shoulder now and then from some huge horny hand to show how pleased they were. And in the end, with a drum beating, a small bullock was led out and sacrificed, falling with slit throat into the hot dust—a strange welcome, if you come to think of it, for a Bell and Howell Cinema Projector.

CHAPTER IV

CHRISTMAS AT DHALA[1]

There first the North's cold bosom spices bore
And Winter brooded on the Eastern Spring.
(DRYDEN: *Annus Mirabilis.*)

AT Christmas, in 1939, we made a party of six friends and took a short holiday in the small mountain principality of Dhala, north-east of Aden.

The son of the Emir of Dhala, bending over his wireless, did not say: "Peace on earth and good will." What he said was: "Here in Arabia we can listen to all the wars of Europe."

The wireless stood, uncompromising and incongruous, on the harem floor. Around it were spread mattresses where the ladies and the Emir recline in hours of ease; a coloured frieze ran round the whitewashed walls in gay and geometrical patterns, surmounted by a motif of trees, porticoed houses and mosques in repeating sequence. The niches that furnish every eastern room were bright with decoration. The two ladies, wrapped in Indian brocades, veiled with crimson embroidered veils, their throats heavily lapped in gold and pearls, were as brightly coloured as the room they lived in; and from its small windows, thick-set in the wall of the keep, the whole of the little kingdom fell away.

Dhala looks with one eye towards the Yemen and her highland neighbours, potentially ready at any moment to overlap the boundary in raids; and, with the other, to wavelike declining summits that drop through lands of the Kutaibi to the sandy friendly coasts of Aden.

Who has not stood at times in front of some old picture, and imagined himself walking into the artificial stillness of its landscape? It comes to life as he advances into imaginary distance; the donkey trots with panniers in the foreground, the little boy with stick perpetually lifted brings it down with a whack. Fresh dust is on the ruts of that track that

[1] Reproduced from *The Times*, March 28th, 1940.

winds into the background by towns perched there on small
and naked hills. The painter has put them in clearly, one
by one, diminishing as the track winds in smaller perspective;
in his faithful rendering you can see specks of people—men
with sashes and rifles, teams of oxen ploughing in the
fields. You can see the Emir descending from his castle,
by a steep path that cuts diagonally to the small town below;
the chestnut pony whisks its long tail, his bodyguard are
running all about him. Smoke rises; the tiny whitewashed
windows look out like eyes of owls from their dark walls;
sparse trees are dotted in the fields. Something is always
happening in this landscape; one can see the brown kites
wheeling, one can hear their sweet shrill voices and the rush
of their descending wings; one can hear the many little voices
from the town; for the fact is that it is not a painting at all,
but the everyday, incredible landscape of Dhala.

Since 1928, the Emir of Dhala has been a safe, wholehearted friend to the British, jealous of his freedom, but ever
ready to take advice and give help or receive it; and no sooner
does the smoke rise from the kitchen of the little guest-
house for Aden officials, than the Emir can be seen stepping down from the gate of his castle, through his stone-built
town with whitewashed minaret, threading his way across
the intervening fields of *kat* (*cathula edulis*, a deplorable
but not intoxicating drug), till he comes with a great
jingle of presenting arms among his barefoot bodyguard to
call.

As one rides about the little principality, one never gets
away from that strange sensation of being not in real life, but
in some picture or story. It has the quality of things read
or told in childhood—the feeling that anything might happen
at any moment; it is far more like a tale of William Morris
than like anything in Europe to-day. If one climbs the mountain beyond Dhala, the rocky mass of Jihaf, 7,800 ft. high,
one can see the whole land with its pointed hills and tiny
settlements, a tomb of Job on a summit two days westward,
and the little square towers that sit on every height. They
are built of cubes of dark stone whose varied colour gives
them an iridescent look; and they have rough fortified devices,
shotholes and machicoulis and embryo battlements. They sit
as if stitched in tapestry on the summits of rocks in this

pastoral highland whose scanty grass has died away in summer. The unshod ponies climb like cats over the tilted slabs; the tiny harvests make yellow patches stacked in trees or rocky holes; from their small forts the few inhabitants gather to watch us ride. Great cacti grow here like tabernacle candles, raising clusters of straight prickly shafts higher than a man on horseback, and the air is as sharp and pure as the cry of an eagle. Here from this summit of the principality one looks across to the wall of Yemen, where withered streams are trickling far below.

We came riding up one morning and found the tribal army gathered to meet us in an open hollow below the highest fort of the Emir. There were about two hundred men, barefoot, in two long rows, their turbans and tunics discoloured, their thin legs and arms and rifles moving like fringes in the wind. In front of them the Emir's son caracoled on a pony, young, thin, well-bred and nervous as himself; he wheeled; the slender hoofs made patterns in the dust; the army banged its drums and led away with daggers playing in the sunlight; on the summit above, the battlements were thronged with watchers. The sun shone white on bleached boulders; the landscape fell in rifts and open valleys to other fortified summits far away; the long snake crawled upwards with short steps, dancing to its drums, with the Emir's son and his guests in the middle; until, between the swarthy hillmen, we dismount at the gate of the fortress, stumble up the unlighted winding stair, and enter the guest-room. The Emir's son, standing to receive us with outstretched hand, says: "May your holy day be blessed here among us."

So far from Europe, our speech unknown and our civilization scarce understood, the ideal of peace and goodwill seems not so unattainable after all.

CHAPTER V

MEDIEVAL ARABIA: IN THE YEMEN

"Is not the border of the monsoon rain the just division between Arabia Felix and Arabia Deserta?"
(CH. DOUGHTY: *Arabia Deserta*).

To the north of Aden, at the top of the plateau, falling sheer on one side to the shelving Red Sea sands and gently on the other to the central deserts of Arabia, the land of Yemen is ruled in an absolute way by its Imam. And when I say absolute I mean it, for he holds in his hands the spiritual as well as the temporal affairs of his people, and for two generations has led their armies in battle and their spirits in prayer and their wealth, such as it is, into his coffers, and has attended to their diplomacy, and their domestic life, their trade, their dress, their journeys; so that his hand is felt everywhere and his holiness is loved in the mountain part of the country where the people believe in it (along the coast they are Shafe'i Sunnis who think the Zeidi Shi'a of the hills quite wrong and have to be kept down by carefully selected governors).

The mountain region of the Yemen is a pleasant country, different in many ways from anything else in Arabia. It is fertile, for one thing, and touched by the monsoon, with streams —some permanent—that fall from the summer rains of the plateau eight or nine thousand feet above the sea; and drop from precipice to precipice where coffee bushes grow on walled terraces and make the name of Mocha familiar to the world; until with dwindling waters they reach the sandy Tihama and the Shafe'i coast, and the shallow sand-dunes drink them.

You would not think, as you sail in and out of the little Gehennams that go for Red Sea harbours, that the outline of mountains which every afternoon the heat haze swallows holds in its jagged gorges such green and shady places—waterfalls tumbling from high shelves, and a luxuriance of trees and creeping plants, and birds dipping and singing; and at the top of it all like a roof, broad bands of tillage binding a rocky horizon ten thousand feet high, whose pinnacles like pencil points shoot into an atmosphere pale and luminous as mercury. In spring and summer the silver-slippered rainstorms scurry by, shining and beneficent, casting shadows and green patches on the clear, sparse, open land; and its villages, clusters of huts small-windowed and dark, by cultivating ever the same fields in the same places, and building themselves over and over again on their own ruins, have grown immutable almost as their landscape, islanded as it were on themselves.

The peasants weave blue homespun cotton—gowns for the men, and for the women trousers like jodpurs under a loose long shirt which they tuck into the waist for field work, except at the back, and there it falls from the shoulder like crumpled angels' wings. There are no nomads here; the camel caravans move from village to village, loading agricultural produce, busiest at threshing time or harvest; it is only in the eastern desert fringes, where few travellers go, that the Beduin carry on their Biblical way of trafficking and raid. Here in the middle strip of Yemen one sees neither the ancient desert world nor the modern world of the Arabian north; one climbs into medieval Arabia and the sort of life travellers found in Palestine or Syria from the Crusades and onward, until the Mediterranean lands became westernized at heart.

His Majesty the Imam Iahya in his high capital of San'a might just as well be living in the crusading days. His long life looks back on the same chequered light of warfare, guerillas and pursuit in the mountains, and—at the end of the first world war—the final driving of the enemy from the land. The enemy was Turk, not Christian; that is a small difference to hill folk who, whether it be Yemen, Scotland, or Judæa, resist imposition from the outside and in the long run usually maintain their freedom. The Imam fought for it, and has held it ever since, and his conservative dislike of penetration —whether they call it oil, industry or general improvement— is possibly connected with those many years of bitter fighting at the head of ragged followers in the hidden rocky places of his land. So perhaps is his parsimony, the only fault with which his subjects reproach him, product also of hard and struggling days.

The Turks have gone, and only their finger-minarets, their easy glass-windowed houses beside the medieval fortress centres of San'a, their cypress trees planted by garden walls—only these remain, and a few ancient officers long shrunken inside the uniforms of their youth, marooned here and employed to train the troops they once commanded.

Every Friday they gather and parade their army outside the city walls where dust blows about the windy spaces. Their old ruler drives out to them in a cab with a hood like a concertina, in whose creases the dust settles in swathes. The army marches, barefoot or sandalled, in dusty calico gowns reminiscent of pinafores, kept from sticking out in the pinafore way by cartridge-bandolier and rifle-strap at shoulder. They march four or five in a row and, if one falls out, he makes it up with a skip, not military but endearing. In the equally dusty calico of a cloth wound loose about the head, they will stick green sprigs of their drug, *kat*, which they chew and in doing so forget their hardships, their scant two dollars monthly pay and long terms of service, when the time comes to lounge over a hookah in the guardhouse. They are every age, young lads and grizzled peasants; and in between their platoons they trundle with pride a refuse of old cannon from the scrap heaps of Europe, things made to lure small armies to their death. (I was pleased to find that neither Britain nor America had sold any of these deceitful wares, though losing some popularity by not doing so.)

In the high light remote from the modern world there was a pathos about this little army. Fifty years ago it could have marched happily to and fro with its obsolete guns in the saucer of its hills, and no one would climb to it through the steep ravines; in the age before aeroplanes, it had chased the Turks from its borders. But now—it was scarce a bomber's hour from the Fascists in Eritrea, sitting like falcons with claws already crooked for the pounce. The medieval Arab world, like the ancient world of the Beduin, has little room left to move about in: and if the troops of San'a were able to march and countermarch and kick up the dust with their bare feet every Friday morning, it was entirely due (let us be honest) to the fact that there were still a few Wellingtons in Aden hangars, and H.M. cruiser *Leander* with her 6-inch guns in the Red Sea down below. The age-old dispute of Arab governments with desert borders went on and still goes on between the Yemen and Aden

over a boundary invisible in sand; but one must admit that
if it were not for Aden, the Yemen would, some time before
the year 1940, have ceased to have a boundary at all. Italy
would have moved, with none to stop her. The peasant
soldiers, surrounding with shouts the lurching vehicle that
held their monarch, adding "May God lengthen his days"
whenever they mentioned his name, had no inkling of such
things. The Turkish officer perhaps thought about them,
riding in the press like Belisarius, aged and poor but erect,
with his bare sword held upright from his thigh before him.
He sat an old mule with drooping ears; his harness leathers
had long ago given way and were tied with lengths of string;
his uniform was a synthesis, half blue half khaki, and the cuffs
were frayed to fringes: but he sat rocklike, with a dignity
oblivious of dress, too proud even to glance at what—to his
military mind—was riff-raff swept before him. He too was
the medieval world, going down beneath a modern horizon.

The old King in his high-wheeled cab, swaying over the
hardened ruts in silver and green brocade, with a bearded
son or two overflowing on the box-seat before him, may also
have thought of such things. As he drove through his gates
at the end of the dusty morning his people gathered round
him; they came from their Friday prayers with fresh white
turbans and gowns striped black and yellow, whose ample
sleeves almost swept the streets as they walked. The cavalry
crash before and behind him through the gate in a chaos of
untrained horses, snorting and rearing; the old King drives
to his palace, vanishes through the dark doors studded with
great nails, and reappears at a window to watch his troops
go by. Among these figures, marching more buoyantly than
any flesh and blood, he sees no doubt the days of his
youth and his manhood, the skirmishes and sallies and hard
long marches in the hills, and friendly villagers and ambushed
foreign soldiers.

Now, in 1940, he is seventy-six years old; sitting like a
prophet at his balcony, with a beard that flows over his breast
in silver waves; with various wives and many sons and daughters
and their children; and a land still safe from a grasping world.
In his audience every morning he is accessible to the poorest
of his subjects, and every decision is brought for his final
word. His ministers are about him for advice; his sons are

25

governors here and there; if there is wine-drinking or any
anti-theological looseness, he can put them and keep them in
prison (his favourite wife wore mourning in his presence for
three years, weeping and beseeching, before two erring princes
were released). Yet he is spoken of with love and a great
respect in the palaces of many of his children. Strangers in
the land are his guests, for none can come up without leave,
and it is rarely granted; and when they do come they are
lodged, and served and fed from the royal kitchens for three
days or more according to their favour, and given a guard
of soldiers who see to it that they never move alone.

In this religious fastness of medieval Arabia, pictures and
toys are forbidden that show the human form; they would
be confiscated by the customs in Hodeidah. A gramophone is
matter for diplomatic correspondence, and allowed only after
long discussion; and the young British doctor had left his violin
behind him, having been told that it was an instrument too
frivolous to bring.

Yet the West makes its way. There was electric light of
a pale sort in the palace, and an arsenal where a Danish
engineer tried to manufacture cannon which, fortunately or
unfortunately, burst. Though without cafés or radio or music
in public places, there was quiet gaiety here and there; the
ladies danced among themselves in their harems (unobtrusively) and the great families who enjoyed the royal favour
were allowed a wireless to listen to the news. And hospitals,
which are a medieval tradition and welcomed in Arabia, had
come with strange matters in their train. They were for one
thing the chief vehicles of Fascist propaganda and had settled
Italian doctors in strategic places, at Ta'iz the capital of the
south, and Hodeidah, landing ground of the Tihama. In
San'a itself they established a medical mission of a dozen
people or more, the largest foreign colony in the town.
Technicians, engineers, and such non-medical stuff were among
them. The hospital itself was a new building, bleakly placed
outside the town, and its smaller and shabbier half was run
by the British; in 1940, neutrality wearing thin, Italian doctors
would cast their dying patients into the British wards, and
go about the town talking of the death-rate among their rivals.
The British staff was small, Christian, and urged to conciliate
at all costs; it went to the Fascist tea parties (where there

26

was also the only good tennis court) and tried the hopeless task of persuading Arabs that medicine alone is the business of medical missions. The Yemen, which only heard Italian news and anyway does not believe in discarding from weakness, thought Democracy was losing the war.

Into this antique atmosphere, like a new weapon of iron into the bronze age, I came in February 1940 with a portable cinema packed among my clothes.

CHAPTER VI

PICTURES IN SAN'A

" The British, though redoubtable fighters, were deeply impregnated by a desire to live at peace and by a belief that wars were always caused by foreigners."

(A. BRYANT: *English Saga.*)

"You cannot win, you know," said Raghib Bey, the Foreign Minister, regretfully. He sat on a *kilim* under my almond tree, with his two wives and myself around him, like the modern version of a Persian miniature.

"Britain," he continued, "has always won wars because she held the sea and had useful friends on dry land. Now she has the sea; but she has *no* friends on land. It is a pity; she must lose."

Raghib Bey is an agreeable old man, his short beard trim and white. His eyes are very blue, his turban and white gown and discreetly embroidered over-gown are freshly laundered; his elder and beloved wife is one of the gentlest women in existence, and the younger one is rosy and devoted to them both. He is a Turk, and in his young days had been a diplomat in Rome, Vienna and St. Petersburg; now, strangely brought by his fates to this high medieval land, with his daughter married to one of the King's sons, and the echoes of Europe eddying among the fortress walls as in a vacuum, he still keeps his urbane ways of the world, and if he thinks nostalgically of the boulevards of Europe, there is nothing to show it in his clear unwrinkled face and easy conversation.

He had been a happy young man in Italy and liked the Italians, who were also the most amusing people to meet socially in San'a. On the other hand they were obviously preparing to invade at any moment, whenever Britain might be too busy to intervene. I was their natural enemy, but the Imam liked my coming; he had accepted me when journalists and diplomats were discouraged, and had arranged help and hospitality over all the stages of the journey, where the Ford

28

van bumped and tilted for six days over tracks meant for camels. A telephone wire lurched across hill and plain, looped over dead branches which are walled into small cairns of stones; and it had carried the royal command of welcome. Only once had we collapsed (in a malarial valley where a hyena plodded before us in the dusk). Something gave out in the long-suffering axle, and my Somali driver, his two aides, my Yemeni cook and Syrian servant had all spent the night hammering at it by the light of a lantern, while I slept under an overhanging rock. This was the only good road of the country, built inland from the coast by Mr. Twitchell, an American; he designed it with a number of curves which the road builders omitted, so that its steepness must be seen to be believed. It carries one eight thousand feet from sea level to the plateau, in twenty-four hours if one is lucky. Having over-come all this, I was met at a half-way village on the tilled upland plain; given lunch and rested and brought to where the city's mud walls and rounded buttresses shone red in the sunset with minarets like candles behind them.

I found waiting for me a small house among gardens in the Turkish suburb. An order had been given, and the owner —an old Turkish lady—vacated it for my visit, and called on me with forgiving friendliness next day.

For ten days after my arrival I had been fed from His Majesty's own kitchen—a week above the time which Arab etiquette requires, so that I could consider myself cordially welcomed. And a guard of three soldiers smoked and chewed their *kat* in the vaulted room at the base of my stairs. They sprawled to the salute when I climbed through them to a dining-room and bedroom where my camp bed was settled; I climbed again steeply into a gay and tiny boudoir decorated with red and white chairs and sofas all ranged against the walls. Each had a three-legged black stand beside it to hold cigarettes and coffee. The windows fluttered with white calico curtains against Gothic decorations filled in with coloured glass. They were small, and touched the floor, so that it was pleasant to sit low on cushions, and see the flowering almond tree and cypress of the garden, and the sloping run-way where a donkey and its harness trotted creaking up and down to fill with splashing skinfuls of water the runnel that irrigated wallflowers and roses, black and white bean flowers and lettuce and wheat beyond. Then came a mud wall, tawny and warm, and a dusty road and other gardens shut in by the city wall; and then the open plain with silvery hills, delicate as the background of a Bellini picture. And from the terrace beside my boudoir, or from the flat roof above it, one could see the city itself, the Arab town with fortress houses decorated fantastically like black cakes with bands and scrolls of stucco icing, and Jebel Nuqum, a many-coloured hill where the royal arms and treasure were said to be kept in secret places; and on the other side the suburb of the Jews, where they live in low and unassuming houses, and are closed in by their gates at 9 p.m., and wear foreheads shaven and corkscrew curls in front of each ear, framing their oval faces and soft eyes.

I spent nearly two months here and used to visit all these houses, climbing by the ladies' entrance and many flights of dark stairs to the high sunny rooms of the harem deep in carpets, where the business of the town far below could be watched through carved lattices, and female gossip was brought in with small amber glasses of tea. Here I constantly met the Italian lady doctor, whose smile grew more and more acid as our diplomatic war unrolled in the shadows of a larger world. The Fascists held most of the cards at that time; they were in force and, as all thought, on the winning side; and many leading people were bribed. As I began to be in their way, two ministers did their best to have me restored to the Aden lowland from which I came. But on my side was the fact that the Fascists were personally disliked in spite, or perhaps because of, their domineering ways. Bribery, I am convinced, is the poorest way to the Arab heart and counts for very little in a crisis among people whose typical and sensible point of view is that of the judge who used to take money from both sides and, when the case was settled, restore what had come from the loser.

The Imam, I believe, delighted to see a threatening influence counteracted with no intervention of his own. I never spoke to him; such honour is not for mere women; but my cook could attend his audience every morning, and could answer questions about my health and comfort, and take little notes which I would write—instructed by the Chamberlain—on the lower half of a sheet of paper so that the royal answer and signature could be added above my own; this was always instantly done, in courteous words, in red ink to symbolize the pre-Islamic ancient descent of the royal house of Himyar (the root-meaning of Himyar is *red*), and with gentleness and kindness His Majesty the Imam resisted all effort to remove me. The modern world was with me because of the cinema.

I mentioned its existence casually on my first visit to the Foreign Minister's wife.

"A cinema?" she said. "A cinema in San'a? We *must* see it."

"Nothing would delight me more," I replied. "But as a guest I can do nothing to annoy His Majesty the Imam and his permission will have to be asked."

"I will talk to the Queen," said the Foreign Minister's wife.

I felt quietly confident in the power of unemancipated women to get their way, and in a very few days was asked to give a private performance to the palace ladies. There is no doubt that women boxed up in houses are *much* more powerful than those of us who roam about outside.

After this my life was altered.

I still spent the day either in the female quarters built like rooks' nests into the tops of the fortress houses, or in my own boudoir on a cushion by the window, embroidering and listening to the Fascist Saga as it came to be unrolled piece by piece by an assortment of visitors who gradually increased in numbers. The Chamberlain, with brown beard and gentle inscrutable eyes, came to ask if I was happily settled; the old Chief of Police came, suspicious at first but friendly as he went away, his sword almost too big for my steep and narrow stairway; Sayyids came who said Allah to keep themselves from harm as they crossed a Christian threshold, or even sometimes spat; the old Preacher who read with me would come. He upheld vehemently the democracy of Islam and, regardless of consequences, thought out things to say from the pulpit in its favour; he had a face crumpled into deep folds with eyes bright and bushy embedded among them. He was a brave old man with a charming mixture of theology and Irish fighting humour, and together we started a fashion in the town and greeted every obviously false statement (of which there were many) with the opening words of the German radio: "This is Berlin." The Arabs have a quick sense of the ridiculous; they were delighted with so delicate a way of pointing false-hood out. The time came when the head of the Fascist Mission, growing more and more furious over my presence, openly insulted me, and, as he had a rather piglike profile, I translated for my old Preacher the English proverb that a silk purse cannot be made of a sow's ear; we turned it into a rhyming couplet in Arabic, and let it loose among the harems of San'a. The Italian lady doctor gave up the increasingly hard effort of saying good morning when we met.

But in the evening, as the stars came out, the cinema part of my existence began.

The private view in the royal harem was followed almost every night by a show in one or other of the chief houses of the town. Every family had to sit down to a separate per-formance, since the men of one family could not mix with the women of another, and all wanted to see; and this necessi-tated a fresh royal permission every morning, and a different expedition every night.

My dinner would be over just as some elderly lady stumbled up through my guards in the basement, her head and face shrouded in thin red and black silk and covered with three other kerchiefs that secure the privacy of San'a ladies out of doors; so that they may also breathe, they wear a pair of silver bodkins studded with turquoise and coral to remove the weight a little from mouth and nose. Over all this is wrapped what looks to the uninitiated like a tablecloth of chintz with bright flowers on a black ground; only the very modern wear the Turkish city-black. Out of this bundle, when Naji the cook had safely retired, an amiable face appeared; I would wrap myself as closely as the casual West allows, and arm-in-arm we would go through the starlit garden to where some antique vehicle stood waiting in the dust. The cinema, with screen and engine, were packed inside, and Naji by the coach-man on the box. The lights were out already in the town, or shrouded behind their shutters and their walls. We crossed the *maidan*, a white vague expanse hemmed with darkness, and came to where the gate of the Arab city broods in its pool of shadow and the voice of the sentry challenges as you go. Fantastic houses rise to the faint light of the night that shines on their upper storeys; down the centre of the street wind the unsavoury gutters, and dust hides the ruts and deadens the horses' hooves. Sleeping, curled here and there at random, lie dogs enjoying their brief peace from the Eastern enmity of men; they cringe and snarl at the disturbing wheels. Here and there a faint oil-wick glimmers at some corner or moves, held on a pole by a watchman. "Whence are you and where going?" he challenges: Naji explains: "Peace be upon you," they say. There is no minding one's own business, in San'a.

When we reach the house we do not seek the decorated entrance, but stop at a small harem doorway in whose darkness ajar a maid or a slave girl is holding her braceleted hand out-stretched to guide us stumbling in.

Naji the cook remains below, with the gasoline engine on which the show depends. When we have climbed several storeys to the room where the ladies are, I let the flex down to him through an arabesque in the carved lattice window and unite past and present by this mechanical thread.

I myself am happiest when dealing with the medieval side of things, and the threading of the film, setting up of screen, remembering what results—all different but all explosive—follow the turning on of switches, is a harassing affair made no easier by women and children flitting like butterflies about me, with draperies so many and voluminous that everything gets lost or entangled. I have, too, a feminine mistrust of machinery and feel morally certain every evening, in spite of all the evidence, that when Naji turns that handle in the darkness down below *nothing will happen.*

It always does happen. The ladies and men are finally seated on rugs and cushions round three sides of the room. (There are few men and many ladies and it makes me think of the military dictum that it takes twenty-six in the rear to keep one fighting soldier in battle.)

Anyway, we are off. My cinema is very innocent: it only possesses three news-reels, one for the Army, one for the Navy, and one for the Air Force, and they still keep carefully clear of the grimmer side of war; anything so basic as a dead soldier is not to be shown for months to come. I also have two of those pictures which the Ministry of Information in its early days thought helpful to British prestige—Sheep-farming in Yorkshire and Ordinary Life in Edinburgh. I rather think the sheep farming seemed silly to the Yemenis, who look upon it

33

as a dull and obvious thing one does without unnecessary fuss for the sake of a living; but the ladies were entranced by Ordinary Life in Edinburgh, and I would snap it back on its reel amid applause, thinking that "one never can tell".

But the war pictures, poor as they were, caused a small revolution in the feelings of the town. For six months we had been at war with no particular news and the Fascists and the Berlin radio had found it easy to persuade the people of Yemen that British arms had vanished from land and earth and sky. And here were tanks making straight for the audience, aeroplanes dropping bombs as carefully as a salmon lays eggs, and battleships, *Nelson* and *Rodney*, swinging their huge turrets, ploughing with caps of sea foam their first way down these dark medieval streets. Through the microphone, in Arabic, I told the story; and turned on the sound track when we came to bombs or guns, so that my audience might enjoy the noise of the explosions.

When the show was ended, the children of the house were given a turn at the microphone to say good evening to their friends. I packed up. We sat a little while and revised the European situation over sweetmeats and glasses of tea. The ladies, brightly decorated, friendly, sprightly, and gay in spite of their seclusion, clustered about me; my elder chaperon began to involve herself in the many wrappings of the outer world; and we trundled back as we came, through streets even more dark, more silent, more deserted, over which the Southern Cross reigned with a light softened, it seemed, by the unplumbed gentle oceans of air through which it shone.

CHAPTER VII

GOVERNMENT OF THE OLD SCHOOL

" Vitamque sub divo et trepidis agat in rebus."
(HORACE III, 2-5.)

SIR BERNARD REILLY, our Governor, and his Political Secretary Colonel Morice Lake, were, I think, the two people most beloved by the Arabs among the British of Aden.

Both of them had come to the country as young men, in the Indian political service and in the army, shortly before the first world war. And they had spent their lives here with short intervals ever since, Sir Bernard being the last Resident under the Bombay Government, 1931–32, the first and only Chief Commissioner under the Government of India in 1932, and the first Governor and C.-in-C. when Aden became a separate colony in 1937. Neither of them ever married, and they remained firm friends, Sir Bernard at the centre of government, familiar in club or on golf course and in the Secretariat office near the harbour; Morice Lake more often away among the tribes he loved in the western part of the Protectorate, following tracks that in many cases no Western man has travelled before or since.

When the transfer from India to the Colonial Office was made in '37, the Arab notables of Aden sent a petition asking:

(1) That the port remain free;
(2) That taxes in general remain unaltered if not lowered;
(3) That laws and local rules remain as they are;
(4) That the rights of the people remain and . . . the people to have a prior right to government posts and appointments, etc. . . ."

And they said in conclusion: "We have confidence in our Governor, Colonel Reilly, *as we consider him to be one of us.* If he remained for ever a Governor of Aden, we would accept any Government without reservations; but alas he will have to go from Aden one day."

Such a document is pleasant to remember, for slap-dash

35

criticism is often levelled at colonial officials; like parents, they are easy targets. As with parents, too, one is apt to forget the long and tiresome annals of childhood filled with mumps and measles and the unending solicitude that helps the young to grow. One sees the strapping youth beside his elders, and the solicitude has become fussiness, and the parental mind is perhaps not so elastic as it once was to foster and give wings to young imaginations; the young imaginations in fact have got wings of their own, and the older eye sees with misgiving that in colour and plumage they are no longer of the texture which once bore him sailing into an earlier morning from his own parental home. If the young are clamorous, the parents must hand over a latchkey—but nobody attributes to mere *wickedness* their hesitations and delays.

Not so your colonial officers. If you believe the words of casual reporters, all they ever do comes from the blackness of their hearts. But the fact of the matter is that your colonial officer has the task of a parent multiplied a hundredfold— the task of an *adopted* parent who has no family likeness to help him. Adoption in the first place may or may not have been justified; fortresses like Aden, or Bermuda for that matter, are destined sooner or later for adoption by the inherent inequalities of things; that, anyway, has not been the affair of the colonial official. He does not take up the burden, but he has to see that it is faithfully borne, and in doing so has to wrestle not only with the character of the child itself, but with the voices of all its relations, from Philanthropy to Big Business, many of them influential and most of them wrong. If he were an angel from heaven, he could not please them all; but he is an average human being, striving to fit a foreign civilization on to limbs never disciplined to such restrictive garments. And if he is a British official, he comes from a tiny plot which has spread the Idea of itself, at one time or another, over a good part of the habitable earth; the grown-up children are self-supporting with families of their own;—they have no central obligation, except in time of war (and then only voluntarily): the colonial official deals only with the young ones, and the parental income is necessarily divided into small morsels to feed so many mouths. They are mostly poor or backward places (otherwise they would be well on the way to cease from being colonies); and every school, road, water-supply or other public work must either be cajoled from the parent chest or achieved out of local resources.

This is the task of the colonial official; and if we want to criticize him we may do so, I think, more for the lack than for the activity of his interference. In the time behind him, more roads and schools and suchlike things could well have been produced, and British administrations certainly can be blamed rather for being lethargic than domineering. But even so it is well to remember that all is not wickedness. What the outraged and reforming reporter so often forgets, is the fact that the colonial official *is fond of his people as they are.* He has come among them as a young man, transferred from district to district but always sitting behind some desk—shiny in an office or shabby in some outpost—listening to their most intimate troubles, feuds and affairs. He is not married at this time, so that no family distracts him from feeling himself a part of them all and to him they are not People, oppressed or otherwise; they are Tom and Dick, Muhammad or Ahmed. His slowness is not only lethargy (and the frequent lack of funds), but also the fact that he has come to see good in a civilization other than his own; the fitting of the Western garment—necessary since the whole trend of the world is with it and the colony itself asks for it with no uncertain voice—is to him rather like the cutting of her boy's locks is to a mother; he does it with the same reluctance, and with the same regret for what the progressive shears must snip away. This is perhaps unreasonable, and so are the mother's feelings, and the young are right to struggle away from it all and pull on the leash as hard as they can; but let us see it for what it is, a natural divergence inherent in everything that grows, a part of the transitory nature of the universe, and not an original sin peculiar to colonial officials.

In Aden there was some of this divergence, as there must be wherever ancient and modern live cheek by jowl as they do in most of the Arabian lands. But the lawyer in Crater and the tribesman of the border united in loving Sir Bernard Reilly.

For one thing they had known him a very long time, as a young man in 1912, and as their Resident or Governor since 1931. He had been with them when the Turks in the world war reached Lahej, and even the suburb village of Shaikh Othman; he had been a prisoner with the mission that in 1919 went up to the Yemen from Hodeidah and was captured by the Quhra tribe and held four months in the small naked fort of Bajil at the entry to the hills; he had seen the R.A.F. come to Aden and alter the face of government by opening the roadless mountains of the tribes, and had seen them rescue our small ally of Dhala from the conquest of Yemen; and in 1934 he had negotiated a treaty with that country, and watched the caravan routes gradually re-open, and had held one hundred and ten thousand miles and about six hundred thousand people of the wild Protectorate with a loose rein (having at that time only one secretary and one political officer with which to hold them).

When I first met him in 1934 he was middle-aged, small, plump and dignified—a natural dignity that came from some sterling resolute quality within him, for no governor was ever more easy, friendly and democratic. He had a great fund of European history stored in his mind, as well as the annals of Aden and all the Red Sea gossip; and would tell an amusing story with a sudden solemnity of manner and slight lowering of voice, his eyes watching with a round serious expression while you took it in, oddly engaging. To the desiccated waste where a low and rather shabby Government House is perched on a rib of the extinct volcano, he imported a love of his boyhood, an expert enthusiasm for locomotives; he knew every type of engine on every railway in Britain and possessed little models with which anyone might be tempted to play; and I think it was this disinterested enjoyment of something which could never be of the slightest use (for nothing can be more abstract than railways in Aden), which first drew me to him with a sort of fellow feeling—for what is an artist if not someone who takes such non-utilitarian pleasure in the odd and incongruous objects of the world for their own sake alone?

Colonel Lake was different, dark and lean, shy, sensitive, and solitary; the first time I met him at dinner I never lured him beyond the monosyallabic yes, and I think he was happier with the tribesmen he had known and walked and ridden among for so many years, and trained and turned from wild recruits into smart soldiers, than he was among his own people. He was not clever, and made cleverness seem a minor thing in life. He had a confidence in the natural gentlemanliness of human beings which no amount of experience ever eradicated;

when he found his belief misplaced, he turned with loathing from what most people take to be quite a natural occurrence. He was disinterested and generous; compassion, tender and ready as a girl's for any sort of sorrow, kept young the shy and secret springs that fed his being. When he was about to retire on £700 a year after a life of honours and of service, he told me once that perhaps he ought to have thought more about money; "but," he added quickly, "I might not then have had the life I liked."

No one knew, as he did, the wildest of the tribes, or loved them better or was more trusted by them. The country a hundred miles or more east of Aden is among the most primitive in Arabia, a volcanic country of unvisited hills. Here in the autumn of 1939 a British aircraft force-landed; the three fliers knew no Arabic in which to explain themselves, and the hillmen crept up and shot them. There were no troops to spare then for a police expedition, even if those remote and ambushed gorges could have been reached. Colonel Lake walked with his Arab servant to meet the tribesmen at a rendezvous unknown to any map, and brought away by persuasion alone the punishment fine in bags of silver dollars, and sheaves of rifles carried before him to his ship—a sailing dhow from Aden.

When I arrived the three airmen were being buried. Our small colony gathered in one of the cemeteries that lie at the foot of the cliffs of lava, between Crater and the new town. There in the distance the little procession with pipes crying came under the bright sun, three coffins with the Union Jack upon them, the Army in khaki, the Navy in white, the Aden Levies smart under folded turbans, the new Government Guards like colts first wearing harness, their tousled hair, indigo-dyed faces, and black uniform exotic in the European ranks. There came Sir Bernard alone in white—white feathers fluttering round the spike of his helmet (which he carried, when inside a car, for the bad roads outside Aden were liable to jam the spike into the ceiling.) There came the Padre, his stole flapping in the wind. They walked from the point on the road where all funeral processions have dismounted since the first burials here. Carried by the wind, the thin wail of the pipes and the dead march from the drums beat muted against the immense cliff wall. The little pageant seemed wonderfully small. And the meaning of such pomps was suddenly clear to me—a meaning

39

not made for nor understood by those who live far from the shadow of death, comfortable lives in prosperous lands; but something found in the difficult dark ages of the world to show that the symbol is greater than visible substance, is indeed triumphant over death and space and time.

Unhappy the land that has no symbols, or that chooses their meaning without great care.

It was right, I felt, that our Governor should carry out with such punctilious reverence the honoured etiquette of death, and by so doing stand for a reality with which neither the stray bullet of an enemy nor accidents of human beings can interfere. And when the time comes, the real thing will blossom from its symbol inevitably, like a flower from its sheath.

The time did come, and very soon. On June 10th, 1940, Italy declared war.

Through the spring days before that, the barbed wire thickened on the beaches, annoying Colonel Lake who said it interfered with walking; the searchlights grew accurate as night after night they played and practised and spanned like fencing green blades the wide black-rimmed expanses of the bay. Our Senior Officer, Air Vice Marshal Reid, took the fortress defences in hand. A few troops arrived, Mahrattas and Punjabis, the Black Watch and some heavy artillery,[1] a battalion of each, against the Italian Empire, for the defence of Somaliland across the water. The countries of Europe were falling one by one; and soon the Italian raiders were upon us, scudding high among the clouds through the moonlit nights; and the black-out was dark as the primeval darkness of our volcano, so that I would have to grope my way among the crowd of sailors to find the inn where I dined, and knock on its shuttered door, and hear the Arab doorkeeper inside ask: "Who is there?"

"Open, oh doorkeeper."

"Welcome, and peace."

A tiny crack followed, and I slipped in, to where punkahs still swung their old-fashioned fringes above the dingy tables and men sat in uniforms unfastened at the neck.

The troops left, and soon Somaliland fell; the French had

[1] The 2/5 Mahratta Light Infantry, 1/2 and 3/15 Punjabis, Bikaneer Camel Corps, Aden Protectorate Levies, two Heavy Artillery Regiments, and (for a very short time) the 2nd Black Watch formed the Aden Garrison.

collapsed in Jibouti and the promontory of East Africa was impossible to hold. In the retreat from Berbera we lost two guns, our papers said, and did not mention the fact that we had altogether only four to lose.[1] The Black Watch charged uphill over the rough African ground a mile and a quarter and drove back eight times its own number of men and covered the retreat; and they were all back again in Aden, dusty and tired, and soon sent off to fill the Egyptian gap. We remained, with our Arabian Levies, and our Air Force—five squadrons of old-fashioned machines against two to three hundred on the opposing side; but they went out to the attack every morning, and no Italian guessed how few they were; and our biplane fighter Gladiators which are now museum pieces tackled the big Savoias when they came.

Ships had to be provided for all who wished to leave, and the quayside was one continual chaos of bundles and families and wails. Food had to be secured, for the Navy in those uncertain weeks could not promise to hold the shipping lanes, and Aden has nothing self-supporting on its barren sides.

In the hot sun, with a heavy heart, I went up to see Sir Bernard in the first few days after France had fallen. He told me with a quiet satisfaction that he thought our food would arrive even if the Navy could not help us: he had bought two ships to run the gauntlet of the submarines and keep us supplied. He was also cheered by the fact that the Aden colony had sent a deputation to say they would all agree to be buried in the same graves after air-raids: with so many mixed rites and religions, this saved a great deal of labour.

As I came down, past the Arabian sentry by the ornamental brass gun, who smiled at me with an amiability probably not allowed by regulations, I turned in to see Colonel Lake in his bungalow.

"What does it look like?" said I.

Colonel Lake deliberated; he always took some time to answer.

"It's not as bad as nineteen-fourteen," he said at last.

I came away still with the strange feeling that we were probably going to be annihilated; but with a staunchness added to my courage that was not really mine.

And when the raiders came that night just as the dawn

[1] The 1st East African Light Battery—four 3.7 howitzers.

was breaking, and our old house swayed with the explosions, so that I lay flat on the terrace to watch the magnificence of the harbour lit with guns—I happened to turn my head and saw my Arab servant, steadying himself as he came towards me in the clamour with my early tea on a tray. There was nothing wrong with the morale of Governor or governed in Aden.

CHAPTER VIII

THE RED SEA

" There is a wilderness we walk alone
However well-companioned, and a place
Where the dry wind blows over the dry bone
And sunlight is a devil in the face,
The sandstorm and the empty water hole
And the dead body, driven by its soul."
(St. Vincent Benét: *Western Star.*)

THERE is a family feeling about the Red Sea whatever nation may happen to own this or that stretch of its flat shores. When I close my eyes I can see it, as from the air, a rag of blue with green and turquoise coral-reef shallows surrounded by the bleached monotony of sand, and carrying in small clusters uninhabited islands empty and brown and ridged like veined dead leaves that float upon a pond.

What great varieties of life are woven into so simple and similar a background, its chief ingredients heat and the absence of water. There is Hes, just north of Mocha, a gathering of huts scarce visible so like are they to the earth which built them, and in their midst the square five-storied tower where their elderly Governor lives. I spent a night there on my way through Yemen, and sat in his harem on a blue velvet sofa, listening to stories as he sucked at a hookah whose long coils, encased in crochet lace, stretched half across the floor. His ladies were away, and the tower seemed deserted except for one bowed grey crone who brought our supper; outside, far below the thick-walled fortress windows, the sand-dunes stretched into the night. The Governor left me to a four-post bed piled high with quilts and satin pillows, and woke me in the middle darkness in a far from reassuring way with a musical box played close into my ear; he feared, he said, that I might feel lonely.

There are the towns of Zabid, and Beit al-Faqih, just north of Hes, entombed and languid in the fierce heat of Tihama, their medieval richness still shown by delicate scrolls of brick-work, their people dark and half-naked with long conical dunce-hats of straw upon their curls. And north of them again is Hodeidah, with dhows aslant in the roadstead and spars against the sea like fine black veins in the matrix of a turquoise. Here houses with carved lattices look down on silent streets of sand, the sea-air blows hot and salt into darkened rooms, the women wear long bright skirts and embroidered boleros over naked breasts; in the dim store-houses where coffees and skins from Yemen are piled for export, the Greek or British agent sits with a towel under his arm to mop the perspiration when he writes. There were two Englishmen, four Greeks, and two Italians when I was in Hodeidah; they waged the world war in the morning against each other in the Yemeni courts; but, being so few and so isolated, played bridge and liked each other through afternoon and evening.

There, off the shore of Yemen, is Kamaran island, also low and brown, but with the quarantine station for the Mekka pilgrimage upon it, and Major Thompson running it all with benevolent autocracy pin-pricked by the Italian doctor; both he and the doctor are asking for a cinema and the Major fears the Fascist cinema may get there first.€ When his letter arrives, Stewart Perowne is away, but I offer on his behalf to try and arrange an accident for the Italian cinema when it comes to be trans-shipped in Aden harbour; the war intervenes, and Major Thompson becomes very remote on his island, a fixed target as it were for any Italian airman who likes to shoot: he carries on, however, till the Red Sea is open again.

There at the southern exit is Perim, a naked spur, with ruins of the old station upon it, dismantled as oil superseded coal. When Somaliland was abandoned, a British paper cheered us in Aden with the news that nothing need be feared in the Red Sea while Perim fortifications remained intact: at that time fifty-five policemen under a Somali Inspector lived with a tug by the lighthouse beside the crumbling ruins.

On the African side of the water is Jibouti, where one can find Parisian perfumes and a permanent wave, and a square with plants in tubs, and a café, and agreeable conversation, which all, however, turned Vichy in 1940, leaving General Legentilhomme, fiery, gallant and true to his name, to escape as best he could with British help across the border.

And north of that is Massawa, where seven ocean-going submarines ride, we know, at anchor and the channels are guarded

—we learn later—with a network of traps and mines. That coast, as we pass near it, lies mysterious and forbidding in the silence in which "enemy territory" is wrapped.

The catastrophe of those Fascist submarines is worth recording, for it brought a beam of brightness into our summer of 1940.

It happened in June, when already they had sunk the first ship outside the bay of Aden; we saw it burning for days with a column of black oily smoke. Our destroyers, nosing about, had flung depth charges and damaged the enemy where he lay hiding on the floor of the sea, and—at what he thought a quiet moment—he came to the surface. Nothing was in sight except a small trawler, turned into a minesweeper; it was called *Moonstone* and was close by; it had a very small gun which it trained on the submarine's conning tower, then fired almost point blank, and tore a jagged hole, killing thirteen officers and men: the submarine surrendered, and came with the little *Moonstone* into harbour, the White Ensign at its mast above the Italian flag. It was cheered by the people of Aden at their windows and balconies and by all the assembled warships. Of the enemy officers, only one lieutenant remained uninjured; and he no doubt knew little of what secret documents might be carried on board.

As I knew Italian, I was invited to breakfast in the Admiral's flagship *Leander* to take a look at the papers; they were then brought to me and I began to translate the "operational orders" which had ended so sadly for our captive. Presently I saw that these orders continued; they specified the immediate future plans and locations of two more of Massawa's seven submarines: and they gave us two or three days in which to act. I wrote with a hand unsteady with excitement while Stewart telephoned Admiral Arthur Murray; in a few minutes his Secretary came once more and carried the news away. We watched our destroyers in the harbour begin to raise steam; in less than an hour they were moving out to sea; and at the appointed time the Fascist submarines were found and defeated, one near Jibouti, the other far eastward, off Oman. One of them put up a long and gallant fight of nearly an hour, shooting back at our destroyers and sinking at last.[1]

[1] The commander of this submarine has now written begging to be released from prison "to fight our common enemy".

Aden, hard put to it to accommodate such a crowd, received most of the survivors; and their interrogation took many days. They were friendly enough, and only about one-third of their number were Fascists at heart, while another third disliked Mussolini altogether. I used to interpret their answers and, with the provost-marshal's consent, would take down pencils and paper beforehand and help them to get letters away to their homes and would hear wistful descriptions of the streets or courts, stoneflagged or cobbled, in Venice or Trieste or Bari, Genoa or Livorno, where they lived. I found that this preliminary made the interrogations much easier and more effective, whatever the regulations about prisoners may say.

In July, resistance in Aden settled down, and the Fascists appeared to have relinquished any idea of an eastward invasion. Night-raids diminished, and the harbour was rarely lit by the lights and dark shadows of battle when the warships illuminated each other with every shock of their great guns and the houses of the Crescent swayed like rushes in a wind. In the early part of the month a first small convoy was sent creeping up the Red Sea to Suez past the Italian shores, seven tankers escorted by destroyers and other vessels, in one of which, a converted merchantman loaded with ammunition, I was given a passage. I reached Egypt battened down and in great heat but undisturbed by the enemy. Here I was asked to transfer myself to the Embassy, was delighted by being sent back to settle my affairs in Aden in a Blenheim bomber (a very exclusive way of travel for a woman at that time), and finally set out once more for the Red Sea in the smallest of vessels, M. Besse's *Amin*, smaller even than the ship in which I had arrived ten months before.

In the dawn we joined a convoy, vague superstructures scattered far and near on the wide breast of the water in the half light that gave no horizon. They had come to the rendezvous across the Indian Ocean. We hardly saw them as we travelled all day parallel to the coast of Arabia; but in the trough of the Red Sea we came together, and were forty-seven ships, with troops and stores for Egypt, and we sailed on a flat quiet sea. The wings of an Aden Wellington would flicker a sudden shadow above us, and the Italian coasts came in sight on our port side.

Nothing happened till the third morning and then, like some

fore-runner of fate, an Italian reconnaissance craft flew out and turned back into the morning sun. The skipper, joining me at breakfast a little later, said he thought we should be attacked in three hours or so. The mate, our only other European ship's officer, never came to meals at all, for he had arrived on board hugging in his arms a new toy presented by the Government, a Lewis gun, and spent his time like a mother with her first child, brooding over it to learn its ways.

Our only passengers apart from myself were one British and two Indian officers with a signal company of Sikhs, tall men who spent much time like the Lacedæmonians, combing out their long hair, serious and silent. They were now smiling, and laid themselves out flat in a circle with their rifles among the sandbags, in whose midst, on our cabin roof, the precious gun was installed with the mate kneeling beside her, like some oracle with its priest in attendance, who alone can make it speak.

The skipper stood on the tiny bridge below, obeying orders as they flashed from *Leander*, our cruiser in the van. He suggested that I had better take cover in the cabin, purely as a matter of form, and so I disregarded it. On the smooth sea, gay in the morning sunlight, the varied convoy ploughed its way as if in lines of traffic; we came to have a feeling of affectionate comradeship for the ships immediately ahead or astern, whose movements had to harmonize with ours. The destroyers on our flanks swept about us, sharp-snouted as swordfish, and the sea banked in a green wall behind them, after the hissing foam. And now the raiders came, flying very high, ten thousand feet or more, deep in the gulfs of the sky; it seemed to wash over and hide them with its thin blue waves. They came like gods of the Iliad into battle, swift and unattainable, and huge cones of water leaped from their bombs around our cruiser, as high as the masts above her funnel, and the quiet, secret, sunny depths of the sea were wrenched and stunned with explosions, Poseidon, that slow god, attacked in his realm.

Then I saw the most majestic sight that anyone could witness, for *Leander* answered with all her guns. The great ship was wrapped in a single garment of flame yellow and shining in the sun; so must Athene with her shield have appeared in the forefront of battle. We mortals in the convoy watched and took no part (except for the Lewis gun,

47

which was shooting happily into the sky for its own pleasure and that of the mate, its range thousands of feet below the attackers' track).

Now the cloud came down that the gods can use—a white film of cloud that coiled and hid the raiders, and no doubt carried them back to whatever Olympus in Eritrea the Italian air force could attain; and our convoy, which had obeyed the order to scatter, swiftly gathered itself again together, and in the course of the day reached Port Sudan, where another air raid was in progress, with incendiaries like small flaming umbrellas opening all along the sea-front as we approached.

Port Sudan is another of these Red Sea harbours where the modern life of the West comes to nibble at ancient continents of Africa or Asia with fangs imperceptible against the immemorial background, but very tenacious: where once they have bitten, they rarely let go. Steel cranes were lifting heavy cases, vehicles and explosives, and, when raiders came over, people waited for their departure in trenches which Mr. Springfield, the pleasant and enthusiastic Governor, had induced the military to dig in strategic places, so that avenues of trees could later be planted at small expense, when our blades are turned to ploughshares once again.

Meanwhile he had not even a searchlight, far less a gun of any size, to deal with the invaders. Port Sudan relied, he told me cheerfully, on "the black-out" for its defence. Its fighter aircraft, poised like dragonflies dispersed among the sand dunes, had so practised speed that they could rise in fifty-six seconds from the ground when a raiders' signal came.

Colonel, now Brigadier, John Marriott was here, already preparing the end of the defensive and the opening of attack. But he took a day off while the transports were unloading, and we left our modern preoccupations and all their bustle and danger, and drove by sandy tracks through empty landscape, brown scrub between the mountains and the sea, to Suakin, mirrored in its estuary, a city of dead merchants, whose houses stand on white powdered coral in deserted streets, disintegrating in the sun.

Here too hovers the memory of Kitchener, who in 1886 was for two years governor at Suakin, in a world incredibly remote to-day, an easier world where Victorian values carried by the West were not in themselves so hardly compatible as those we have to reconcile to-day.

The ghosts of the merchants, and that of the young man who loved his remote people and dreamed his dreams here, still hang about the dusty rooms where he lived. The broad verandah, shabby but cool, leans over the estuary, and small *huris*, invisible under a triangular sail, flit in and out to sea. From the balustrade you look down into deep water and see the tiny fish that glitter, many-coloured, like jewels, and browse their short lives away among the streamers of the sea-weed and intricacies of coral; and Time, which has devoured the merchants, and Lord Kitchener, and the infinite crowds of men and fishes, and is now rocking the Italian raiders up and down above us before casting them for ever out of these dawns and sunsets—ceases to be, and only Something remains in our heart, which is behind all the generations of this world. So, drenched in memory and forgetfulness we return from Suakin, and I climb in the evening train to Atbara and the valley of the Nile; and in blasts of heat that beat from its rocky sides as from a furnace, sail down from Wadi Halfa, moored to the banks at night because the river is now unlighted: past the empty gigantic eyes of Abu Simbel, past Phylæ, in whose temple courts one can walk in the summer lowness of the river—where army lorries near by are detraining; and down through the night to Cairo and the Mediterranean world.

PART II

EGYPT

CHAPTER IX

YOUNG EGYPTIANS

" No blazoned banners we unfold—
One charge alone we give to youth,
Against the sceptred myth to hold
The golden heresy of truth."
(J. W. RUSSELL.)

In a country where there is no poverty it is natural not to be a snob; it is equally so in a country where all are poor together: but where the inequalities are such that no rich man can look upon them without feeling an uneasiness at heart, he usually prefers not to look at all, and to forget that there is any other world beside his own. This may be said in a superlative way of many Egyptian Pashas.

For a long time it was largely true that the Arabian world was divided between the Pashas and the Poor (apart from the Nomads, whose ideas on Equality I have spoken of already). And though Egypt is in many ways not typical of the rest of the Arab world, yet it shares its religion and its language, and is the chief centre of its culture; and the difference between the Pashas and the Poor has always, I imagine, been more pronounced here than elsewhere, and has remained so to this day.

In Egypt, as in all the lands of the Arabs, the twentieth century has produced two artisans of evolution—the internal combustion engine and the middle class; and while the former is chiefly at work across the empty spaces of Arabia proper, in Egypt we may, I think, look upon the young professional as the principal agent of change.

For the Pasha of the old days, sitting like a Buddha with chins on the platform of his revenues, not much can be said

to-day; the good he has done can be "interred with his bones";
indeed most of it was not done by him at all, but was accomplished much against his will in an uphill battle waged by
foreign officials in years gone by, and very much was done,
less than eighty years ago, by Lucie Duff Gordon, fragile and
dying in Luxor among the Egyptian Arabs who so loved her
that they offered her a burial among the holy ones of their
own Muslim dead. One may read her letters to notice what
a beneficent change has overtaken the Egyptian villager's life
even in this short time: the lifting of the corvée has done as
much for Egypt as the cessation of Turkish conscription did
for the villagers in other Arab lands.

Much remains to conquer still. The villages are riddled with
disease, and their labourers got an average of $2\frac{1}{2}$ piastres a day[1]
before the war; and the wealth of the Nile still sweeps into far
too exclusive coffers. But into the breach which administrators
from other countries held, not without honour, from Muhammad
Ali to Lord Cromer, there are now stepping young men who,
though they may look westward for inspiration, have their feet
firmly planted on the peasant soil from which they spring.

It is a very remarkable phenomenon, for it is the first time in
centuries that this country has not been governed by foreign
rulers. Like the Arabs of Palestine, the peasants of Egypt are
mostly immemorial inhabitants of their land, a product of many
mixtures, with but a thin sprinkling of the desert conquerors
among them; but the ruling Arabs through the Middle Ages
were a separate and exclusive society, followed by the more
exclusive Turks. The Copts are most like the original people
of Egypt; even now you can recognize their slender profiles
and long-lashed black eyes, opaque and lustrous, in any
Pharaoh's tomb. They still are one-fifteenth or so of the
country's population. They have kept the Christian religion
taken from earlier conquerors, but they have long since
adopted the Arabic language for ordinary conversation; and—
as they are not what is called a "pressure group"—no one
thinks of Egypt as they do of Palestine, or contemplates turning
it back to the Copts to be as it was in the days of Titus, when
his galleys sailed past Roman Alexandria towards Roman Judæa.

The skein of the Middle East in all these centuries has gathered

[1] The minimum pay now, if Government injunctions were obeyed,
would be $7\frac{1}{2}$ piastres a day.

threads of very many colours; and no return to simple black and white will ever be possible again—whether it be the dream of Fascist Rome or Zionist Jerusalem, or that British form of empire which has become obsolete during the last half-century, though we still continue to call something quite different by the same name. Amalgamation, the weaving of patterns, and not separation, must be the task of the future. It is the task which the middle-class young Egyptian is taking over from Britain, and it would be well if this relationship, built upon an identity and not on a conflict, were better understood on both sides. Perhaps it would be, if it were not that the plump silhouette of Privilege blocks the view. The professional young man is a new arrival, and it has taken both the Englishman and the Pasha some time to understand that he is here at all. He, on his side, has seen those two so long together, that he is inclined to think of them as one, which is both inaccurate and unfair—for the Englishman has long been fighting the young Egyptian's battle, wresting now this now that out of the hands of Privilege on his behalf; for many long years he has been fighting the Pasha on behalf of decent government, and now, as he sees him with the new figure of the young effendi beside him, is apt to think of the two as the same, and to feel doubt and hesitation as to what his own supersession will entail. That is how the Past gets in the way; and it is only by leaning out beyond its portly figure that the Englishman and the modern middle-class young man of the Arab world can get a clear view of each other, and become aware of the fact that their pathway is the same.

I like the young effendi of Egypt; and I met him in 1940 at a time when the British cause and that of democracy in general appeared to be at the very nadir of their fortunes. General Weygand with practically the whole army of Syria, on which the defence of the Middle East depended, had followed the Vichy misfortunes, leaving General, now Field-Marshal Lord Wavell, to hold with his few regiments the vital bridge of Europe and Asia. Graziani the Italian general was at the Western desert frontier, advancing upon it with 300,000 men; and there were 80,000 Italians, mostly Fascist, at large in Egypt itself. Their language, usually so pleasant, but ominous at that time, could be heard on any pavement as one walked. And when I settled in a flat in Zamalek, on the small arm of the Nile where slow gyassas trailed their sails beyond my windows, a charming Egyptian neighbour told me how her cook had come to her from the home of the Italian Minister, recently departed, and had told her that he could stay with her two months only, since his master expected to return.

In the shadow of these threats things went on much as usual, except that the people who worked were working twice as hard and twice as long. Pashas listened politely to the news that we would yet win the war, and said little in reply; in the highest circles, where domestic staffs were largely Italian, another tale was heard and naturally believed. Ali Maher, the Prime Minister, had long been known to be in Fascist hands: he was removed, and by July 1940 Hasan Sabry was in his place. The fact that Ali Maher was a Fascist partisan has been widely spoken of as a sign of Arab unfriendliness at that time of doubt and trouble: the firm loyal friendship of the three Premiers who succeeded during the years of crisis, is hardly ever mentioned; yet there can be no doubt that, on the whole, opinion in Egypt swung over towards Britain at the time when Britain was most obviously alone.

I first began to be made aware of this fact by a visit paid me by two young students of Cairo University. They came to me, sent by Colonel Scaife who was then an assistant professor of English literature, and their wish was a simple one: they believed in the principles of democracy and were anxious to help in the defeat of the Axis. Simple as it was, it seemed strangely difficult to do anything about it. Egypt's neutrality was being stretched to breaking point by unofficial help behind our lines; but she *was* technically neutral and her people could not be drafted into a belligerent army; and there is very little besides fighting that a young man of slender means and no experience can find to do in war-time. The two lads sat on my terrace in the sun, balancing little cups of coffee in the blunt thick hands their peasant forbears give them. Muhammad came from a Delta village and had the thick-set figure that early puts on weight, and a round face with round features which Time will finger into quaint furrows and ridges, like those wooden faces they used to carve in the Tyrol, but with so much good humour and homely quickness that one comes to have an affectionate regard for this Egyptian plainness. Kemal his friend was from Shubra, a suburb of Cairo, and was a youth like any other, with dark hair and sleepy eyes and eyelashes enviably long. They wore blue suits, and there was nothing to distinguish them from the same sort of young man anywhere else—not even their youthful honesty and the dream of a world they can alter in their time.

Muhammad was a Wafdist, and Kemal a Sa'adist, which was an honest party under Ahmed Maher eager for intervention in the war; and they were both students in the faculty of arts. In the afternoon sunshine we abandoned the idea of helping democracy by force of arms, and laid instead the foundations of a little society that should work for the same end through persuasion; I had already been a member of such a thing in Aden, and we called ourselves the "Brothers (and Sisters) of Freedom."

Every week Muhammad and Kemal came and sipped their coffee and brought new members among their friends and gave me the more damaging news invented by the Axis since our last meeting; and I for my part would try to find what information I could to help them, and we would sit discussing the whole position for an hour or so, and its meaning in the centuries of history past and to come; and when the sunset had smouldered down to its death behind the pyramids, and the white egrets with their sloping shoulders had flown across it in twos and threes to their resting-place in the tree over the river, the young men would go off to catch a tram in the dim blue-lighted streets, with their tarbushes aslant on their heads and a feeling of companionship warm in their hearts and mine.

I think it was useful work, for it helped them to realize their own beliefs at a time of their life when the supports of school and college were slipping out of sight. At such a time it is the forces of tradition, the gradual evolution from one generation to the next, that alone help the young traveller pushing in his untried boat from shore; they give him, as it were, a coast-line with anchorages ever in sight. But the youth of the Middle East, brought up in a Western way, has no such coastline: he steers into open sea; and the passion of devotion with which he looks back to the days of guidance, to teachers (very often American) in school or college, can best be realized when the loneliness of his further journey is borne in mind. We find this hard to understand; for British traditions are deep,

54

flexible and strong, and their help carries most Englishmen from youth to age; and America is building towards an unimpeded horizon: and neither has to face the difficulty and solitude that lie in renouncing a past, and in building—not in clear space an edifice of our choice—but a house designed by strangers, in the midst of cumbered ways.

This is why it seems to me that help in school and college is not enough, and that we should extend to these, who strive so earnestly to come into our heritage (for better or for worse) something of that invisible background of support and cohesion which is ever about our own path, and is not a relation of pupil and teacher, but a companionship and a help from fellow travellers who happen to know a little more about the way.

This, apart from our confounding of the Axis, was what I hoped to do, and our little democratic body grew apace. It was a simple organism; it just met, and drank coffee and talked; and everyone paid a few shillings a year for the privilege of doing so and to defray expenses; for we soon outgrew the accommodation of my terrace, and met in various groups in many other parts of Cairo as well, and wrote a small bulletin of our discussions so that all our members might think over the same things; it was written in Arabic by Mr. Samaha, a journalist who joined us in these very early days and gave his time and labour as a free gift. I do not imagine that any Fascist or Nazi in Cairo at that time believed that these people were helping us from mere love of the principles we fought for; yet it was so. Few, in the autumn of 1940, thought ours the winning side: and when sceptics asked me how we kept our ranks uncontaminated (for they were collected in a haphazard way, and I have been accused of leaning out of my car and asking a total stranger if he believed in democracy) I was able to explain that we discouraged the insincere by offering no advantage of any kind to those who joined our flock.

Our chief difficulty was to avoid local political feelings, and on this account it was perhaps as well to have a woman among the founders, in whom a general dislike of party politics is not only natural but decent; even so I had to argue strongly and often, so as to allow neither parties, nor nationalism, nor any other -ism beyond a wholehearted dislike of totalitarians to interfere with our interest in more fundamental things.

CHAPTER X

BROTHERS IN THE AZHAR

" Dishonour not, then, the transitive virtue within you, be it feeble or great, for it is a portion of that yearning which fills the world with thought and with deity, as with a hum of bees."

THE Brothers of Freedom gave me a number of happy days.

Their small centres sprang up spontaneously in unexpected places, and sent pressing invitations; petticoat advice if not government was what they seemed to like, and I would look through my crowded time-table for a few free hours and would find some young brother or sister waiting at the appointed moment on my doorstep, ready to guide me through intricacies of Cairo few tourists come to know.

Sometimes we sat round silver and napery at a tea-table such as you find anywhere, in London, Paris or New York, and the interest was one of friendship or curiosity more than any abstract fervour. Many friendly and disinterested Pashas helped, and gave to our Idea their blessing and to me personally encouragement and friendship from the first. But they were busy, and Brotherhoods do not walk very freely past doorkeepers up carpeted stairs; it was in shabbier places that the longing for Service blossomed, disinterestedly like the gentians my father once brought from the Alps and planted in his garden and—because they never flowered—threw away on to a flinty bed, where they flourished in unencumbered poverty and covered their stony heap with stars of their hills.

One of our members was a typographer, and ran a little business of his own in two dark rooms off the long dull street that runs to the mosque of Muhammad Ali; he was ill and eventually died of consumption, and his sister helped him and then carried on his work; and I sat at a meeting with them and their workmen, half a dozen men or so, with the cylinders of the machine they lived by dark in the gloom behind us, and loose type scattered all about—and in that Rembrandt setting listened to what the Egyptian craftsman thinks on Freedom.

Often they were students, or teachers, or clerks in offices. We climbed to them in some small room with chairs round three walls and a sofa at the end, high above streets and screeching trams, and drank milky tea in shallow cups with coloured cakes—all against our restrictions, for we wished to keep our meetings simple enough for anyone to join, however poor, and tried to banish competitive entertainment; but this was the most difficult of all rules to enforce, since the Arab thinks hospitality and charity are benefits to the giver and not the taker, a means of practising what is good for his own self— and it goes against his deepest instinct not to offer the best he has to anyone who steps across his threshold.

One of our centres was very poor indeed, a gathering of the smallest of shopkeepers, of the kind who stand behind an empty booth on dingy thoroughfares of the outskirts of Cairo; a few sweepers, and a watchman, and the servant of a mosque belonged to this particular branch: they had no place large enough to meet in, and I first invited them to my flat, where they all made speeches in turn on democracy and its meaning, with good sense and pleasant manners surprising in the dim, emaciated figures that stood in ragged cotton gowns. Their chairman was a university student; he had gathered them and came to ask how they could now keep their weekly meetings, for they had nowhere to sit except the open benches of some café at the corner of a street, where each member would have to spend a halfpenny on one of the small cups of sticky coffee. Their means did not reach so far. We collected a Founders' meeting and discussed the point; but everyone was adamant against the principle of a subsidy; and I finally gave a (very small) private present which infringed no rules, and which remained the only money ever paid out to the Brothers of Freedom.

Many among them were wealthy. Their numbers grew astonishingly fast, and one or two personal friends, British or American or French, who had a little time to spare, joined this or that circle. Mr. Fay, who is still at our centre in Cairo, gave his scanty leisure from the Fuad-al-Auwal University; Prof. Scaife came now and then, and took my place when I left; and Mr. Fouracres from the Sudan Agency would attend a central meeting and help the inexpert founders in the chair. Mr. Reed, of Victoria College, had a group of young men

57

devoted to him, and Mr. Murray of the Egyptian Survey sat in a prosperous upholstered office lent by a merchant, with a circle of substantial elderly men from government offices about him.

Our great majority remained Egyptians; and while the Fascist armies marched and radio from Bari acclaimed the capture of Sidi Barrani on our doorstep, our democratic members grew from tens to hundreds and then to thousands, and many young Arabs found a pleasure which is not purely occidental in standing up for what they thought at such a time. Officers from the army came, Major Shauki and Major Amin Zaki; and Dr. Awad, professor of geography, who could speak equally well in Arabic or English; and the Emir Amin Muhammad Haidar of the Sherifs of Mekka, who came at the first and never neglected us; and doctors, both medical and others, such as Dr. Al and Dr Moughy, and his inseparable friend and ours, Mr. Kilani, who wrote story books for children. Copts came who had to be kept off politics; and Mubarak, who is a dragoman from Mena and brought his whole village behind him, and also his nephew, Magoob Effendi, a lawyer, who started centres of his own. There were female centres, whose hearts were democratic but their attendance irregular; there were young circles in the post-graduate club for men and girls, where one received warm-hearted welcome as a friend; there was a Persian group in the Muski, which Christopher Sykes or Prince Ali Khan would visit now and then, where Yezdi Bey gave us tea beside the goldfish of his fountain, where carpets and brocades are stacked round patterned tiles, and flagons of perfume look down from their niches, and his sons stand respectfully to serve him and us and the Persian journalist and the stout amiable poet who was a merchant in his spare time.

Close by, down a narrow lane of crowded shopping and across a square, is the Azhar University, the stronghold of tradition, founded in A.D. 972. Because of its influence, a great deal of Nazi and Fascist effort had been directed at this fortress, and apart from this, its body of learned men—who are drawn chiefly for the study of religion from all over the Islamic world —had been embittered against Britain by her pre-war policy in Palestine.

The Azhar is no longer a purely medieval institution, as

it once was. The account of it given by Prof. Muhammad Khalil Hasanein Bey (in the Arabic weekly *Al-Ithnein wad-Dunya*) best tells the story, typical of what is happening in the old Muslim world.

"When I was a student," says Hasanein Bey, "I remember that I read in the newspapers of that time exciting news of a strike in the noble Azhar. . . . I remember that that strike was started because it was in the minds of the Azhar students that the science of geography was to be introduced into the Azhar. They considered this an innovation which should be stopped. . . .

"These conditions went on in the Azhar till the year 1925, when the students rebelled again, but on this occasion their rebellion was to *demand* the introduction of the new sciences and their teaching in a serious, useful way. . . . It is most probable that the cause of this rebellion was the students' desire to open a way for themselves to obtain employment, because they saw that since the Azhar had cut itself off from any association with these sciences, it had ceased to touch on practical life . . .

"I was at that time . . . in the Ministry of Public Instruction, when the Egyptian University was started" (i.e. the modern university in Cairo founded in 1925. There is also an American university in Cairo now doing excellent work). "So King Fuad commanded that I should . . . take up the post of Inspector of New Sciences in the Azhar . . .

"In the year 1930 another board was formed to . . . amend the programmes of instruction in such a way as to fall into line with scientific changes and include all stages of instruction, primary, secondary and higher."

In spite of all this, however, and although the Azhar now enables a young Egyptian to take modern exams, it still remains the citadel of old-fashioned thought, and in its cool wide courts where the stones are rubbed and polished by many hundred years, under the pillars of the portico, the white-turbaned Learned still talk to their pupils, gathered in groups around them on the ground.

Mustapha Habib came to us from the Azhar. He himself belonged to the modern Egyptian university, but he was one of the teachers of "new sciences," and he soon started Brother-hoods of Freedom in the ancient house of learning. When we met every week, Mustapha would arrive with one or other of his disciples, and soon brought a brother of the Shaikh al-Maraghy, the Rector himself, a tall, decided, friendly man in neat white turban and grey cashmere gown, who had studied in the London School of Science and spoke excellent English. Other friends too came from the Azhar, such as Shaikh Yusuf, who had heard about me in the South and came to call one day late in 1940 anxious to do something for the civilized world; it was always pleasant to see him, small and earnest, with white gown and fringe of beard, and wide light eyes, and passionate belief in the one-ness of mankind.

Soon I was invited myself to meet some teachers of the Azhar, to discuss and answer their questions; and from then onwards at intervals would go down with Pamela Hore-Ruthven, who assisted me, her gold hair tied up under a kerchief to mitigate the exotic appearance among the Professors of Islam.

We would make our way gingerly, for I was only beginning to drive a car and it was the crowded part of Cairo where most things, and particularly the traffic, are left in the hands of Allah; but we arrived, and were surrounded by the "modern" young men, with smiling faces under their tasselled tarbushes, and yet a little anxious over the innovation; and were led to some quiet room near, but not within, the centre of theology, and sat there while it gradually filled with a mixed crowd of learning. We would spend an hour or two in talk, and it was here that I came to realize, from the theologians of the Azhar, on what democratic foundations the theory of Islam is built: text after text they would quote, from Quran, or Tradition, or history of the first Caliphs, the Guided Ones; and this appeal, of the original democracy of Islam, would time and again brush away all the arguments of our enemies, which at that season were being poured like a deluge over the Arab world. I believe indeed that it was this fundamental tradition, so opposed to despotic doctrines, which chiefly kept the Arabs on our side.

Here too was confirmed the immense emotional influence of Palestine spread out so far beyond its geographic boundaries. Practically every expression of antagonism would centre round that small country, whose power for trouble, like that of

Cleopatra, age apparently cannot wither nor custom stale. When the subject was broached, the two currents of education, ancient and modern, the turban and the tarbush, united; it monopolized nine questions out of ten, and kept me clinging, like a garrison to its flag, to our Government's White Paper. We have there promised, I explained over and over again, not indeed an end to immigration across the Palestine borders, but an end to its imposition by force and against the majority's consent. I have always held that force is a monstrous thing to use against a people long settled on its lands to induce it to accept immigration; if the arrivals are angels from heaven, it makes no difference—the habitation of a land for two thousand years gives one a right to close or open the door. And to say that a country's "absorptive capacity," or "inferior efficiency" give other people a claim to rearrange its populations, whether it be Italians in Abyssinia or Zionists in Palestine, savours too much of what we have spent these five years fighting against to be acceptable to a civilized mind. Let us by all means try to help those we care for—and in these I wholeheartedly include many sons of Zion—to obtain their wish, and revisit the home of their childhood which is now the house of our friends: but let us do it by asking, and give to the present owner the privilege of yes or no which is his right, and not stand with a bludgeon on the doormat. And as for all this talk of inefficiency—where, I should like to know, is it permissible to be inefficient if not in one's own house? We have suffered a little too much from herren-people who come on the plea of superior efficiency jostling us out of our own homes.

Feeling as I did, and with the word of our Government behind me, it was not difficult to reach the hearts of the Azhar teachers, who asked their questions with none of that rude battering aggressiveness of which one gets so weary, but with a wish to know.

There would be anything between twelve and twenty in the room, crowded down both sides; young faces, pleased to see a way made for the beliefs they shared; middle-aged, bull-necked teachers of Law, with heavy eyes surprised and slowly gentler, and rough cheeks shaved with scissors (a traditional practice which always seems to me a carrying of religion too far); Pamela's gold head with a sunbeam on it, radiantly inappropriate; and some old ascetic faces with clear eyes, such as you might expect to see in any cloister, in Plato's grove or by the Ganges, in quiet monastic walks, in Oxford or in Harvard, wherever men in their variety commune with their God.

They came, teachers in one of the oldest institutes of learning on earth, where women and Christians and foreigners have ever been excluded, to meet a woman, a Christian, and a foreigner whose abstract principles, which they had learned by hearsay, it interested them to know: it seemed to me an eloquent proof of the liberality of knowledge.

When we parted, the Young World took us back to our car into the sunlight and smell of spices, the cries and jostlings and flapping cotton gowns and sub-stratum of children and bundles, the suave Levantine merchants at their dark rich doors, the military groups in battle dress led to their clients by dragomans, like sheep to the shearing, the colour and noise and millennial gaiety of Cairo.

CHAPTER XI

THREE PRIME MINISTERS

" Cyclop-like in human flesh to deal,
Chop up a minister at every meal."
(DRYDEN: *The Medal.*)

EGYPT shares with the United States the advantages and disadvantages of not possessing a governing class. The old Turkish ruling officials, who draw their origins from the blue blood of the Ottoman Empire, are becoming either outcasts or undistinguished in the land they dominated; they live in a sort of Faubourg Saint Germain society of their own and speak of the disintegration of the social order as English landowners used to speak of it in the days before the Conservative Party grew revolutionary.

It is this Turkish society which may reasonably object to the British in Egypt—if one considers that it is their privilege, power and riches that have been curtailed since 1882. Whether this would have happened in any case is a moot point; but the fact remains that the improved status of the native Egyptian, from peasant to Prime Minister, has come about with the decline of the Turkish ruling class; and it was therefore natural that the most fertile nursery for Nazi or Fascist doctrine should be among those dispossessed, who still own great estates and are the only aristocracy in the land, but whose political powers are steadily disappearing. Like objects illuminated by the sunset, they throw a shadow greater than themselves. There *is* an Art of government, a little more tangible and a little less important than the Art of living, and in a land otherwise largely composed of peasants or alien merchants, they alone possessed what there was of it; the Effendi is only now acquiring sufficient education, experience, and authority to take over; during the interval of his doing so, the official intercourse of foreign nations with Egypt has very often been carried on by means of this diminishing foreign crowd, and their voices, or the voices they inspired, have often been taken, by British or others, to be the national voice.

Some of them, as I say, remain in their seclusion, with ideas and outlook gradually becoming as immobile as those petrified forests in the desert beyond Mena which once were trees; but others, breaking from their past, are being drawn into and absorbed by the new Egyptian stream.

Of the three Prime Ministers who have ruled the country since June 27th 1940, two, Hasan Sabri and the last premier, Mustapha An-Nahhas Pasha, came from that peasant stock which has tilled along the banks of Nile canals for century upon century, regardless of the coming and going of dynasties above their head. Now education has come, and the peasants' children go to school; the Egyptian is reconquering his land.

Hasan Sabri was born about 1875, and took his degree in Egypt, studying both Islamic and foreign law. He was the first layman to be appointed as inspector in such subjects as mathematics, history and geography in al-Azhar University. He was first elected as a Wafdist deputy in 1925, and in 1933 became Finance Minister, was Egyptian Minister in London in 1934 and returned to be in every Cabinet as Minister either of Communications or War between 1935 and 1939.

He became premier in 1940 when Ali Maher, the friend of the Fascists, was deposed. He undertook, with great good faith and directness, a very heavy burden; for Egypt in those days was quivering like a horse in a bog with Britain's very existence shaking beneath her. Hasan Sabri had barely time to prove himself in office, however: as he stood reading the speech from the Throne to the opening Parliament in November, 1940, with the King and the diplomats and the Cabinet before him, he fell into a faint, and died. After an interval of little over a year, Mustapha An-Nahhas Pasha, another peasant son of the Nile, came to power, bringing with him the strongest party of the country, the Wafd of the small people, of Egypt for the Egyptian; it represented about eighty per cent of votes, and Makram Pasha, a close friend and adviser to An-Nahhas at that time, brought him the good opinions of the Copts.

I am not a politician, and could not write with authority on the subtleties by which people get around and above each other in this game. My liking, and what training I have (it is not much), is for the more stable science of geography, whose interest is in historic change but not in the immediate moves of knight or pawn or bishop which it determines. I had the pleasure of meeting An-Nahhas Pasha in 1943, and saw him in the pomp and bustle of his power, an emblem of the Egyptian change—a man of sixty-four, with rugged face, wall-eyed and rather sad, beneath a narrow shiny skull. The lines were deep, the face not very sure or strong—as if life had got the better of it. He has his dreams; and loves his people as well as or perhaps better than himself. A strict Muslim, he neither drinks nor smokes. And for twenty-six years now he has belonged to or led the Egyptian party of which nationalism is the keynote. He has thrice been Prime Minister, and I can remember in years gone by railway stations crowded with shouting people because Mustapha An-Nahhas was in the train. This is heady wine; and it is hard to come from a small town among the reeds and see the crowds hanging upon your lips, and to remember that it is not *you* but only the idea of which you are a symbol which that applause acclaims.

In the great temples of Egypt the huge stone figures stand, and beside them, no more than knee-high, the figures of their wives. I think it is rather a depressing picture of conjugal relations, but it is an excellent type of the Idea, gigantic beside the smallness of the Man, and a model to all politicians. Perhaps it is because this relation is maintained, the agent so little visible, the idea so great beside him, that the structure of the Catholic Church has stood so many centuries unimpaired. It is the lesson women learn, who hold all heaven in their hands for someone at some moment, and must watch the power depart. It is this knowledge that marks the divergence of statesman and politician; and the tradition of government must teach it, if it teaches anything at all. The man is nothing, the idea he wields everything: it is the chief lesson which the Effendi, coming newly to govern, has to learn.

For this reason it seems to me that a democracy does well to collect and cherish and use such of its remnants as possess the tradition of government, and not to despise their service merely because it objects to their control. The people in Egypt who belong to the old ruling class and are willing to step from that superannuated enclosure and take a hand in the new business of the country, are doing useful service. Husain Sirry Pasha, himself of Egyptian peasant stock, entered this Turkish aristocratic society through his wife, who is pretty, charming, and kind, and related to the Queen. He became

65

Prime Minister in November 1940, on the death of Hasan Sabri, and held the post till February 1942, during the difficult year of the war, before the entry of the United States.

A son of Ismail Sirry Pasha, he studied in England, at Cooper's Hill, became an engineer, and entered the survey department in 1925; in December 1937 he became Minister of Public Works, and remained in the Cabinet almost continually in one post or another, until his resignation and election to the Senate in 1942.

I used to meet him at dinners here and there, and was always pleased when the luck of the table placed him beside me. He had a substantial Pasha figure whose shadow was growing more rather than less; a heavy face and sleepy light eyes; and it was only when the conversation was well under way that one noticed a fine fencing quality of wit and observation playing unobtrusively among all that solidity. As I was English, he would rely on my not noticing a hidden meaning, counting on that obtuseness which the Mediterranean expects from the Atlantic. But I have had a continental education myself, and would usually perceive the target, and he would look pleased, as if over a click of the foils.

For the art of conversation, it is an advantage, I think, to belong to a small nation in normal times. There is a detachment, an ease of letting the gaze wander, over the audience, over the platform, anywhere it likes, while the Exalted—banked up there with bouquets—can hardly screw their necks to right or left. The Exalted can only be happy or amusing if they refuse to take themselves seriously, and how few of them do. What was more insufferable than the Victorian manner abroad? Now, in the Middle East, we watch the British grow less rich and far more pleasant, but the Americans begin to share unpopularity; there is no getting away from it; it comes of sitting on the platform.

The people of the small nations are spoilt only by preoccupations about money; if they have too little, they think about it, and this thought is ruinous to conversation. But if they happen to be independent, either with money or without, and care not one atom about the world they mix with, and are free from that incubus of setting an example, and therefore can—not perhaps *say* but at any rate *think*—what they like—those are the people to sit with and be happy.

66

So I would reflect while talking to the Egyptian Prime Minister who, even in war, had some of these ingredients, and could dispose himself in his narrow ribbon of river-land as at the Opera, watching the storm beyond the meagre orchestra of our guns. Everyone was then promising everything to Egypt. She was the key of Asia, and knew it, the door between the Axis and Japan. All she need do was not even to relinquish her neutrality; she could interpret it in a way less amicable to the democracies, and our slender resources could scarcely have weathered the storm. At this time she was helping us with the guarding of concentration camps, with the watching of roads and bridges, with transport, with the hundred and one things done by those twenty-six who are said to furnish the rear behind a fighting soldier.

At no time in 1940 did General Wavell's forces exceed thirty thousand front-line combatants; they took four times their own number of prisoners alone, fighting an enemy whose equipment was superior. Only in October did our first Hurricanes come from Britain, and they were only six. I was told at an officers' party to get up early to see them fly over Cairo, when they were intended to show that we had something in the air. In the early dawn I heard them, and snatched a dressing-gown to watch from my terrace, where the lesser Nile crept under mists stagnant among the palms and suburbs and vegetable fields: and there in the rosy-petalled sun they flew, round and round the awakening city, six blunt noses catching light or shadow, playing like dolphins, filling the morning spaces with their noise; and so little had we seen of such things, and so great had been our need of them, that I found myself weeping as I watched them.

About this time, while the Fascist armies were advancing, G.H.Q. issued a bulletin which finally goaded our political people and made them insist that journalists and not the military deal with publicity and the arrangement of the news. Our forces, the bulletin said with a soldierly disregard for anything like gilding on its pill—"our forces are able to cope with ten times their number: the enemy, unhappily, are more than ten to one." Bulletins or no bulletins, the Egyptians knew it: and their help in this critical year must be regarded in the light of this knowledge.

So far as one could see there was nothing to make Husain

Sirry believe in our victory unless it was some perception of unbeatableness he may have acquired together with his other knowledge at Cooper's Hill, his personal liking for our cause as against the totalitarian, and that trend of Islam towards the democratic principle to which I believe the friendship of the Muslim world is very largely due. Some months later this could perhaps have carried Egypt into the active war had we so wished it. But there was, among a complexity of other things, the fact that we could not afford her as an ally; we had no equipment to spare, and to lose unofficial helpers in the rear so as to acquire men in the front to whom we would have to give the weapons already insufficient for ourselves, was an uneconomic policy. Political advantages and military necessities were weighed and balanced. But this all happened after the winter in 1940 had brought a triumph which General Wavell wrested out of an almost unbelievable inequality of numbers.

I spent Christmas in Luxor, with Pamela, and Sir Miles and Lady Lampson (now Lord and Lady Killearn). The pendulum of the Desert was swinging for the first time to the West, and we were as happy as birds out of our cage. We danced with the Pashas in the evenings, both the good and the bad ones who looked as if they had backed a favourite and lost. We galloped on donkeys all day in the winter sun, taking tombs and temples in our stride (and theirs). Sir Arthur Longmore, A.O.C.-in-C., a steadfast leader, a true companion, a good friend, was there, between one victory and another; Australians, New Zealanders, young men of the Hussars released by the Palestine truce, were in and out from battle. As we returned to Cairo, they were taking Benghazi; it was our first great advance of the war. And when I met Husain Sirry Pasha at a luncheon party he looked happy; he looked like someone who has backed an outsider and won.

CHAPTER XII

LULIE

" The state of bondage is overcome through perfectly maintained discrimination."

(YOGA SUTRAS OF PATANJELA.)

IT would be impossible in a short sketch to give a picture of the kaleidoscope of different worlds which was Cairo in the first three years of war. The continent of Europe was cut off, and there was a strangely Napoleonic feeling about the Mediterranean, where Admiral Cunningham criss-crossed on Nelson's routes and kept the same flag flying in the same way about the same hostile shores.

The air roads of the world centred like the spokes of a wheel round Cairo, and brought a stream of interesting people, bearers of varied news; and in one wave after another came the diplomats of Europe, projected by the advancing German tide; royalties, legations, refugees, their offices sprang up everywhere, and the click of typewriters grew so loud that one began to wish the war could be won with such machines.

In and out of all this, the colour of khaki grew in the streets; a mere trickle in 1940, with slender young officers making their way diffidently among the tarbushes and civilian clothes, it swelled imperceptibly into a mighty torrent; Shepheards and the Continental and their immediate neighbourhood were first submerged; then the quarter where G.H.Q. gradually gathered itself out of a labyrinth of villas into one huge edifice built with grey pillars as if to house a Sphinx, whose encircling barbed wire and Cypriot guards I seemed to hit whenever I lost my way in the little car which, in my novice hands, turned itself about only with jerks and noises, humiliating in the presence of lounging military drivers.

The stream of khaki grew not only in numbers but in quality: the fresh complexions from Europe turned to bronze toughness of the Western Desert, to the hard keenness which came on leave (shipped in the night by the Navy under the nose of the enemy) from the hot summer epic of beleaguered Tobruk in 1941. And with the army came its traffic. Army lorries were rare and guns scarcely seen on the streets of Cairo in 1940; and with what warm feelings were the first American trucks welcomed as they clattered by the policemen's truncheons, amiably and indiscriminately waving.

This was not my world, but I went into it and out of it, chiefly owing to the kind and easy hospitality of the Lampsons, of the Wavell family, of Mr. Kirk the U.S.A. Minister, or such pleasant houses as those of the Russell Pashas, or Mrs. Otto Kahn and Mrs. Marriott, or our own Embassy staff who were all charming and all friendly. Nominally I belonged to the Embassy, and first Reginald Davies and then Owen Tweedy under Sir Walter Monckton were my chiefs: they were all personal friends as well as the pleasantest people in the world to work for. But in fact my path lay among the Egyptian effendis and their wives, and the Brotherhood of Freedom took up more and more of my time. It was a small but stout pillar of the democratic cause, and as such helpful to the British war effort, which at that time needed all the help it could get; and because of this usefulness, Mr. Davies and the Ambassador—both imaginative men with minds refreshingly unorthodox—allowed me to devote my time away from official duties and even permitted Pamela to be picked out of the severe grey marble arms of G.H.Q., to help with the Egyptian democrats whose numbers threatened to submerge us.

Very few people could understand the success of the little society, and most were inclined to attribute it to the powers of propaganda. Now to my mind there is only one way of conducting lasting propaganda, and that is to work wholeheartedly for the people whose goodwill you are anxious to obtain; in the long run there is no other way of insuring goodwill. Pamela and I felt we were doing this, and none the less so because the values we dealt in were not material values. The young people of Egypt were watching on their very doorstep the war of their age, waged not for this or that particular place or nation, but for ideas which every one of them was called upon to believe or disbelieve. In such a moment who would not wish to take a part, whether to help or hinder? What we gave was not to be counted by any standard of coin: we offered a share in an adventure, a chance for disinterested effort, an escape from that frustrated feeling which every generous mind must have when the things it cares for are being fought for and its own land is neutral (and in so saying I am casting no slur on neutrality as such; after September 1939 *every* nation outside the German orbit remained neutral until it was attacked. The appeal of our Brotherhood was made entirely to *individuals*).

What young Egypt felt about it was shown by the response we met, and Pamela and I, as secretaries, were soon snowed under; our committees might have been mushrooms they multiplied so fast.

It was then that Lulie joined us.

It would be unfair to write about the Arab world of to-day or to-morrow and not mention its women. I am not a "feminist" myself, and always think this a strange word by which to describe someone who wishes to make women more like men;—women who, even in a world at peace, are busy with the fundamentals of life and death, who look Eternity in the face with the birth of their children, and Time with the passing of their youth. Their feet are set far deeper than a mere man can gauge except in time of crisis or by the use of his imagination, two contingencies which he tries to eliminate by Regulations. Woman has spent many thousand years watching man make a mess with regulations, and the sight seems to me to offer no great reason for trying to grow like him. But education is another matter, and there appears to be no advantage in making reading, writing or even arithmetic a matter of sex.

Education is pouring in upon the female Arab world like a tide, and the young girls are frisking in its foam. Among the débris which it rolls in a short clamour of waves and casts away, is the veil, already discarded in the town society of several Arab lands. Madame Sirry Pasha told me how sudden this revolution was to those who, out of their young seclusion, stepped into the open, feeling as you would in a walled garden if the walls fell down. She ran the Red Crescent in Cairo, corresponding to our Red Cross, and many of the Egyptian ladies worked there. Other friends of mine had for years been busy with a sort of welfare society for poor people suffering from tuberculosis; it was now developing, and there were several hundred girls, with classes for the study of social services.

There was also Madame Fahmy, who ran one of the pleasantest girls' schools I have ever seen, quite modern, but with a feeling of gentle affection about it. All these things had been started as it were under the veil, whose swathes of black chiffon seem to me to have banked and preserved rather than suffocated the fires of the now middle-aged pioneers. The young generation have a clean start and an easier task. School is a matter of course, and university—where boys and girls mingle as in America or Europe—is growing very general.

Lulie went a step further and asked for an Oxford degree. Her father, a distinguished Syrian Arab who was Prime Minister in Transjordan and whose own father had been advisor to the Sultan Abdul Hamid, died some years before the war; her mother belongs to the Turkish families dispersed all over the Arab world; and Lulie, apart from an incredible number of influential relations spread over the Islamic East, has one sister, Lima, less animated but equally pretty and a year or two younger than herself. Lulie uprooted mother and sister and, by sheer force of will, induced them to establish themselves in Oxford while she took a degree in history and enchanted the undergraduates: she used to appear, her pretty bronze hair dishevelled, her fingers covered in ink, books in sheaves carried by her or her devotees, to catch her lectures like cricket balls as they sped by. Mr. Davies told me about her, for they lived in the flat next to mine, and all through the winter that charming family and I became closer friends.

It would be difficult to know whom to love best, but perhaps my heart goes out most of all to the mother for the gallantry with which, in her middle years, she plunges into the strange and modern world. She once showed me a photograph of herself dressed in a fancy Beduin gown, a girl slender as a cypress with beautiful eyes, holding with one gentle rounded arm an earthenware water jar upon her shoulder; the picture managed to convey the impression of someone innocent and beloved. Most of this has gone now, and of the girlish image, the eyes alone remain, with some of the softness of their black depth lost, and a very fine wisdom added. Her figure, about which Lulie's mother cares not a bit, is now full and sober, and she manages it with immense dignity and a quiet economy of effort, and clothes it in handsome black loose gowns, so that one notices chiefly the sallow strong face above it, unadorned

72

by any make-up, whether material or spiritual, for Lulie's mother is one of the most simply genuine people I know. Every year she travels to Transjordan to spend a few weeks of remembrance beside her husband's grave; the loss of that beloved one has left her with a serene tranquillity, as of one who has had the best gifts of life and now is safe. Her own story so happily accomplished, she enters into the lives of her children with a calm mind, and a zest whose edge has been kept intact by her own sequestered youth and later ways. Having gone to Oxford with Lulie, she returned with the two girls by aeroplane, and thought nothing of it, knowing well what is and what is not important in a world full of changes.

The real home and proper setting for the girls and their mother was an old palace of the time of Muhammad Ali or perhaps about 1840 in the very centre of Cairo: there at the end of difficult and tortuous streets you came upon them in a labyrinth of rooms, so numerous and disused, and divided by such unending lengths of corridor, that no bell or telephone could ever reach them unless the old retainers drooping at strategic corners happened to hear and carry the news. But the house had great character; its branching double staircase and Aubusson carpets, its chandeliers and painted walls, had the wistful charm which the Cairo of Muhammad Ali possesses, an elusive echo of a Rococo Europe, dim and gay and very far away.

But it was much too cold and difficult in war-time to live in; and in the flat next to mine the three were happily installed —two young lives pushing out in every new direction, and the old one there to help and not to hinder, with a mixture of authority and service most pleasant to see. One was welcomed at any time of day or evening, and the house was always full with a varied stream—Egyptian cousins and girl friends, young English soldiers, a gaiety and vivacity of youth, with here and there, sitting in the shadow and talking to Mamma (who anyway spoke very little English) some wraith-like figure in long black gown, or grizzled tasselled tarbushed head, the old-fashioned, dominated, disappearing world.

It had a great deal of influence, however, and Lulie's Mamma was between the upper and nether millstone, Lulie and Lulie's relations grinding their opposite ways.

"So long as *I* approve, it is all that matters," she would say to me with her serene and dignified common sense, when the relatives had been uncommonly critical, and added kindly that while Lulie was with me she would always approve. For Lulie, who loved Oxford and therefore took in the British as well, went daily to help as a volunteer in Mr. Davies's sadly under-staffed office, and would there be found combining—in the eyes of her conservative relations—the practice of an un-ladylike occupation with the support of a losing cause.

Neither Lulie nor Lima nor their mother cared one atom about victory or defeat where their friendships were concerned; their advice, labour, and enthusiasm when the dark days came were always a comfort and a tonic. In the stronghold of the most exclusive set, where the Nazis chiefly flourished, Lulie's mother would sit over silver-handled cups of tea or coffee, fighting the fight of democracy with urbane but telling phrases: Lima spent her days at the Red Crescent: and Lulie, having joined Pamela and me in the Brotherhood, soon became one of its most convinced gospellers, and, when Pamela had to leave me, my constant companion.

She would flash along in her half Syrian Arabic at committee meetings, the words tumbling over each other in their eagerness, demolishing any Brother who had the bad taste to show himself timorous over rumours that came pouring in. The fact that our army was retreating, that "in these operations three generals were missing," that the Egyptian frontier was violated, left her as confident and only a little more combative than before. Her pretty head, the narrow pointed face with lips pouting a little, the tilted nose and glinting waves of gold-brown hair that matched her eyes, shone with a Renaissance richness against many a dim committee background; and when the long talk was over, and our questions collected for next week's bulletin, she would take my arm and we would walk back through the murmuring streets, while three or four of the stalwarts among the Brothers, Dr. Abd-ul-Al, or Alphonse, or Mr. Fay, would gather round and see us home in the starlight.

Lulie is not Egyptian and is proud of the Arab ancestry that goes back to medieval days; it connects her with the holy Rifa'a Dervishes of Baghdad, and with the great families of northern Syria; in Palestine, where all this counts a great deal, she is now building up among the women a social help organization which has grown out of the sort of things we founded in Cairo. I met her there last year, living independently in Jerusalem, a circle as ever about her. Her mother was staying with Lima as a guest in the harem of H.H. the Amir Abdulla in Transjordan, so as to be near her: through the door which H.H. the Amir alone, among men, may enter, I went in to lunch with her, and found her exactly the same in this seclusion, serene, interested and affectionate, as she was amid the coming and going of the flat in Cairo.

"I hope you can persuade Lulie not to spend the winter in Jerusalem," she said to me. "It is so cold for us all; it would be much pleasanter in Cairo."

This is the only complaint I ever heard her make over her emancipated children; and Lulie is still in Jerusalem, and her mother's plans are arranged accordingly. But this year, in the malaria epidemic which swept over upper Egypt, Lima went to the infected zone to nurse with other Red Crescent workers; Lima's mother followed this second duckling, became horrified at the misery of the villagers and the supineness of their landlords, and—having become interested in their cause —is now deep in social work among them. Lulie writes that she is becoming rejuvenated by leading an active life.

CHAPTER XIII

THE MAYOR OF DERNA

"It is liberty alone which fits men for liberty."
(GLADSTONE.)

THE language of salesmanship was no doubt born with the first fashions in fig leaves in the garden of Eden. A strange concept has grown around it: if something is to be sold, inaccuracy is not immoral. Hence the art of advertisement—untruthfulness combined with repetition. The cliché and the slogan appear, people hear a familiar sound, and take it for granted to believe. What we have not yet fully realized, is the depth to which this salesmanship language has crept into the spiritual realm, into politics, religion, and even art. It is a blot on any civilization; for words are poor enough anyway to express the thoughts behind them, and only the most devoted care can make them even approximately exact: to think lightly of their perversion leads to a perversion of the thoughts behind them, and hence to cataclysms, war and death. Mussolini discovered the salesman language and used it in a country still innocent of the advertising art. And it is not unknown in the circles of Democracy. With the exception of the Christian Science Monitor I know few centres of public expression from which it is entirely banished. By it our palate of truthfulness is blunted. In New York stores you will see tawdry muslins "cool as summer breezes" or underwear draped on simpering plastic, guaranteed to be "your lover's dream": every decency or intimacy of life is used to sell something, and who minds that it is all bogus? After an hour or so among these blasphemous labels, my companion remarked that I looked ill.

"I think it is the adjectives," I said.

One does not feel very different after reading many public speeches, whose underlying principle (if that is what one should call it?) is growing to be the same.

One of these slogans is that of Arab unfriendliness during the war. There is little solid substance behind it.

76

Eygpt, with large foreign and Axis elements, was partly isolationist (so was the Middle West); yet no one who was there in command would minimize the importance of her help. The peninsula of Arabia, except for an organized pro-German clique in Iraq and an isolationist Yemen, was all friendly: King Ibn Sa'ud, from the earliest moment of war, and indeed before it, never missed an occasion to prove himself so in words that echoed all over the Islamic lands. The Palestine Arabs—as I have mentioned—chose the time of our difficulty to propose a truce which perhaps tilted the balance of the Middle East; in Syria it was the Vichy French and not the Arabs who helped the enemy; Transjordan never wavered in its alliance; and Sayyid Muhammed Idris es-Senussi, in August 1940 when France had fallen and the British Commonwealth stood alone, offered all he had in men and money to fight in the Western Desert.

The Senussi are one of those strange phenomena which religion produces in times of weak government or disorder, when—in the absence of other management—the spiritual takes over the temporal conduct of affairs. They began as a purely religious sect under Sayyid Muhammad Ali es-Senussi, who was born in Algeria in A.D. 1788 or thereabout. He was, it is claimed, a descendant of the Prophet, and later of an Idris al-Alawi, who first came to Africa in flight from the Abbassid caliphs, and was poisoned by an agent of Harun ar-Rashid, from Baghdad. His descendants, however, prospered, and one of them, a Spanish Emir, came to settle near Jebel Senus in Algeria, and gave the family its name.

Sayyid Muhammad Ali, in the nineteenth century, began to teach religion in Mekka, and founded the Senussia, a return to a primitive and simple faith. His disciples spread to Cyrenaica, and in 1842 Sayyid Muhammad Ali returned to Africa and settled first at Beida in Cyrenaica and then in the oasis of Jaghbub, deep in the desert, where he died in 1859. His son, Sayyid el-Mahdi, retreated into the still greater remoteness of Kufra, and the religion spread from Tunis to Darfur; it was still a more or less non-political movement. He died fighting the French, probably in 1905.

The Senussi centres of teaching, called Zawias, had gradually —from being purely religious—become tribal. At the time of El-Mahdi's death there were over fifty of them in Cyrenaica.

77

They were places of refuge, instruction, and justice, living on their own resources of tillage, water and grazing, granted to them by the tribes. They would consist of a Shaikh, who collected tithes, of teachers, pupils, and servants, and would usually be the monopoly of some tribal family with an appointment, a "blessing," from the Grand Senussi in Kufra. The people of Cyrenaica look back to this simple government, evolved in their own midst, as to a happy time.

There were too many pressures in Africa to let it continue. The Turks first saw it with suspicion in a region they considered theirs. But then, when Sayyid el-Mahdi's nephew, Sayyid Ahmed ash-Sherif, succeeded him, the Italians attacked Libya in 1911, and Senussi and Turks (hitherto not very cordial) were thrown together to resist. Mustapha Kemal Ataturk came out to help in this war, and I have been told that an English lieutenant, recognizing him when the Italians had set a price on his head, allowed him to flee across the border into Egypt, and so laid the foundation of a national friendship which Ataturk never forgot. But Sayyid Ahmed remained, helping the Turks through the Great War. After tying down at least two divisions, he was defeated by the British and escaped in a German submarine, dying later in 1933 in the holy city of Medina, a constant enemy of the Italians.

His nephew, Sayyid Muhammad Idris, succeeded him, and tried to come to terms with Italy in 1917; but the flimsy treaty did not long survive the Fascist rise to power. In 1922 the Sayyid retreated to Egypt, leaving his brother and Omar Mukhtar to carry on a guerilla war which ended with Mukhtar's execution in 1931.

Mukhtar is the hero of Cyrenaica. Innumerable stories are told of his ten-year war, of his heroism, and final death in the presence of thirty thousand or more spectators whom the Italians gathered under the foolish impression that Arabs are ruled by fear. One of the stories tells how the guerilla leader, exhausted after battle, lay asleep in a tent, and the women crept out from behind their curtain and looked at him, and marvelled at seeing so small a man. One of them stooped and measured him from the feet upward with the outspread span of her hand; but when she came to the span that measured the heart, she heard Mukhtar's voice (for he had awakened) say: "This alone (of the heart) is the measure that matters."

Sayyid Muhammad Idris remained in exile in Egypt, and I first met him there in 1934.

He was living in a very modest, inconspicuous way a little west of Mariut, which is forty miles west of Alexandria. I go there when I can to stay with Wilfred and Phyllis Jennings Bramly, who have retired and built themselves a house out of the blocks of some forgotten Ptolemaic structure, on a stony ridge from which you look upon the sea in triangles of sapphire between the yellow dunes. They built a town too, at the request of the Egyptian government, to make a centre for the Beduin, and two thousand are now living behind fine walls built on a Moorish pattern of the time of the Crusades, which will no doubt puzzle archæologists in millenniums to come. When the war swept along the coast, the Bramlys refused to move: the Beduin of all the district were devoted to them, and if they came with any fears, Wilfred would point to his wife and say that when she left it might be time for them to go. Alamein was only thirty miles away; Wilfred wrote to me that their domestic heroine of that time was a hen who, sitting on eggs, had been blown off by the blast of a shell and stripped of her feathers; she gave herself a shake and returned, naked, to her eggs, obviously infected by the same steadiness which controlled the household and encouraged the Beduin.

In 1934, the British eye appeared to be shut, though anyone who looked could see an Italian war on the horizon. Sayyid Muhammad was being quietly wooed by unobtrusive, suspicious people. Wilfred, however, believed in his friendliness and took me to visit him in a square and small suburban sort of villa alone on an eroded hill, sparsely furnished with shoddy, respectable upholstered things that wilted in the pitiless light of the desert, under the driving sand which whispered and piled up on window ledges, like the minutes of one's life pressing in upon one. A white mare snuffed at a meal of chaff in an earth-walled paddock; and a steward, faithful in the Sayyid's misfortunes, showed us in with the dignity that sees no difference in hut or palace.

This beautiful breeding, the sheer ignoring of a material world, was the delight of that visit, and is pleasant to think of now, when Sayyid Muhammad is, one hopes, returning to his own. He sat and talked in a gentle voice, unhurried and detached, with his long slender fingers resting on the arms of his chair as in some Elizabethan portrait; the narrow face and pointed beard and dark eyes might also have belonged to that time, and the outward gentleness run, as it were, on a thread of steel, unpitying and unflinching.

"I have been trying to go to Aix to take the waters," said the Sayyid (who was ill at that time). "You cannot imagine how difficult it is when you belong to no nation. The Italians would give me a passport—but that would be to admit myself their subject, so it is out of the question. The Egyptians, having them on their border, are afraid. And the British"— he smiled. "I asked the British for a temporary pass to take the cure at Aix; they have been thinking it over for some months, and now they reply that they cannot send me to Aix, but will let me go for two months to Mekka instead. It is not quite the same."

I was shocked by this story; but I knew nothing of Government departments at that time.

When the war turned badly, in 1940, Sayyid Idris, still in exile, offered us the Libyans, over whom his word continued to rule. Four Senussi battalions enlisted, and under British officers were sent to the Western Desert. But apart from this, and more important, one may say that every single Arab in Cyrenaica who had the chance, served the Allied army as he could. They guided our raids and furnished our intelligence; and thousands of lost or wounded men owe their lives to the Arabs in Cyrenaica (who practically all belong to the Senussi sect). In two British retreats, every Arab camp was a refuge, and the fact that this might or did entail shooting by the enemy never made a difference. A friend of mine wrote:

"A gunner recently arrived in Derna with a letter from his commanding officer asking that he should be helped to find an Arab who had befriended him. With our help he went out and found the Arab living in a tent in the hills behind Derna. This Arab had rescued the gunner when he was wounded during a retreat, and had carried him back to a cave where he fed and nursed him for six months. Then he took him on a camel, all the way back to Alamein, made his way through the lines, and having handed him over, returned to Derna. He did not leave his name or claim any reward."

Very many stories of this kind might be collected.

The Italians are out now, and these lands are "occupied enemy territory" until the Peace Conference decides their fate. The Allies will then have a chance in Cyrenaica to see what they can do, free from many of the obstacles that make things difficult in other Arab lands. There is no town and nomad problem, for Benghazi is the only biggish town and there are not even any villages to speak of. There is no minority problem, the four thousand Jews have for centuries lived in easy amity with the Arabs. The whole population is solidly devoted to the Senussi and friendly to the Allies. And as the country is underpopulated by the removal of the Italians, there is no population problem.

All that we need to remember is the right of human beings to manage their own affairs. Their incompetence, at any rate when it endangers the general comfort and peace, may, and does, require assistance; but it does not give us the right to take things away from them. And this will have to be remembered, for the Italians have made it difficult. They allowed only minor Arab administrative officers in the districts. There has been practically no secondary education, and many of the young men, though speaking and writing Italian, are poor in Arabic. Even in agriculture, they were denied a share in the work of the new colonies, except for a few labourers. Craftsmen and skilled workmen are lacking.

And yet with all these drawbacks a good start has been made. In the hill farms the Arabs are taking over, pruning the vines, protecting the trees, planting vegetables; and the crops of corn last year did not fall very far below the total produced by the Italians, one of the best agricultural peoples in the world. In the two principal settlements, ninety per cent of the farms are now occupied by Arab families.

Sayyid Muhammad Idris last came to see me in Cairo, in the summer of 1943.

His fine black beard had a few streaks of grey in it, his cheeks were a little more hollow; but he had the same detached and beautiful manner, with a gleam of real pleasure running through it, over the happier prospects of his land. As a consummate politician, he was not giving much of this away, and referred in passing to the Senussi of French Africa, farther west.

With him came the mayor of Derna, a youngish man dressed in a grey striped tweed suit; except for the red tarbush, his tall figure, broad shoulders, and straightforward, rather full-chinned face might have been that of some Ohio farmer. As he was leaving, he said:

"I hope that all will be well. I hope they (the Allies) will not think that because we are backward, and have had no opportunity, we are not fit to keep our own land. We have everything to learn: but we *will* learn; our heart is in it. Give us our chance, give us protection, give us twenty years, and we will have learnt to govern ourselves as well as other Arab nations have learnt it."

I think the mayor of Derna expressed what every greater power could remember—the duty of the stronger to *help people to look after themselves*. The theory of Mandates, whatever may be said against it now, had the great virtue in its day of declaring such a principle: it tried to safeguard the weak or undeveloped from being swallowed or handed over; in the Arab world, in a short twenty-five years, it has already produced four independent powers. One hopes that this fundamental respect for human right on its own soil may be the seal of any future jurisdiction.

Footnote: I have been indebted for many facts in this chapter to the notes of Mr. John Reid and Mr. M. Foote, to both of whom I am most grateful.

CHAPTER XIV

COUNTRY VISITS

"Il faut être léger pour voler à travers les ages."
(ANATOLE FRANCE.)

1. *Minia*

IN the winter of 1941 I once reached Cairo after a short journey. The usual dilapidated porter took my luggage, lifted it on to the shoulder of his blue cotton gown, and flapped away before me in the crowd. When we reached a comparatively open stretch of platform, he stood still, put down the load, and turning back to me: "Peace be upon you," he said. "I too am a Brother of Freedom." We shook hands, he re-lifted my load, and found me a taxi.

This sort of thing was always happening and added to one's enjoyment of life. But the pleasantest parts of the Brotherhood were the invitations it procured us to the country.

Very few tourists have any idea how agreeable the Egyptian country is; neither have the Egyptians, at any rate in the north, and you would think them unaware of anything between Cairo in winter and Alexandria in summer. It would perhaps be a blessing for the landlords themselves if their incomes were so reduced as to make it advisable for them to live in some garden beside their own brown villages, where the water buffaloes come slowly home along the tow path by canals in the sunset light, and the date harvest ripens in brazen clusters, avenues of Byzantine carved capitals close to the columns of their trees, whose serrated spiked fronds above are motionless and sharp against the sky.

As you go further from Alexandria or Cairo, the well-to-do people do lead a more country life, clustered round some smaller provincial town. One of the pleasantest of these was Minia, about half-way to Luxor, in the country which is called the Sa'id. Mr. Serafim, a wealthy and friendly Coptic landowner, ran a committee there, and invited us to visit them, and Lulie and I spent one of our happiest week-ends among the Brothers of Minia.

Whether it be a human being or a town, it is pleasant to meet one that has no rivalry in its heart, but lives, enjoying its own relaxations, without the gnawing feeling that some admired neighbour would probably be doing it all differently. Such a little town is Minia, a prosperous agricultural centre, with a club set in a large garden among electric lights and casual flowers, and a long, wide, well-kept promenade with green clipped hedges, where one can walk on summer evenings and watch the rising or the falling of the Nile.

For some reason which I have now forgotten, the whole town was built on one impulse in 1902. There is an older and very dilapidated Minia adjoining, but the one that matters, with straight streets planned round a centre, with markets and all the oddments of civilized life, is the Minia of 1902 built apparently by Italian architects who brought a florid stucco washed with pale pastel colours, an ornamental style of an earlier generation from Europe. The Serafim house showed this exotic influence, with white marble heads decorating grey marble stairs, and ceilings painted with lace canopies and roses, of great solidity, charming to me because they reminded me of my childhood in old-fashioned North Italian villas.

All this lived comfortably, quietly and contentedly for itself alone. Luxor, with its winter fever and summer sleep, is far up the Nile, and the nearest antiquities to Minia are neglected pyramids scarcely ever visited, that squat among cotton fields on the right as one follows a straight dusty road south from Sakkara.

The mayor of Minia was a fresh-faced, alert, twinkling Muslim in a dazzling loose snowy gown which he rightly refused to exchange for hot and ugly Western clothes. He dined with us in the garden of the hospitable Coptic house, at a long table on a strip of gravel under sweet-scented jasmine; his friend, the chief lawyer of the town, was there also, a handsome, grey-haired, cultivated man; and a number of other leading people of the town. They were evidently in the habit of seeing each other every day, and formed a friendly little oligarchy without distinction of religion, consulting in amity over the municipal affairs on which their lives revolved. There was an Englishman, they told us, then living in the town; I never heard his name, but he appeared to be one of those unhappy British whose manners are a small international catastrophe, and we avoided him; a pleasant young couple opening a British Institute promised happier relations. More influential than any of these was the Egyptian governor from Cairo, who lived in a formal modern villa with a sentry at the gate, and gave us a kindly reception.

But the real life of the town was in the group gathered at table about us. They all had houses and lands in the immediate neighbourhood, low rambling houses whose gardens melt into the fields, so that one scarce can tell where the roses end and the crops begin. To these, their country residences, a mile or two out, they go in summer, returning to Minia for the winter season.

Every extension of road, irrigation, street lighting, every municipal amenity, affects them personally. I have seen the same in Prairie towns of the West where the citizens look with feelings of achievement on improvements as they come. And this indeed is the happiness of any

"Little town by river or sea shore"

from the beginning of time. In such a way the municipal authorities of Epidaurus no doubt rejoiced in their new amphitheatre, and the elders of Mycenae congratulated Agamemnon, or whoever it was who put those ornamental lions up above the gate. There is much to be said for the little town, and all around the Mediterranean shores it came to its perfection, with life very similar, whether in the square at Tarascon, or under Tuscan plane trees, or round the café kept by some Greek in Egypt. You can see ruins in Algiers, in Cyprus, in Syria, of the same civilized provincial life—the pavement at Tipaza with the shops below, looking out over the sea; the long fashionable street at Jerash and colonnaded piazza where young men could turn their chariots and show their skill in driving; the columned ways of Salamis which were followed by the walls of Famagusta; the mounds of Apamea deep in asphodel.

Some are in ruins now, but most little towns continue through the centuries, and their charm is that nothing of universal importance ever happens to them; the cataclysms of history sweep over and leave them, with another name perhaps, but much the same at heart; if the storm is very severe, in a few hundred years the municipal affairs will be discussed in another language; and Mr. Serafim, whose roots are with the Pharaohs, talks over the new road with the representatives of his Muhammadan conquerors in the streets whose Italian architecture of forty years ago already looks mellow, ready to melt into that long vista of small municipal events and excitements which is the history of little towns like Minia.

2. *The Fayyum*

Near the Fayyum there was once a series of such small civilized towns in the Hellenistic age; but the sand has covered them and they have vanished.   Professor Ruthven, of Michigan University, spent some years in excavating among them, and the house of that expedition when they left was taken over by the Lampsons, who made it an enchanted retreat from Cairo, where one spent happy Sundays as remote as was possible at that time from the urgencies of war, riding over forgotten hummocks whose iridescent glass and everyday utensils lie now in dead boxes in museums.

There we rode, mindful of nothing much except the beauty of the sunsets over the lakeland below, while Lady Lampson flew like a small Valkyrie up the slopes of sand; and dotted about with sleepy eyes, on camels, like sphinxes on the ridges, the mounted police kept guard at a distance.

Beyond this house in the desert and below it, the Fayyum lies, with a wide lake visited by waterfowl, between one desert and one garden shore.   It is a large fertile oasis, with many villages that live their island life, among lush groves, and vegetable plots, and fat poultry, and many-windowed domes of clay that look like temples but are really dovecotes, at the entrance to every group of houses.

Here one of our Sisters of Freedom owned a village. She was a quiet, earnest woman, who came regularly to a committee which her more sophisticated sisters of Cairo treated with deplorable irregularity; but there she sat, saying little, reading Mr. Samaha's bulletin with thoughtful care, and her face— no longer young but very gentle—lit by a sudden glow when she spoke of the wickedness of the despotic doctrine that was being broadcast through the land. The Fayyum, she explained, lies open to the Western Desert, and no effort was being spared across that empty stretch to prepare the minds of the oasis for a Fascist entry into the Western gates. And one day she asked Pamela and me to go down with her to talk to the peasants there.

This we did, in Pamela's dilapidated car, with Mme. Bey Wali, hooded and veiled, beside us; and found her house in the uneven village street a little higher than the other houses, and furnished comfortably with electric light, mosquito-curtained beds, and running water, but otherwise unpretentious, opening to farm and garden at the back; for no town is more than an overgrown village in Fayyum, and everyone lives on or by the land, in a peasant society neither entirely feudal nor patriarchal, but tinged with both, and touched by urbanism only through the narrow dark ribbon of the asphalt road to Cairo.

Here we ate fat delicious chickens from the yard, and in the morning met the assembled elders in a room next the dining-room. They were gnarled old peasants, with shrewd doubting eyes festooned with wrinkles, and a few effendis, banker, post-master, village clerk, etc., among them, who all listened to what their president, our host, had to tell them as he introduced us. It was a perfunctory performance; the ardour came from his wife, standing there with her sister in the shadow of the door, unobtrusive; and as I saw the two figures, with the ageless garment of the black veil draped around them, I thought how little women seem to have been impeded by their seclusion. When a new world began to spread about the shores of Galilee, they took their part; and in Mekka, later, the wealthy widow was first to accept the doctrine of Muhammad.

In the Fayyum, our husband was a prosperous man, with an eye to business and a house in Cairo; compared to all that, democracy was a shadowy ghost in his eyes. And yet there was a new warmth in him by the end of the morning, when we had answered questions, and quoted teachers, and satisfied the old headmen of the peasants, and seen a stirring in some of the young men, and refuted the rumours of the Fascists; and we felt that our new little settlement was safe, with a gentle but constant pressure of its womenfolk behind it, nor did we

87

make the mistake, in the land of Cleopatra, of underestimating that influence behind the veil.

In the afternoon, we saw a less happy aspect of female seclusion.

We had done our work, and there were some hours to spare, and our hosts took us driving through the soft roads of this Arcadia, on which orange trees and mangoes and the feathery peppers threw their shade,—to where a small slope has the distinction, they told us, of generating the only water power in the flat Egyptian land. An engineer was in charge, and lived with his young wife in a brown detached villa as new as a new pin, with everything modern about it. We called, and found a drawing-room as polished as all the rest, with satin cushions of every size, shape and colour scattered wherever a cushion could be. On the middle of the sofa sat a doll, almost life-size and very richly dressed; we were left to admire it for a long time, while the engineer's wife got ready to receive us—not an everyday labour, as we saw when she came in, resplendent in Cairo fashions, with waved hair and face made up to match, and tea approaching behind her, in thin Japanese cups, shepherded hesitatingly by a very small maid.

As we talked, she told us what a lonely life she led: there was no one to call upon at all.

"Do you ever go walking?" said we, trying to find a bright side.

"Sometimes, when my husband has time. I could not go alone in the fields."

There seemed nothing to be said; we admired the doll on the sofa.

She gave it a wistful little glance. "I had it before I was married," she said (I suppose she was about eighteen). "I keep it. It is a sort of company."

Poor young effendis. Their professions oblige them to live in country places, and when they marry, their wives, surrounded by exported modernity in chilly splendour, have nothing in the world to do. No wonder they all ask to be transferred to a metropolis, where they may once more see a smile by the domestic hearth, and not feel that the whole social existence of their dear ones depends on them alone. As for emancipation, I often wish there could be less of the committee or group variety, and more of the sort that requires stout shoes and a non-snobbish interest in country neighbours.

3. *Alexandria*

During the early months of 1941 I made many small journeys of the kind I have been describing. There was always a long list of invitations waiting, and time alone prevented the visiting of every district in Egypt.

We spent a pleasant week-end with the tribal people of the north-east, the Hanadis, who still keep to the traditions of Arabia, and deal in horses, and hunt with falcons, and keep the feudal hierarchy, though they have long since settled in villages as tillers of land, and their chief men have become effendis, members of Parliament and such, in the towns.

I stayed on in Luxor, when the Ambassador's Christmas party had left, and visited old friends among the Senussi, who are settled there in villages round about. It was an amusing contrast, for we had lived in great splendour during that week, and I had driven to the station in a luxurious car with everyone else, and seen the Ambassador and Lady Lampson on their special coach, with red carpets and red roses all about, and an array of dignitaries to see them off in an official manner tempered by cordiality (for their natural pleasantness made them very popular). When all this was over, I looked round; the car had vanished; the red carpet was being rolled up along the platform; I found a one-horse garry with a hood, picked up two Brothers who were hanging modestly on the outskirts of the grandeur, and went to encourage a Coptic committee that was venturing in a timorous way to declare itself democratic, like a cautious swimmer with one eye on the Fascist wave ahead. Sayyid Mahdi el Idrisi of the Senussi and a young Muslim school teacher had started our society in Luxor, and it was a diplomatic success to bring the Coptic community in as well. It was chiefly due to a jaunty neat little old gentleman in a grey suit and stiff high collar who had (he informed me candidly) been consul for the Germans: he would have been consul with equal nonchalance for anyone who was socially desirable: what he collected was not principles, but people and curios, a panoply of photographs and promiscuous blue idols plastering his room until there was scarcely standing space: but he found means to settle a committee of Brothers in among the knick-knacks and Mr. Todros Shenooda and Iskander Mahrous, both younger, nervous and

> "Like one that on a lonely road
> Doth walk in fear and dread,
> And having once turned round, walks on
> Nor turns again his head,"

shepherded the little flock along.

One cannot blame a minority in the East for being cautious about its step; the fact that they are so often intractable when co-operation would pay is far more remarkable (and regrettable sometimes); and one of the reasons for welcoming the movement towards unity in the Arab world to-day is that it tends to minimize the very narrow nationalistic and also the bigoted religious boundaries.

The Copts of Luxor did not hesitate long, and their Bishop never hesitated at all. I was taken to see him at the moment when, with jewelled hand and long robes, he came across the stone flags of his palace to take a service in the church below: he spoke kindly and asked me to go with him. Through the dim aisle, quietly filling, we walked, in procession, and a chair was placed for me in the chancel, in surprising proximity to the episcopal throne. It was an afternoon service, and it ended with a sermon; and when the preacher came down from the pulpit, the Bishop asked if I would like to ascend to speak to his congregation about democracy from that elevated and conspicuous place. I have regretted my cowardice ever since, for I do not imagine that the chance to address a congregation in church will ever come my way again; but it had to be done in Arabic, and I felt myself unworthy. I went instead and met the ladies of Luxor at tea.

*　　*　　*　　*　　*　　*

The most remarkable turn taken by our Brotherhood was in Alexandria.

It was begun there by a wealthy contractor, Abd al-Khalil Kinawi, who is now our most valued collaborator. A tall, sallow, drooping man, he was brought one day to my flat in Cairo by a Syrian member. We were by this time so cramped for room, that I had to buy benches which were kept stacked on the balcony between our weekly meetings. At the end of an animated discussion, Mr. Kinawi came up and told me that he was going to start a branch in Alexandria. We did not expect very much, for contractors are usually busy making their fortunes; but he told me that he had made money and wished to spend it in a good way, and we accepted him with pleasure. He began, and after a while I visited him in Alexandria, and there—welcomed with the most generous hospitality—I found the Brotherhood already blossoming among the foremen and labourers with whom Kinawi dealt.

There is as yet practically no organized Arab labour in the Arab world, for the more westernized of its nations, Egypt, Palestine, Syria, are still at the beginning of their industrial development. The elements are there, however; the establishment of factories will produce a working class, and the spread of education will give it a voice. The last war increased the textile factories of Egypt from two to eighteen; the process is accelerated now. The secretary of our Society in Alexandria, an energetic, strenuous little Muslim called Muhammad Isa, seemed to be a predestinate leader of labour in the coming age.

Alexandria is the sort of place where such movements begin; its huge docks employ scores of thousands of workmen, who lift the bales of cotton on their backs. They come from the Sa'id, and have their own courts and customary law, and are a tougher, healthier, and more difficult people than the peasants of the Delta, their vitality not sapped by bilharzia and malaria. They live in Alexandria in a region of their own, of drab streets where huge lorries clatter under the compressed bales, in and out of sheds of long windowless walls and clanking gates revolving on iron, that give a look of prison to the whole neighbourhood. Sad, that the wealth of the world must look so dingy in its origins.

In the middle of this desert of commerce is the Sa'idis club, a charming building with Quranic texts upon its walls, to which everyone belongs. It is of the docks and its workers, and practically no foreigners except those interested in cotton ever visit it. I met its Elders, and drank tea there, charmed with the dignity with which, wherever the Arab civilization reigns, the spirit still triumphs over circumstance, and the most unlikely place develops a ceremonial drawing-room atmosphere of leisure.

In about a year's time, when already I had left Egypt and was there again only on a visit, after a pressing invitation, I again saw our Brotherhood in Alexandria, and drank tea in the dockyard club. Our members had grown to thousands, and only half the heads of committees could be invited, and they were more than eighty. Some were teachers, doctors, business men from the town—but most belonged to the workers from the dockyards, and I sat at a long table spread with cakes and decorations, with a bunch of roses in my hand, and listened while one after another stood up with speeches and poems. There was a strange feeling about it all, as of something emerging, the wings of a creature without eyes or voice, but instinct with life, beating for a way. The workers, as they grow in importance, will gather themselves together, in Egypt as in other lands; and much depends on who leads them by the hand before they come to their strength. The Pasha will do well to think of it while he still has the power to give.

But I was busy with principles and not with politics, and could listen happily to the genuine kindness of all those voices. The last to speak was a sort of Rienzi of the docks, an effendi with thin keen face; the tassel of his red tarbush danced about as he edged his way to the front among the handshakes of his friends. He made a fine speech, using the lovely flexible Arabic as a fencer uses his foils; and when he had finished he walked up to me round the table, and pressed my hand in both his, and with no manufactured feeling said: "Tell them, tell them in England that every working man here is with them." This was in the autumn of 1941, when our garrison was beleaguered in Tobruk.

My own belief in the genuine quality of this democratic feeling, which we found scattered all over Egypt among all sorts of men, was shared by Mr. Fay and Colonel Scaife, who were elected to the secretaryship that I had to abandon and ran it with the same devotion and far less amateurishly than ever I did. And in the summer of 1942 our faith was justified, as all our hearts were tested, when Rommel's Army marched along the coast towards us, seventy miles from Alexandria, and the Fascists in the town bought up the red, green and white bunting, to be ready for the triumphal entry when it came.

At that time we had over twenty thousand members, and half of them were in Alexandria, in hearing of the guns; they worked like slaves in those days, or rather like free men, contradicting the already triumphant Axis rumours, printing leaflets at their own expense, and even fighting the Italians in the streets. When it was over, and Alamein had turned the tide, the Egyptian Government thanked us for our help. The Brotherhood was justified in its existence.

It has now moved to an old and beautiful house in the centre of Cairo, with eighteenth-century lattice work and carved ceilings unspoiled. The members are over forty thousand. Mr Ramzi, who first came to help with accounts (Pamela and I wrote them on the backs of envelopes and they always got lost), now keeps the office, and other clerks have been added to our little Christian Azmi; apart from Colonel Scaife and Mr. Fay[1] there are about a dozen British and other foreign members; the rest are all Egyptian, and when I passed through Cairo last year, I still met the friends of the beginning, flourishing in their new surroundings.

[1] Since my departure Miss Mary Berry and the Hon. E. Gathorne Hardy have joined us in Cairo.

PART III

PALESTINE   SYRIA   TRANSJORDAN

CHAPTER XV

THE CHANGING ROAD

"Ever a little further—it may be
Beyond yon last blue mountain barred with snow,
Beyond that angry or that glittering sea."
(FLECKER.)

IF one were given a single window from which to look upon the changing Eastern world, it should face, I think, the traffic of the road.

Borodin's "Steppes of Asia" show in music the magic of primitive journeys, the dusty, grassy tracks of caravans. The camels lurch from horizon to horizon, with a thin clank of cooking pots and other metal utensils hitched for use to the cords that tie the bales. The noise, mingled with bells, is washed by radiant air; it comes pleasantly, diminishing in distance, with the rhythm of slow, padding steps that have carried merchandise for unrecounted ages across the Asiatic stretches of space and time. I have seen the long caravans, in Persia, and Baluchistan, and in the Arabian South. In the nearer East the hard road has come, to split the caravan into shorter pieces, herded at night behind parked lorries in dusty, shabby places the casual traveller now no longer knows.

When I first went to Syria and Iraq the caravan still held its own, and the mechanic driver waited while, at some sudden corner, camels were slowly cajoled to the inside of the road. In and out of the new smooth curves, wavelike bales could be seen bobbing from short cut to cut, along the old and stony, unengineered, dilapidated way. On the road itself, in Persia, the high-built horse-carts went swaying, hooped, and covered in with canvas; I have watched eight horses pulling them abreast up the Paitak pass.

94

During the war, the traffic of the road has acquired a new and heavy beauty of its own which fits with strange familiarity into landscapes that have seen so many centuries of marching invasions. Military engines of the Crusaders were not unlike, in looks, to our moving armour; and every column here, through all the ages, has been shrouded, blurred, and half obliterated, by the same Asiatic dust.

I have seen, along the Palestine coasts, between ancient Philistine cities, at the edge of small and rocky sunlit bays, our low, cemented turret for guns—a shallow dome in the landscape—and a sentinel standing, his steel helmet and dusty battle dress coloured like the rocks, his rifle alone catching the light, his face turned to the sea.

And travelling after dark along the shore of Syria, the head-lamps of the car have caught a column of tanks, cresting the brow of a hill. The sudden light has silhouetted them against the blueness of the night; the riveted panoply of steel, the slats of the treads and broad squat wheels revolving, the figure of the captain with his jaunty béret seated on the turret rim; —they have shown with every detail etched for a moment, and passed, like the days of their history behind them, again into the dark.

On the desert road between Cairo and Alexandria I have seen the Western convoy hooded and stationary against the sand-storm. The huge, top-heavy lorries loom by the roadside with every canvas fastening battened down in a yellow twilight made intolerable by the sharp and stinging arrows in the air. The sand of the Western Desert must be made of some harder substance than that of Iraq; in three hours, while I waited, it polished the windward side of my car as with emery, and left the shining metal with not a layer of paint upon it; and pitted the glass of the windscreen with small indelible notches; and clotted itself up under the bonnet. I have been told that this western sand has driven its way through the cork of a bottle into the liquid inside.

Perhaps the most romantic of the Middle Eastern roads were those of Persia, that took supplies to Russia in the hard-pressed days of 1942 and 1943. The one from the Persian Gulf, turned over to the Americans, I never saw; but I drove in the spring of 1943 from Delhi to Teheran, by Quetta and Zahidan along the British-kept stretch to Meshed, and then—thwarted by floods and the appalling strip of the northern road that was attended to by the Persian Government—back through the Salt Desert, by Kerman, and Yezd, and Isfahan. Gay and irascible, Johnnie Hawtrey of the R.A.F. came with me, snatching more than his share of the driving and wading in his thigh boots through the puddles to see if we could get through. Here, over the sleet and slush of the passes, across immense and shallow stretches swept by torrents, American lorries travelled day and night, loaded to the brim. Two thousand miles of loose gravel along which the life-line ran were manned with Persian navvies like footmen along the red carpet to a ball: every strip of two hundred yards had a worker attending to it, with a flying squad ready for repairs at any point where a flood broke through. The surface was kept by merely throwing gravel upon "the desert's dusty face"; and the road ran in easy loops from range to range through the remote provinces of the eastern marches, and in a straight grey line across the central, bitter desert of salt. There were some dangers; in 1942 men were shooting among the passes; in 1943 we were still warned here and there to keep away at night or twilight from some passage of the hills; the Kashgai tribes on the western road held up the help to Russia for twenty-nine days against the Persian army. A more serious danger was that of tyres, for the gravel ground them to shreds, and their replacement price in Persia at that time was £300, so that bandits from the Afghan border were beginning to look upon them as desirable, and one might run the risk of being left with a wheel-less car. But the petrol was there in tins in dingy village houses, round which the grinding traffic churned mud and oil into a greasy sea; and Colonel Busk of the Sappers kept a workshop for repairs at Zahidan, to whose kind help we owed the continuance of our journey.

The roads lead from curve to curve, from skyline to skyline, from frontier to frontier into the highlands of Asia, and already I am beyond the boundaries of the Arabian world.

I come back to Palestine and Syria, through which, in one way and another, I travelled nine times during the course of the war, so that the memories of roads and stopping places are too various here to be written down. Of actual traffic of war the happiest picture is in the Sinai desert, along the black asphalt patterned with yellow sand-drifts, in the summer of 1941 on the day the Syrian campaign began. Here, in dazzling light between wind-bitten ridges, a train of guns came gaily rattling along the valley floor, wrapped in loose covers, camouflaged pale green canvas, with long snouts jolting behind the lorries, each one almost touching the radiator that followed; with a feeling of buoyant courage in the brilliant day, and the quick pace, and the fitness of machines and men. One did not see many guns at this time: it was the campaign in which, when General Sir Maitland Wilson was asked for three tanks to send on show to "improve the morale of the villages," his answer was that: "The sight of three tanks would improve my own morale."

I think almost everyone who met him was devoted to General Jumbo, as he was called from his good stout size, his capacity for quiet listening, his eyes—that looked like those of an elephant, small, shrewd and wise. They have an engaging way of peering up from under lifted brows and wrinkling when he is amused; and his laugh would ring out with such full and infectious enjoyment that no one hearing it, even in our worst days, could ever believe the war news to be bad.

I was in Jerusalem, and lunched with him a day before the opening of the Syrian campaign which he commanded.

It might have been launched by the King David Hotel, so electric was the atmosphere there, so thick the press of scarlet and gold braid, so busy the coming and going through the super-decorated halls to G.H.Q., which incongruously inhabited the top floor. General Catroux was there, looking ten years younger as he prepared to cross the border with the six thousand or so Free French who took part. Prince Ali, the son of the Aga Khan, was there, ready to make for his own Ismaili sect among the hills and villages of Hama. John Shearer was there, and Brigadier Clayton, a wise and quiet man with many years' knowledge, of head and heart, of the Arabian world. Half G.H.Q. from Cairo seemed to be there, silhouetted against the conversational background of international people with financial faces who hang about the lounges of King David.

But as you drove down to where in a little square house in the valley General Jumbo lived with Patrick and Mark, his son and military secretary, and a handful of soldiers about him, you came into a domestic atmosphere of quiet. The C.-in-C.'s flag, drooping in the sun above the red tiles and

97

square suburban beds of flowers, looked overdressed. So did the big staff car beside the gate under dusty cypress trees. Inside the house all was plain, undecorated and easy, with a sense of leisure and summer pleasantness through open windows. I was just out of prison in Baghdad. The General had come from Greece whence—someone told me—he succeeded in extricating "eighty-five per cent of our army and seventy-five per cent of himself": he was thinner, placid, full of most excellent common sense, and as ready to be amused and to talk of this and that as if the quietest life on earth lay all about him. We talked, I remember, about military missions.

"The extraordinary thing," said the General, "is that they are nearly *always* wrong."

I had been thinking this myself, in Iraq, but was delighted to have it authoritatively confirmed.

General Wilson and Lord Wavell are the only two commanders I have known, so to say, in action, and both have given the impression of calmness and efficient leisure—the quiet which is said to be in the heart of the tornado. On the day when the winter offensive of 1940 was launched, General Wavell was invited to dine with the American Minister, Mr. Fish, in Cairo; with such preoccupations the C.-in-C. was expected to cancel; but he arrived punctually; the great machine was set in motion, and he had time to spare. Only once did I see him deflected by the thought of trouble. It was at a wedding in the spring of 1941, when he gave away the bride in the absence of her father. It was a Roman Catholic ceremony, and the Apostolic Delegate (an Italian Monsignor) officiated in purple robes in a chapel full of flowers, with a gloomy expression in face of a congregation consisting mainly of the British army. Barbara, the bride, had gold hair from which an immense veil of tulle billowed down the steps of the altar and around her, and heaped itself like surf round the feet of our commander, whose profile showed very firm, kind and invincible against this airy frame. During the party which was given afterwards at his house, I saw him standing with no ear for the buzzing talk, eyes far away and a paper in his hand. It was, Peter Coats told me later, the news of the Desert, where the pendulum was once more swinging against us.

This absence of fuss is in the main stream of British tradition (with the Duchess of Richmond's ball). It had, among other advantages, a tonic effect on Arab opinion, which always responds to steadiness. At the peak of Rommel's advance, the British Ambassador in Cairo arranged for new paint on his garden railings, more encouraging than many a public speech.

To return to Palestine.

On my way through, I would often spend a week or two in Jerusalem, an interval of peace due to the kindness and hospitality of Sir Harold and Lady MacMichael, who allowed me to make a sort of visiting home of Government House—perhaps the most beautiful modern building of the Middle East. Austen Harrison, who designed it, has placed it, with a massive austerity, on the grey hillside, to be the expression and climax of its landscape. In its seclusion, surrounded by descending terraces of rosemary and lavender, with the steep walled city of Zion catching the sunlight on the opposite hill, Sir Harold held the reins of his difficult team, insulted, respected and unperturbed.

"I cannot be doing so badly," he once told me. "If I get abused on *both* sides."

I think history will show that he "did not do so badly." His dignity, courteous and remote; his impish, biting and delightful sense of humour; the rather elf-like look of the dark eyes and black eyebrows under grey hair, were all accessories to a great fund of judgement, experience, and indeed wisdom. It will be a rash statesman who rushes into Palestine without listening carefully to what Sir Harold can tell him.

This is no controversial work, and I have no wish to enter the Palestine arena or to take up any position beyond the very simple and fundamental one that it must be wrong to make a country accept immigration *by force*. The people of Palestine, after two thousand years or indeed longer, are attached —like all the Middle Eastern peoples—to their soil; and they have already admitted close upon half a million Jewish immigrants within the last twenty-five years. The Arabs now number roughly two-thirds, the Jews one-third of the country, so that in proportion of populations the Jewish immigration would correspond to sixty-five millions in the United States. If America *had* admitted sixty-five million Jews, or Gentiles, or indeed Angels, all in one lump in less than thirty years, and it were proposed still *to coerce her to keep her door open*, it is easy to imagine what her reaction would be. The Palestinian reaction is exactly the same.

The British position is a recognition of this fact and a promise that future immigration is to take place only by consent of the Arabs who are the majority in the country. This is the basis of the White Paper of 1939. The British Government, through Mr. Eden, has given the assurance that this policy remains unchanged; but if there were to be any change, it could take place only *with the acquiescence of the country, whose future this change will affect.* The whole question indeed hinges on the fact that agreement and not force must be the basis of the future. If this were not so, the Atlantic Charter for one thing would look remarkably silly. There would also be a general explosion and revulsion throughout the Arab world.

Why a reasonable recognition of these facts should brand one as an anti-Semite I do not know. Many of my best friends of Jewish nationality feel deeply on this matter. To them it is a tragedy to see a narrow and bigoted nationalism threaten that world-wide torch of civilization which the Jew has held up through every darkness and behind which the array of the world is at last slowly gathering.

Even for the Zionist himself, for whom one has great sympathy, there is no eventual alternative to Arab conciliation but failure. In a notch of a country surrounded by totally Arab lands which are growing every year in capacity, self-consciousness and geographic importance, the choice is between a friendly compromise or eventual expulsion. British or American bayonets might force the issue for a time, but not for very long; and it seems to me that the fact to remember about Palestine is that there are *only two* alternatives—agreement or force. If the people who write manifestos, whether for Democrats, Republicans or the British Labour Party, really prefer force, it would repay them first to study carefully the history of the last twenty years in the Middle East, so that they may have some idea of what loss of life, sacrifice, exertion and failure their choice entails.

CHAPTER XVI

VIEW FROM THE HEBREW UNIVERSITY

" Thus saith the Lord unto the house of Israel :
'Seek ye me, and ye shall live :
But seek not Beth-el,
Nor enter into Gilgal, and pass not to Beersheba.'"
(Amos.)

ONE of the most charming people in Jerusalem is Professor
L. A. Mayer, of the Hebrew University. He has a full, square
and curly beard, speckled grey and white like Dartmoor rocks;
and above it are gentle, lively and honest eyes. And he lives
far from the venom of politics, enhancing the reputation of
his University with his studies in the history of art.

I met him in England years ago, but I spent again a summer
morning with him last year, under the aromatic pines which
the University has planted, visiting the fine new buildings, the
open-air theatre, the libraries and laboratories, on Mount
Scopus, with Jerusalem below, and a landscape falling from
loveliness to loveliness, bare in all except its garment of colour
and tender simplicity of lines.

I have visited agricultural colonies round Galilee and Hule,
in the plain of Esdraelon and under the heights of Nazareth,
and have seen the remarkable industrial development near
Haifa and the ruthless vitality of Tel Aviv; but of all the
Zionist achievements of the last few decades—and they are
very numerous—this pleasant University speaks to me with
the gentlest and most humane voice; and although this book
deals with the main Arabian stream and turns regretfully aside,
not for want of interest but of space, from the minorities,
Christian, Jewish or even Pagan, of the Middle East—I cannot
resist the record of this summer morning, with the Holy City
shining below, in a sun that seems to gild without healing
the scars and passion of its history.

Seen so from a hill-top, Time looks like a living water, flowing
with new drops through channels basic to the world. There,

grey among clusters of houses wrinkled with slits of streets, is the dome of the Holy Sepulchre, for whose roof repairs King Edward IV sent lead from England in 1492. A 'gentlemen's agreement' between the Bishop of Salisbury and Saladin in A.D. 1192 arranged for the attachment of two Latin priests and two deacons to this church, and to Bethlehem and Nazareth also, when the Crusaders left the Holy Land[1]; a typically Anglo-Saxon talent for compromise seems to have achieved some success, even then.

It is strange how little the public hears about Christian Palestine. On the wall of St. Helena's chapel, where the wooden relics of the crucifix were believed to be found, the Crusaders signed themselves with small crosses cut into the stone; there are hundreds of them, clumsily wrought and touching, each the record of perhaps a dedicated life or at any rate a great and high adventure overseas. When Lord Allenby had entered Jerusalem in 1918, the bells of Bethlehem were dug up by the returning monks, whose predecessors buried them and handed on the tradition of the hiding-place, when they fled after the battle of Hattin, more than seven centuries before.

So many things are woven in this land "into one faggot of time"; so many different paths wind up the hill to Zion. Below there, not far from the dull gleam of the Dead Sea waters, is the little desert sanctuary to Moses, whither the Muhammadans descend in pilgrimage every spring. Bethany is on the left. The new wisdom of the Hebrew University overlooks the site of Solomon's temple, now the third most Holy place of Islam. Solomon himself built altars outside the gates, "for all his strange wives, which burned incense and sacrificed unto their gods" (1 Kings xi. 8), a conciliatory policy towards the Palestinians of that day: perhaps if it had been persisted in, the Edomites and others might not so have gloated over the city's ruin.

As I sat in the sun, listening to Professor Mayer on Islamic art of the Middle Ages, I wondered what gave the feeling of peace so absent from the Zionist atmosphere of the cities and farms of the plain. I think I know what it was, but it is difficult to put into words. It is perhaps toleration, the opposite of the feeling of *exclusion*. This feeling of exclusion

[1] From the Poetic Chronicle of Ambrose.

haunts one through all the Zionist endeavour in Palestine: it spoils the atmosphere of the agricultural colonies, where Arab labour is nearly all shut out; it spoils the hotels where Arab service even in laundry or garden (I have been told again and again) would be "disapproved of"; it infuriates you if you happen to dislike the Jewish wine and ask for the Catholic, which is hardly ever obtainable; it is only forgotten in the earliest colonies, established before the modern political movement began, whose concern was of the spirit, and whose friendship with the Arab population has remained unimpaired. Even the University might have become, I reflected, a beacon for all if it had made itself bilingual, gradually to unite instead of dividing (for the Arabs who cannot go to the trouble of learning Hebrew are now very naturally anxious to increase the status of their own College on an opposite hill).

At the level of pure learning, in Professor Mayer's company and that of Dr. Magnes and his kind, this exclusiveness is forgotten and one can taste the atmosphere of peace. But it is something very ancient, and one may remember how St. Paul, who knew his nation, puts his hand, perhaps, on the trouble of Palestine, and writes[1] that Peter "was to be blamed" because, having eaten with the Gentiles, he then "withdrew and separated himself, fearing them which were of the circumcision" and, rising to his climax, promises that "they which are of faith the same are the children of Abraham," Jew or Greek, male or female, bond or free. "For, brethren, ye have been called unto liberty; only use not liberty for an occasion to the flesh, but by love serve one another."

This may still be said with profit to those who have found freedom here from the sorrows of Europe and have been given as their home one third of this land; and must, for better or for worse, live with the people of this land who have, as it happens, no racial prejudice against them, and will live peaceably if the fear of their dispossession is removed. And when Professor Lowdermilk promises to harness for industrial purposes the waters of the Jordan, it is comforting to reflect how there is an older Faith that also could move mountains, and walked upon the waters just below us, and was rejected, and lives, and was dedicated by a Jew not to a national exclusiveness, but to the gentleness and universal service of Mankind.

[1] Letters to the Galatians.

CHAPTER XVII

PALESTINE EFFENDIS

"Let us keep it a Holy Land. Let us make sure that we do not transform it merely into another nation, jealous of its own national rights, heedless of those who, for the past two thousand years, lived within its borders."

(ARTHUR SULZBERGER in the *New York Times*, November, 1942.)

"WHILE Mr. Churchill was speaking from Washington in English, we were already repeating his speech in Arabic, and when he ended we were not so very far behind."

The Arab announcers, and Squadron Leader De Marsac, who organized them and Sharq al Adna, the broadcasting station, were showing me over their premises in Jaffa. They worked in low, whitewashed, modern houses, built on corrugated rocks that jut into the water, where the suburbs of Jaffa end in sunny, salt-bitten walls and narrow lanes powdered with sea-shell dust.

The whole thing began in 1942 with a staff of four in a three-roomed farmhouse; but over a hundred Arabs were at work there when I visited it in 1943, and five houses had been taken over; and they ran a practically non-stop programme of twelve and a half hours on the air, covering news, music, drama, religion and children's talks. Every day about thirteen thousand words were translated into Arabic (and Kurdish) from English.

This was an achievement for the war, meant to counteract the Axis who at that time were giving the Arab world twenty-two daily transmissions in its own language. But what most interested me was the fact that Squadron Leader De Marsac had avoided the turning of it into a British or Allied station: it was done by the Arabs, for the Arabs, and no one, walking through the offices and rooms, could mistake the cheerful enthusiasm of all these young effendis, who felt that they were running their own show.

I think the same sort of person who likes the Arab, likes

the Irish, or Italian, or the Greek for that matter; they respond to something that is unregimented and individual, that discovers a reluctance in organizing its soul for worldly good. The people who do *not* like them, who incline to the regulated and German way, are apt to call these people inefficient: but they *are* efficient, only they think that other things are often more worth while. So do I. The call to Efficiency is being sounded all the world over, and, like medicine, is good in reasonable doses; one can only hope that pleasant people may not be addicted to it to the exclusion of all else. In the broadcasting rooms at Jaffa they still kept a happy equilibrium; the coffee-pot was on the hearth and a social welcome offered with the little hexagonal cups to the broadcasters as they came for their appointments: and the broadcasts were none the worse for being sent with a holiday happiness across the wireless space.

    *   *   *   *   *   *

One feels a rather touching quality in the Arab effort in Palestine, due to its financial background which differs so very much from that of the riches of Zion, drawn from all the world: it is rather like David and Goliath, the other way round.

There is, for instance, the orphanage of Deir 'Amr, in the hills between Jerusalem and the sea, just off the Jaffa road.

I went to visit it with its chairman, Ahmed Eff. Khalidi, Principal of the Arab College, and his charming Syrian wife, and they told me how the first £1,000 was collected among fourteen Arabs of Jerusalem who founded it at the beginning of 1940, and built the school, and the farm, and the director's house, in strong stone at the top of a stony hill, overlooking the bare and waterless shoulders and forget-me-not triangles of sea. The Egyptian Government gave a present of £5,000 and the Palestine Government made a grant of £500, and the rest continues to be voluntarily collected among the Muslim and Christian Arabs; and when I went in the summer of last year there were already forty boys learning the art of agriculture, to take back to their villages in the future.

It is an excellent work, for it aims to produce farmers and not theoretical officials: and everything that is done on the place is done by the children, except the heavy deep digging of the yet uncultivated hill. They have got their vines and vegetables planted, and have terraced here and there, and

have put in olive and apple and fig as well as ten thousand
forest trees. A new cistern is there, and four ancient Roman
cisterns have been repaired and are in use; for it must be
admitted that the Arabs have been left with the poorer and
stonier portion of their land, and the crops of Deir 'Amr rely
almost entirely on the heavy dews "which fall," Ahmed Khalidi
told me, "most profusely in all the holy neighbourhood of
Jerusalem."

The agricultural director was a kindly, fair young man,
fond of his work and his children. These live a school life
full of variety: one was feeding the poultry, two others were
cooking the vegetable stew for dinner in cauldrons almost
bigger than themselves. It was August, so the class-rooms
were empty; the neat dormitories were clean and bare; a new
portion of the untamed hillside was being taken into cultivation. Nothing they dealt with was such that, when they leave
their school, they cannot reproduce it in their village life.
They hope in future to increase their numbers, to start a
girls' country school in the dip of the hill below, for which
they have already collected £3,000—and to build themselves
up to three hundred or so in time; but always to keep small
individual groups, so that they may merge imperceptibly into
the village life for which they are intended.

The Arabs' passion for education is, I think, one of the most
interesting things about them. To it we owe much classic
culture, that has been saved and handed down. There is a
typical lament in one of the most charming memoirs of the
Crusading time, the reminiscences of Usama ibn Munqidh (a
Syrian, and a friend of Saladin), who saw his library looted
by the Franks upon the shore of Acre.

"Al Malik al-Salih transported my family on one of his
private vessels to Damietta . . . and from there they sailed
on a Frankish vessel. When they approached Akka, the King
sent out some men in a small boat who broke up the vessel
with axes . . . and the King looted all that was in it. But the
safety of my children and the other members of my family
lightened for me the loss of all the property that was lost . . .
except for the books. For there were 4,000 volumes of the
most precious books and their loss has left a heartache that
will remain with me as long as I live."[1]

[1] Usama ed. Hitti 34–35 trans. Hitti 50–61.

The Turkish occupation threw a blight on this love of learning, and in 1838 there was not a single bookshop in the whole of Damascus or Aleppo.[1] The first political journal, the *Clarion of Syria*, was started in 1860. But love for the beautiful language remained latent, and in the first half of the nineteenth century two great leaders of culture, Nasif Yazeji and Butrus Bustani, both Christian Arabs of the Lebanon, inspired and helped by the early American teachers, once again brought it into the open.

The years of war have helped this Arab renascence by flooding the Middle East with money. It is inflation, and economically it is I believe a disaster, but in the meantime the Arabs have more money in their pockets than ever they had before, and a strong awakening of social consciousness, and especially of the desire for education, is visible in every one of the modern Arab lands. In Palestine the example of their Jewish neighbours has given an added impulse. A few notes and figures taken at random may show something of the spirit of the time.

The little town of Nablus in the hills raised £10,000 towards a private secondary school, to prepare for matriculation. In Jaffa, £12,000 was collected about two years ago to start a school of midwifery for twelve nurses, with twenty-four beds. An Arab doctor in this town established a private hospital at a cost of £15,000. Sitt Amin Khalidi, a lady of Jerusalem, left £150,000 for a hospital and for a welfare centre in the old city. In Gaza, near the deserts of the south, another Muslim lady gave £30,000 and nearly 2,000 acres of land. Damascus has collected £100,000 for a hospital. Many years ago, in 1928, I became interested in a girls' school in Damascus. It was started by a handful of Muslim young women of good family, who still lived strictly behind the veil; they collected the capital among themselves, and with infinite difficulties rented a small house and started.

"We wanted a Syrian headmistress of our own, and there *were none*," my friend said to me: her name is Amatellatif, which means the handmaid of Allah. "We had to take one who had none of the university degrees asked for by the Government; but she was very well educated, and no one asked questions, and she carried us on until the increased

[1] G. Antonius: *The Arab Awakening*.

number of trained women allowed us to find one with all the
necessary qualifications."

The school is now flourishing, with two hundred girls or
more.

In Haifa, an Arab committee collected £12,000 in one week
for the building of an industrial orphanage. Beginning as a
voluntary movement, and now taken over by Government,
10,000 children are given free meals in Jerusalem and various
other towns; and there are children's clubs, like that for a
thousand boys in Jaffa, to which the Government advances
£1 for every other £1 voluntarily subscribed. A Government
school for the blind in Hebron is run by a blind Arab
headmaster, and volunteers have subscribed for the support
of twenty-five boarders. Less spectacular, but possibly even
more significant, is what happens in the villages, where they
are gathering small funds and building their own schoolhouses,
so that the Government may send them a teacher. The result
of all this is shown by the fact that in 1920[1] there were 10,662
Arab pupils in Government schools, and in 1941 they had
increased to 54,645.[2]

This development is quite separate from the Jewish system
of education, which runs under its own regulations and along
its own lines, helped by Government grants but not otherwise
financed by the State. Apart from voluntary efforts such as
those I have mentioned, Arab education receives more of the
taxpayers' money than does the Zionist, and is a cause of
constant protest from the latter; but it should be remembered
that the Zionist population draws financially on a world supply
of Jewish contributions, while the Palestinian Arab has little
beyond the resources of his own stony land; every comparison
between the two must bear this essential difference in mind.
As the entrance of the Zionists in such numbers has been forced
on the Palestinian against his will, the Government find it
desirable that he should gain as many advantages from it as
possible. Moderate people, like Dr. Magnes, voices crying in

---

[1] *Statistical Abstract of Palestine,* 1942:

	1931	1941	Increase	
[2] Arab population	794,000	1,023,000	28 per cent	From J. Katul, Assist.
„ pupils	50,000	93,700	85 per cent	Director of Education transl. Al Muntada

the wilderness, agree. The most elementary wisdom might have prompted the extremer Zionist himself in this direction, and one wonders again what a different history might have been written in Palestine if the instinct of the newcomers, with their wealth and their experience, had been to *share*. The chance has gone by for the moment. Soon after the last war, a Jew of Baghdad (where they have remained as Benjamin of Tudela found them in the twelfth century, a powerful, rich and non-political community), bequeathed a sum to Jews and Arabs alike for education in Palestine; but it was found impossible to amalgamate the two, and the agricultural schools of Tulkarm and Tabor again perpetuate the principle of separation.

In the fields of industry it is the same. The Arabs now make soap, cigarettes and matches, and have looms for weaving in Nablus; they have looms in Gaza and a thousand looms in Majdal; they make marmalade in Jaffa and have oil presses everywhere; their citrus plantations in fact preceded the Zionist ones, and are more successful owing to cheaper labour. The machine age is advancing slowly upon them, encouraged by their dislike of the flourishing factories of their neighbours.

Jewish progress in industry has of course been incomparably greater, and very helpful to the Allies during the war. When the war ends, the natural markets for these Palestine factories must be the surrounding Arabian or Muhammadan lands; so that there is also a strong economic argument for conciliation. The Zionist starts with great advantages, of experience, of organization, of industrial knowledge; the Arab is only beginning, but has on his side the weapon of cheaper labour. For the Zionist to encourage a weight of political hatred against him, is folly; it is to his interest, as well as to that of everyone else, that whatever is done in future may be done with the consent of the Palestine majority, and not in conflict against it.

There is no doubt that, indirectly, if not directly, the presence of the Jews among the Arabs of Palestine has greatly accelerated the advance towards the West. But it has not been the mainspring of that advance; in my introduction I pointed to more general causes to which this is due. As we are in a chapter of statistics, we may glance at some of those of Transjordan, a purely Arab country, where the few Jews there were have wilted away under the pressure of unpopularity caused by their Zionist brothers throughout the neighbouring lands.

Transjordan in 1918 had three elementary Government and six private religious schools; it now has about fifty primary and four secondary schools, in which it teaches over 11,000 boys and 4,000 girls. It had two small hospitals, and no health department: it now has twenty-five either hospitals or clinics. Its population has grown from about 200,000 to just under 400,000 souls and the population of the town of Amman, its capital, from 2,000 to 43,000 in twenty years. Its revenue has increased 700 per cent. Apart from the Arab Legion, of which I write later, the Transjordan Frontier Force—half Transjordanian and half Palestinian and 98 per cent Arab in its personnel, has been helping the Allies in Syria and Iraq. With Palestine, with Iraq, with Syria, Saudi Arabia and Egypt this little country is taking part in the general resurgence of the Arab lands.

Armies, moneys, the accelerated transport, the new demands of every sort, have made as it were an avalanche of Progress. The young effendi can hardly be turned out in sufficient numbers to cope with it all. He is keen enough, and I have before me some examination papers of the Government Arab College in Jerusalem which ask him to write, among other things, an account of Rome in the days of Alaric and a summary of "Lord Chesterfield's Letter to his Son on the Employment of Time."

Poor young effendi. When I was sitting in a crowded tram in Cairo one day, an old woman stumbled up the step just as we were moving.

"You might have killed yourself," said the conductor.

"I have saved an hour by catching this tram," said she.

"An hour?" said the conductor. "What is one hour? One wave among the waves of the sea."

But no doubt Lord Chesterfield has his uses; and the young Arab is grateful for his advice. In Palestine, where we had been fighting him for so long, he contributed £5,000 to the British Soldiers' Welfare Fund; £1,700 to the Red Cross and for the Arab prisoners of War; and £3,000 from Jaffa alone for Allied soldiers' comforts. He knows, and is grateful for, friendship; but he will fight for his own land.

drove alone through Palestine in the summer of 1941, when the loss of Crete and other things made our fortunes none too bright. As I went, I would give a lift to villagers trudging along the roads of Samaria or up through the hills behind Acre; and, every time, I made a point of asking what they thought about Palestine, and whether they meant in the future to live in peace. I always had the same answer though it would be turned in various ways. Sometimes they would begin by saying that they liked the British, or that they had no quarrel with the Jews as such: "They come from Abraham as we do," they would sometimes say. But then two sentences invariably came into the answer:

"We cannot fight you now, while you are *busy*" (as if war with them were a relaxation) and:

"We will fight again later, if we must."

CHAPTER XVIII

LUNCH ACROSS THE JORDAN

" Years of Arab courtesy spoil us for the rough and tumble of the
Western World."
(From a British Official in Transjordan.)

I MET H.H. the Amir Abdulla of Transjordan five or six times during the course of the war. Sometimes at the Lampsons' luncheon table, when the whole party would afterwards go on to watch His Highness win at the races on anything he backed, for he has an excellent eye for a horse; sometimes at receptions given when he came to stay with his nephew, the Regent of Iraq; and twice in Amman, his capital, the ancient Philadelphia.

It is the sort of small capital that Walter von der Vogelweide and the minstrels of his day must often have visited: not in looks, for all in Amman is either very ancient, or Hellenistic, or extremely modern; but the actual life is medieval in its roughness, comfort and independence. It is small enough for everything to be a family affair. On an early spring day, the damp, green highlands smell like the English moors; in their narrow valleys, blossom tosses against slate-coloured skies, and puddles lie in the roads, pleasant to us who come from the unchanging silhouetted palms.

The town is really one long street in the cleft of the valley, with the stream and the amphitheatre and various shreds of the old Greek masonry on one side out of sight. The ancient citadel is above, a grass-grown shoulder, with temples half submerged and blocks of stone, and a Byzantine-Muslim *qasr* still standing, decorated with wind-worn reliefs and shaped like a cross. Beside it, near a cistern built by forgotten forefathers, boys of the town are playing football; caves where Ammonites lived long before Greek or Roman came still keep some poor gipsy inhabitants on the shelving slopes around. The Arabs, says Professor Hogarth in the *Penetration of Arabia,* have "assimilated to their creed, speech, and even physical

112

type, more aliens than any stock before or since, not excepting the Hellenic, the Roman, the Anglo-Saxon or the Russian." These descendants of the Ammonites are fine people, sturdy, tall and with colour in their cheeks given by the climate; they are manly and friendly, and there is a feeling in the town of a healthy poverty, not too hard to be easily borne.

Its population has increased, as I said before, from two thousand to forty-three thousand in twenty years, and new houses have been spreading with new roads, like the fingers of a hand from the valley to the surrounding heights. From the blackout of Palestine one came to lighted streets which, with all the usual municipal services of a modern town, have also been produced out of the little country's own resources since the last war. A central square has blossomed with flower-beds, and a band that plays on Friday afternoons; a tiny house of Parliament has been built; and on the high ledge of the plateau, with the houses all below it, stands the modern palace of the Amir.

The Amir Abdulla was the second son of Husain al-Hashemi, Sherif of Mekka, and—like many of the foremost Arabs of his generation—was educated at Stambul. Before his thirtieth year, he represented the Hejaz in the Ottoman Parliament, and became interested in Arabian liberty. It was in his name that correspondence first with Lord Kitchener, and then with Sir Henry McMahon, was carried on, by which the Arab revolt was planned.

After the vicissitudes of the war and his brother Faisal's short-cut reign in Syria, Abdulla entered Transjordan in February, 1921, with the intention of attacking the French; the then Colonial Secretary, Mr. Winston Churchill, interviewed and persuaded him to abandon this plan, and he remained, at first to keep order among the tribes, and from May 5th, 1923 onwards, as ruler of a virtually independent state. He has never wavered in his friendship to the British or his dislike of the French; after 1940, when I expressed my sorrow over France, he waved it away with both his small and well-kept hands: "A good thing," he said. "Let it be so. It will mean a year or eighteen months longer, but England will be alone at the peace." In his family, the game of politics is in the blood.

He is now sixty-two years old. His idea of democracy is an old-fashioned one, of a ruler who listens to advice and does with it what he thinks. He belongs, indeed, to the Arab world which is passing, with its high breeding, its absolute self-reliance, its great charm. To him the Middle Eastern map is one of dynasties rather than nations, and the coming reign of the effendi as surprising as was the development of America to George III; and he never forgets that he is not only the ruler of a small Arabian kingdom, but also heir to the greatest dynasty of Islam.

I was invited to lunch on my last visit to Amman (in 1943) and—having been driven to the palace—waited a few minutes while His Highness finished the midday prayer in his garden. He came, small and slight, and exquisitely neat. Behind his easy friendly manner is the whole line of his ancestors, to the Prophet and beyond. His gown, striped satin grey-and-white, might have been made by Lanvin; a gold dagger was in the sash, and a white cloak fell from the shoulders, stitched at the neck with gold. His head-kerchief too was white, held by a white silk cord. I made my curtsey, but he took my hand in both his and led me into the dining-room, a modern room with big windows round a polished table. It was a European meal, with a small and easy family party, and we talked in Arabic about poetry and hunting. The Amir has the love of his ancestors for things of the open; he knows the names and ways of animals and flowers; and is himself able to compose a verse, with that feeling for poetry as a part of every-day life which still makes the charm of the East.

I was planning a little box at that time with an inscription for General Wavell, and asked him what he thought of Mutanabbi:

"The night, and the horse, and the desert know me:
And the sword, and the lance, and the paper, and the pen."

"I never like Mutanabbi," said the Amir. "A poet must rank by what he makes one *feel*, and Mutanabbi speaks nothing to the feelings. He is all courtier. But that particular quotation is right for General Wavell."

He looked across the table at Shaikh Hamza al-Arabi, who was sitting there as it might have been Walter von der Vogel-weide, but in appearance more like a Persian miniature, with a wide pale face surmounted by a huge turban.

"Add a line to the quotation," said the Amir.

The learned man obediently sank for a minute or so into meditation; at the end of it he was, like Mr. Rogers, "delivered of a couplet."

The Amir himself had now fallen silent.

"And the East and the West and the Germans know me,
And the Greeks, and the Turks, and the banners.

"What about that?" he said.

"Yes," I said. "But perhaps as the Turks *are* still neutral? . . ."

"True," said the Amir. "We will put India instead. Write it out, Shaikh."

The Shaikh copied all the four verses in a beautiful calligraphy, and brought them to us as we sat over coffee in another room. His Highness looked over them carefully, crossed out and substituted a word that did not scan, and the devoted Shaikh once more retired with his pen to copy.

It was one of the pleasantest luncheon parties I can remember.

CHAPTER XIX

TRANSJORDAN AND THE ARAB LEGION

" Men are the heartbeats of Man, the plumes that feather his wings.
Storm-worn, since being began, with the wind and thunder of Things."
(SWINBURNE.)

THERE are various ways in and out of Transjordan across
the river, but perhaps the most beguiling is the one which
climbs from Galilee, through Ramoth Gilead which is now
ar-Remthe, a low-roofed little town among downlands of
corn; and south under twisted oak-woods, whose branches
caught Absalom by the neck (not the hair),[1] when he came
there unused to forest country from barren Judæa; by Jerash,
still sleeping like a long lizard in the sun, its mellow street
a street of ruins, its Greek air of civilisation undestroyed; to
the medieval age of Ajlun, where the mosque has Roman
foundations, but the shell of the castle still stands overlooking
the southern menace of dead crusaders from its hill.

One can drive through all this in an afternoon, and I did
so, listening to Stewart who, having left Aden for Baghdad,
was travelling about, elaborating Biblical scenery and the fact
that Ruth, the most agreeable of all the Old Testament women,
was a Transjordanian.

What interested me even more was the progress of the woods.

They have grown enormously in the last twenty years, and
the little country now possesses 510 million square metres of
forest land, a gift from the population to the state. Mr. Kirkbride, the British Resident in Amman, told me how this
remarkable present came to be made, for which he was himself
chiefly responsible: for there had been a Turkish law which
prevented landowners from cutting down their trees, much
resented by the independent Arab villagers; and in 1933,
Mr. Kirkbride and Mr. Mitchell spent three months touring
the country from end to end, asking them if they would grant
their barren, "useless" patches of land to the Government in

[1] Sam. II. Ch. 18, v. 9.

116

exchange for the repeal of the law. The two officials had only their personal word as a guarantee; but the Arabs knew and liked them, and the forest question has caused no further trouble; the Government are now planting out the treeless parts of their 510,000 hectares from nurseries that have already issued 200,000 fruit and 500,000 forest trees; and the forests are growing so high that future Absaloms can safely ride beneath them.

Urban governments seem to be extraordinarily reckless in their dealing with land; they look upon it as something to be bought and sold like any other property, and hardly realize it as the blood and bones, the livelihood and the deepest love of men who have had it from their fathers and have watched their children grow there with the corn. The owner in the city may lightly sell his scarce-visited acres; but he who for generations has gathered in the harvests of one particular field, has got its substance bred into his soul. Italian expropriation in Cyrenaica, so as to make room for colonists on Jebel Akhdar, "made the Arabs much more bitter even than the executions and concentration camps; for land with an Arab is more important than life itself."[1]

In Transjordan the Turks had been working it on a system which was bound to give a minimum of production with a maximum of trouble; it was largely based on communal ownership, with a re-allocation of the separate plots every three years or so. In 1933 the Government began a great work of permanent settlement of claims, with registration, and survey of village boundaries: it is not yet finished, but already lawsuits are reduced by ninety per cent: and it has been done with the advice and help of the villagers themselves.

Mr. Kirkbride lives quietly in Amman. Tall, slow of speech, devoted to these people, he has piloted them through a number of their changes. He first became a friend of the Hashemite dynasty in 1918 when he joined the late King Faisal in the attack and capture of Damascus. He has lived in Transjordan and Palestine ever since. He has no authority except that of wisdom in his advice; if that were doubted, his advice need not be taken. But it never is doubted, for no one can help feeling that the life of this little country, which he has watched from its cradle, sits at the very centre of his heart. One would

[1] J. Reid: *Report*.

like to think that such a happy exchange of friendship and service might be the new and only meaning of "Empire" in the world.

Transjordan is fortunate, for it has had devotion from its foreign servants from the beginning of its separate existence, twenty-one years ago.

Some, like Mr. Kirkbride and Mr. Foote, are still there; some like Colonel Peake of the Arab Legion, have handed on to their successors; the whole number altogether are a small handful; and the country is chiefly run by its own children in an atmosphere of equality pleasant to people who have no exclusiveness of race or caste. Over ten years ago, when I was lunching in Transjordan, I sat next to H.H.'s A.D.C., who happened to be a negro from Nigeria, and in the course of conversation told me how shocked he had been by a party of Western ladies who had come from Egypt and walked down the High Street in trousers.

This complete absence of racial self-consciousness, this real devotion of Arab and British working together, the proof of a practical possibility full of infinite promise, makes Transjordan one of the pleasantest countries in existence. In the Arab Legion, which represents both army and police, the second in command is an Arab, the third British, the fourth and fifth are Arabs; there are about ten times as many Arab as foreign officers, and whoever happens to be senior gives the orders. At the head of it all is Brigadier Glubb Pasha, a small, blue-eyed man with a gentle manner and a persuasive voice; he has been known in all the deserts that lie between Iraq and Syria since his first coming out there in 1920. Fourteen years ago I heard of him "in a ruined castle of the wilderness where the Jinns bring him the desert news";—it was an Iraqi policeman who told me, and his legend had already taken root. In 1930 he came to Transjordan, and was given command of the desert area, with a magistrate's power over the tribes. In 1939 he took over the Arab Legion.

This is the only independent Eastern army between Gibraltar and India which has actually fought for the United Nations and is still serving outside its home territory; (Palestinians, Sudanese and North Africans have fought, but under direct European command). H.H. the Amir lent his little army to the British for the duration of the war, and though their active fighting is over for the moment, they are still manning a number of garrisons, and freeing Allied troops for service elsewhere. They now wear khaki battle-dress and steel helmets over short hair, and manage their modern devices, their wireless and artillery with smartness and ease. But when I used to meet them in the desert, racing at speed across the scrub in their trucks or in one of the six armoured cars they made for themselves when the British were too hard-pressed to send equipment, they still wore the dress that gained them the affectionate name of 'Glubb's Girls' throughout the desert armies.

Half-hidden under belts, cartridges and bandoliers, their cotton gowns like nightgowns had long white sleeves wrapped for action round the khaki cuffs of the battle coats they wore. Their hair lay in plaits on each shoulder; their eyes, black-pencilled with antimony, looked very dashing under the flowing red fringe of the head-dress and the jaunty black circlet, lopsided, that held it on.

They are a gay, devoted little force, half-police and half-soldier and their spirit is the most remarkable thing about them. From 1926 to 1938 (Britain having agreed to attend to the external defence of Transjordan) they were policemen only, recruited partly from the nomad tribesmen and partly from the villages. Their commander is automatically also the Governor of the desert, and the desert administration here is entirely staffed by tribesmen (so that there have been no tribal raids in Transjordan since 1932).

In 1938 the Arab Legion became also an army. But it had not got very far in extending itself, when war broke: France, and therefore Syria, had collapsed before the training of a motorized regiment was agreed upon. By 1941, four hundred and fifty men were mechanized and joined the less-than-two British battalions who fought across the desert to Baghdad.

"At that time," Brigadier Glubb has told me, "every single Arab was convinced that Britain was done for."

Loyalty, fatalism, and a complete devotion to their leader, kept them in what they thought a losing cause. Their services were far greater than their numbers would make one imagine, for they alone knew the desert with its treacherous dips and sandy low ridges and sudden lacerating outcrops of sharp stone, and were able to guide the mechanized column across five hundred empty miles to the river lands of Iraq. They also, while the main body fought for the Euphrates at Fallujah, led a northern column to cut the Mosul road and descend along the Tigris to Baghdad by the golden domes and four gold minarets of Kadhimain, the holy city; and it was fear of this force, and its possible march eastward across the road to Persia and the way of escape, which—we were told—induced the rebel commanders to flee while yet they could across the border. The Syrian campaign against the Vichy French opened in June 1941 as soon as Baghdad was relieved, and the Trans-jordan army—turning round to accompany the attack on Palmyra—again led British troops across the desert. Chancing upon a French mechanized column, they enjoyed a small battle of their own, in which they took eighty prisoners and three armoured cars, and brought them back with half a dozen captured trucks and shouts and cheers to the Allied camp.

Gay, swaggering, dusty and nonchalant, incredibly cluttered up with garments, these were the second people from the out-side world to reach the invested Embassy in Baghdad. The first to arrive in early dawn on May the 31st, was an Iraqi car with officers, bringing the British representative, Colonel Gerald de Gaury, who stepped over a sleeping servant athwart the Ambassador's doorway to rouse Sir Kinahan and take him across the lines to the signing of the Armistice. By the time he came back, the Children of the Desert in their armoured car were with us. With a fine untidy arrogance of the wilderness they strolled about the decorous but weary purlieus of Chancery, glancing at us—pallid and rather deplorable effendis—with friendly and tolerant amusement. There is no doubt that the Desert considers itself superior. So do we, for that matter, thinking of all the gadgets we have made. But perhaps an unshakable gaiety in the face of Life and Death, an acceptance of the universe with all its accidents, and a love of adventure are just as solid causes for satisfaction.

CHAPTER XX

SYRIA

" Beyond the village that men still call Tyre."
(FLECKER.)

MEN still call it Tyre, and it is off the main highway along the Syrian coast. At the cross-roads, notices and policemen tell the military what to do; they show large signs by stagnant rivers, among banana and sugar-cane plantations—saying that here is no camping but only malaria: they point out car parks under olive trees whose trunks are speckled like vipers, their leaves silver and dark as moonlight: and the road winds through villages with roofless houses and shot-spattered walls, where the French so strangely fought their friends in 1941.

But Tyre, on her headland, listens to the waves. Her columns are lost or carried away or lie in the sea where they fell broken, and the water, clearer than glass, lisps over them or under, singing an old song learned in the mornings of Time; and the causeway built by Alexander is flanked with fields and crops; and the streets and markets, leisurely places, keep the Roman rectangular shape unwittingly, and the forgetful children of the Phœnicians still build small clumsy boats on the open beaches. There is nothing left in Tyre except this forgetfulness, a life of little things quieter than silence, an essence of oblivion woven with the sun and sea.

In spite of the traffic of the greater harbours, Haifa and Beirut and Jaffa, this remote atmosphere clings to the Philistine and Phœnician coasts. As you go south from Athlit you meet it in sun-bleached coves, where villages that once were little cities look down from the ridge of Palestine on to their bays. You find it drifting with the sand and the swallows in and out of the Gothic arches of Tartous; and in Latakia, where sailing ships are moored to shafts of columns sunk into the grass-grown quays; and in Ruad the island of sponges where Phœnician walls, half eaten away, stand on sea-wet ledges, like Titans made undistinguishable by time. All these cities have somewhere in their neighbourhood the ruin of some yet older city: through languages now forgotten or unknown, they go back to days before the record of language; their tombs, their rude cyclopean gateways, their earliest caves in the limestone, make a strange, silent tumult to the mind; and all along this coast the sea wind, and the smooth waves with their undertone and the humming particles of sand seem to exult with a fiercer gaiety than elsewhere, with a ruthless loveliness, constantly triumphant over the works of men.

History built on history behind him gives to the Syrian effendi of to-day a civilized and slightly tired charm. A long unity, not of race but of life, has set a seal on the river lands of Iraq and Egypt, and on the desert lands that lie beyond; but Syria dips to the Mediterranean, and every wave, whether of ideas or nations, has washed along her shores.

Out of such diversity the idea of unity can grow. It is the homogeneous nation that finds it difficult to amalgamate with others, and a degree of fusion, already well advanced within her own borders, is beginning to appeal to the modern Syrian as an international adventure with his neighbours. Religious toleration is the test of success or failure. If the cleavages of centuries between Muslim and Christian, between Shi'a and Sunni, between Orthodox and Maronite, or Druse, can all be overcome—there should be no great difficulty in extending the process across merely political boundaries.

In the summer of 1943 I visited various people in Damascus, Arabs both Christian and Muslim, and was surprised to see how much unity of outlook has already been attained. The leader of the Nationalists, Shukri al-Quwatly Bey, now President of the Syrian Republic, I had known already and liked and admired in Baghdad. He is a tall stooping man, built heavily and with a heavy, powerful face; everything about him droops as if with some invisible load that presses the flat dark eyebrows over heavy-lidded eyes. The forehead is low and broad. He is impressive even in the dull suitings which are our Western contribution towards the unification of men. He has the ease of someone used to an audience, and a pleasant smile, and an air of integrity which his life and reputation have sustained.

Member of an important Muslim family of Damascus, owners of land, like many of his class and generation he was educated in Stambul, and became an official there before 1914, but was soon imprisoned by the Turks for his interest in Arab freedom. He was in King Faisal's Syrian government from 1918 to 1920, and played so great a part afterwards in the anti-French movements which flared up into the Druse revolt of 1925, that the French excluded him from their amnesty, and he lived from 1928 to 1930 as an exile in Egypt. After his pardon in that year he returned to Syria; held office; withdrew from politics rather than compromise on the matter of the treaty with France; and re-entered with immense popularity in the summer of 1942. When I saw him in July, 1943, he was just being returned to the Syrian Chamber with a smashing majority; as we left his house, a procession of students and other young men came to congratulate him; they stretched from the end of his street to the top of his stairway, and cheered as he appeared with his visitors, saying good-bye; I had to edge my way down past the smiling and shouting crowd, and thought that the French Sûreté was probably putting a most inaccurate interpretation on a harmless unofficial visit that ended in this vicarious blaze.

What with foreign education, exile, and dealings with a number of governments, Arab public men have many opportunities for broadening their minds. Shukri Bey has a statesman's outlook, and shows its tolerance in the questions that most interest Syria, federation, minorities, Palestine and the French.

For these, as for the Jews, there is no basic animosity in the Arab world. Indeed I have often admired that flame of France, which works into the very marrow of other civilizations, so that it becomes a part of them, impossible to divorce.

After 1940, whatever the feeling for her policies may have been, the French *complexion*, in those lands whose culture she has kneaded, remained practically unimpaired. I have wondered if British influence would so survive the loss of Britain herself? And, speculating on the cause of this tenacity, believe it to lie in the fact that *ideas* have an importance to Frenchmen which in Britain they lamentably lack. If you place him between a theory and a locomotive, there is small doubt which the average Englishman looks upon as the more substantial: the Frenchman recognizes and serves the intangible, and lives at ease in a house not built with hands.

In other sorts of building he has a future filled with obstacles,

123

particularly in Syria. He has been pursuing an old-fashioned policy, the exploiting of a zone of influence in which the population tends either to become assimilated and deteriorate, or to rebel; he has been doing this in Syria, which is, as it were, a small island among lands where for the last twenty-five years Britain has been trying out a new policy of advice and suggestion, with as little interfering as possible: this means constant adjustment, frequent bad government, and a great deal of friction over the exact measure of interference, but it *stimulates*, and its result is beginning to appear in an *active* friendliness among the Muslim peoples.

There are arguments for each of these systems, but they cannot work side by side.

The keeping of Syria back, while all the rest of the Arabian world advanced towards independence, has caused a great deal of bitterness and has become impossible for the future. It has been made worse by the fact that French management has gone down to very small officialdom and has been frequently corrupt; there is a possible choice between a *good* foreign and a *bad* native government—to be governed badly *and* by foreigners is desperate.

At the same time one may sympathize with the French dilemma, for the progress of Syrian independence is bound to re-act on North Africa, where policy is tied to a large French population settled on the land, liable at any moment to produce the sort of racial problem which the United States are facing in their south. Incidentally the effort in Syria to run counter to the general current of Arabia is bound to foster continual French animosity against Britain and America, who are encouraging the independence of the neighbouring lands.

The feeling about all this is practically unanimous and was shown unmistakably both by the elections in 1943 and by the disorders of the Lebanon among the Christian Arabs. That such a nationalist movement should come from the stronghold of French influence shows how much religious divisions are giving way, and not so very slowly, to national and international cohesions.

Shukri Bey al-Quwatly has established and is manager of a jam factory: Naim Al-Antaki, Foreign Minister in 1943, is lawyer to the Syrian Petroleum Company: Faris al Khuri, now President of the Chamber of Deputies, is director of a cement factory; in Syria perhaps more than elsewhere one notices how the Middle Class is coming to its own.

Naim al-Antaki is a pleasant civilized man in his forties, educated in Beirut University and excellent in his English. His family—Greek Orthodox Christians—migrated from Antioch to Aleppo about three centuries ago. He has spent a busy life in travel, politics and law, and, when I saw him, had returned from a discussion on Arab federation with Nahas Pasha in Egypt.

We came to this, as one comes to every subject in the Arab world just now, by way of Palestine.

"It seems to me a strange thing," he said, "that in every other country your Anglo-Saxon theory is to carry out as far as practicable the wishes of its inhabitants: for Palestine alone there seems to be a general idea both with you and with the Americans that the voice of its inhabitants should not be heard. They have been there two thousand years. Does that give them less of a title than that of most other nations?"

"I couldn't agree more," said I. "But don't you think that the whole question may become easier from a practical point of view if the Arab nations come together into a Commonwealth. What does Syria think of it?"

"We can't federate until we have something to federate *with*—and that is why our national development comes first. But I think we are now on the way, each of us towards our own national status, and in sight of a general union, economic educational, and perhaps military, at any rate between the northern countries of Arabia. The actual form will probably be a very loose one, and would have to be settled by delegates from each of these nations."

"Shukri Bey al-Quwatly has been telling me exactly the same."

"The whole of Syria is agreed on these basic points," the Foreign Minister assured me.

I came to this conclusion myself, for I talked with a number of people, including Jamil Mardam, who was back in politics. Khalid Mardam, one of the leaders of the Damascus Academy, a learned man-of-the-world, said the same from a more abstract angle. So did Ernest Altounian, who lives in Aleppo, and knows northern Syria better than anyone I know; half Armenian, half Irish, and a poet, he can see things in a light of his own. The family of Dr. Shahbender, old friends of mine, are living apart from politics since his murder—the loss of an honest man grievous to think of. I saw him last in the first months of the war, tall and tired, with long face and features, and blue eyes, conscientious and careful, looking as if for some answer far away.

Another charming blue-eyed Syrian, white-haired and acute, with a sort of Hans Andersen benevolence about him, is Faris al-Khuri, a Protestant lawyer from the hill country of Hasbeya, which is shared between the Christians and the Druses. He too was educated in the American University of Beirut. He retired from the Professorship of the Faculty of Law in Damascus on reaching the age limit in 1940, but was elected President of the Chamber of Deputies in 1943.

"The merit of the British," he said to me, sitting at his desk with eyes twinkling, "is that wherever they govern they have *trouble*. They teach freedom, and naturally that makes everybody restless, since one learns to wish to be free. Other countries keep well away from it, and their people are obedient and quiet—like the dead."

"As for us Christians, in Syria and Lebanon," he continued, "I think we are going to make a better business of it than Palestine. We have as old a claim to our land as anyone else anywhere, but we are taking our share in the general life of the country, and its unity comes on, however slowly. And our Jews are as much a part of the Syrian nation as any other: their chief men in Aleppo have been imploring the British not to allow Zionism across the border. It is not fair to think of them as Zionists. Zionists," he said with another twinkle, "are *Nazis*: they base their system on *race*: they let no one in from outside: they have the same chosen-by-the Lord attitude: and the same regardlessness for anybody else. We Arabs have a lot to complain of: you make fine gestures in countries that do not belong to you: but if you stick to your White Paper, we are glad enough to think of the future and not of the past."

At this moment a deputation of learned men in turbans trooped in and draped itself over the office chairs: we made a circle suitable for conversation, and went on from where we had stopped.

"We would be satisfied with the White Paper," said a mulla

with black beard and gown, "if we thought the British would keep their promise. The one to the Jews they have kept; they have given them one-third of Palestine; but ours they always break."

"There is no breaking up to the present," said I rather crossly. "We stick to what we have said and Mr. Eden has confirmed it in Parliament in so many words. It is no use to worry about people's sins before they have been committed."

This sounded like theology. The mullas looked at me, and nodded their heads.

"I may tell you," I said, "that I am a Government servant myself while this war goes on: and if we *did* break our promise, I should resign to-morrow, and so would lots of other people. You mustn't think that the Arabs have a monopoly of honour."

A murmur of agreement greeted these words, and I left, escorted to the door by my delightful host and thinking what a godsend for conversation it would be if only the Palestine question could be settled. One cannot get away from it, and it is not as if the Syrian effendis had not plenty of other things to think about. On their old foundations they have to build a house of very many mansions to accommodate the variety of their people, so closely intermingled, so deeply different, so strongly individual. And above all, they have a sort of interior, psychological revolution to accomplish, for the day is coming when they must no longer sit back and criticize the governing efforts of others, but in the dust of their own arena must build their own edifice themselves.

CHAPTER XXI

THE DESERT TO BAGHDAD

"A Dry Wind of the High Places in the Wilderness."
(Jeremiah.)

In the spring of 1941 I paid a short visit to Baghdad; the interesting events of Rashid Ali's rebellion prolonged it, and when that was over Sir Kinahan Cornwallis asked for my transfer to Iraq. I returned to Cairo for a few weeks only, to settle my affairs as I could, and hand over the care of the Egyptian Brothers of Freedom to the hard-working, devoted and much beloved hands of Mr. Fay who, with Lulie and his wife to help him, wrestled all the year with the increase of committees as remarkably and as successfully as Hercules with the pythons.

In 1942 Major Scaife, who had been led away from us by the siren of the Western Desert into a Senussi battalion, was invalided and returned, and is still our president. The army and its conventions have passed in vain over his intellectual head; and he wears his uniform with an air of Oxford ease. He reads the poets delicately, as if they were expressing the meaning of his life; he is interested in ideas, so that young men love him (and so indeed do we all); he is a sensitive actor, devoted to beautiful things, and our house in Cairo with its old loveliness has been awakened by him out of its dusty sleep. Yet his heart is away with the armies, longing for the routine of camps, and he clings to his uniform with the feeling one might have for a flag hanging by some altar—badly in need of pressing but symbolic.

He was away in Tobruk while I prepared to leave Cairo and all its friendships of war, and all the worlds which revolved there in a planetary system of unbelievable entanglement. One would miss these visitants that sailed in and out of one's orbit; the Free French star, whose hard heroic course one met in charming places, at the table of Professor Wiet and his wife, well-remembered friends; in the circle that joined young Egypt to listen to her teacher, Dr. Taha Husain; or in the beloved house of Esther and Michael Wright, where one might meet General de Gaulle with his strange, sad face, or General König, most charming and kindly humorous of all the Frenchmen.

There was the world of the Italians, contacted at unexpected points, through Bernard Burrows of the Embassy, or Christopher Sykes, who was usually to be found scribbling it down in caricature in office hours—or John de Salis dealing with the Apostolic Delegate, or Colonel (now Brigadier) Thornhill, who struggled to make military directness a match for the tangle of animosities with which he had to deal. One felt with the Italian patriots as one does with a zig-zag river—what a lot of ground it might cover if only one could make it go in one direction only—and I would come away full of sympathy and affection for the bluff old Colonel who struggled so gallantly (and not at all unsuccessfully) with things alien to the military mind. The most charming of the Italians was Mme. Terni, who loathed Fascism and all it stood for, and worked for our radio station with a sad and disinterested devotion and a bleeding heart, and many a rebuff too from words she must have heard about her country, all the more bitter if she felt them true. We in our darkest days have not had that misery, to be ashamed of the land we belong to; it has surprised me to see how rarely this is recorded for what it is—the deep fountain of our life at this time.

There was the world of supplies, which kept Charles Empson awake at night, wondering how half a dozen lands could be fed while most of their public men insisted on hoarding things in cellars. There was the Women's Club, with Zinette, and Dorria, and Mme. Ragai and the Coptic sisters, and a number of charming Egyptian ladies. There was the Anglo-Egyptian Union with John Hamilton and Walter Smart too often the only Englishmen there. And days at Mena, and John Shearer, the D.M.I., to breakfast on Sundays, and a few hours off now and then walking with Tom Boase or Austen Harrison in the Zoo, soothing a jaded mind with simple pleasures such as the sight of the hippopotamus at lunch, or visiting mosques with Mrs. Devonshire and the young men from New Zealand.

On the morning of July the 8th, 1941, I drove with Sophie Shone to say good-bye to General Wavell. He was being sent away from us, as C.-in-C. to India, after directing four victorious campaigns through four countries and in two continents, and evacuating our army from Greece with twelve aeroplanes and a handful of troops. He looked tired, and sad, and kind, and the huge and empty aerodrome, the sandy edges of the hills, the pale colour-wash—ochre and blue—of the early day, seemed all to lie attendant as a frame to a picture, round the group of uniforms and the weather-beaten faces, and the solitary figure who was handing over the defence of all this world and what it meant. He stopped first with one then another, leaving a trail of affection unspoken but glowing, warmer than the pale sunshine of the morning. Admiral Cunningham and some of the Navy were there, and a few Air Force with our new A.O.C.-in-C., Sir Arthur Tedder, a great leader and a charming human being; and Lady Wavell and two daughters, and Peter and a number of the Army. The little group, the buff and scarlet and gold, lonely in the bright morning where only the kites were flying, with the camouflaged Lysander lying like some French brig ready to take off into the sea of air, made me think strangely of a Highland farewell in the Stuart wars; the image was not inspired by any thought of lost causes, but by an atmosphere of loyalty and personal devotion that hung about the scene, and with it an acceptance of all that comes. Sometimes it is given one to see men greater than all their fates, through some accidental rift, as it were. Here it was perhaps the loneliness of the sandy aerodrome where so little coming and going of aircraft lay at our command: the handful of men who stood there were holders of the bridge of Asia: General Sir Claude Auchinleck, with his fine head like a lion, had his foot already upon it; the watch on the bridge was being changed: and far away the landscapes of Asia and Africa, widening from their meeting places, the ranges and deserts and ranges, and pale green intersecting valleys, lay waiting; and the greater pincer claws of the enemy, at which in their advance we were so desperately hacking, were beyond, on the horizon of the Caucasus, of Libya and of Crete. All this was visible, if one looked, on Heliopolis aerodrome that morning.

A day or two afterwards I left for Baghdad in a little car, a Standard Eight, regardless of friends who said they knew more about my driving than I did and called it unfit for the desert.

There was a great deal of military traffic to come to one's rescue at that time, and I took a day's supply of food and water and an extra tinful for the radiator, and hoped nothing would happen to make me change a wheel (which I know I am incapable of doing).

A wheel did behave strangely on the way through Sinai: it made a noise and began to sway from side to side; a friend to whom I was giving a lift to Jerusalem tightened it with a spanner. I hope he never guessed my anxiety when we rose from Beersheba to the backbone of Palestine, for—having learned to drive on the flatness of Egypt—I had never met a hill before. To start down those shining curves of asphalt, disappearing round sharp corners frequently cluttered up with sheep, was rather like the breathless painful joy of the débutante when first she ventures on to a dancing floor.

I left Jerusalem and began the solitary part of my journey, and the self-starter came out in my hand in a long piece of wire before we were well out of the suburbs. A red-bearded Arab travelling in a truck stopped to show me how one manages without a self-starter, by putting two little pieces of metal together inside the bonnet and keeping out of the machinery when it begins to go round. The great gift of Arabs with motor-cars is that they know how to get along *without* any vital part. In a hollow of the Samarian hills we stopped again, this time with no apparent reason; we just panted and settled down; and after waiting half an hour or so, a party of effendis going home to their village gave me a push and we went on again. This, I thought, promised badly for the desert of Syria, and I reached Haifa and left the car to be overhauled while I spent two happy days in Naharia, a tidy prosperous little colony of Jews from Germany where, in a touching piety of exile, an old-fashioned, non-political atmosphere from Europe gives a friendly welcome to all.

My little car, the garage told me, was as fit as a race-horse, and I took it up the steepest slope of Palestine to Safed, coasting in the middle morning down to Galilee in a new and happy intimacy with hills. There was time for a bathe at Tiberias; a seaplane was brooding on these waters that seem to hold for ever their secret peace. I went on after lunch, and picked up a young communist from Poland on the way to his colony at the south end of the lake; as we went, he told me of the life there, its aims, its beauty of sharing. He was a happy lad, and he had found his Philosopher's stone.

"How do the women manage for clothes?" I asked. This has always seemed to me a difficulty.

"They are distributed by our elders from a common stock."

"Do you mean that one can't choose what one likes to wear?"

"One has a small choice—not very much. Nobody *cares* for such things," said he proudly.

"That," said I with real admiration (but I would have believed it more if I had heard it from a woman), "is quite wonderful. I have always thought the trouble with Paradise would be that all the Angels are dressed alike. And you have got over that?"

"It never occurs to us," he assured me.

I set him down at his turning, and wished him well, and drove on, thinking how easy all would be if everyone enjoyed being like everyone else. Instead, we have this mosaic of little pieces that must be made to fit with the pieces of other people. But, dash it all, I *prefer* a mosaic. I was still in the middle of these reflections when, in the lowlands of Jordan, the car stopped again.

It was 2 p.m. of the 12th of July and so hot that if one left the steering wheel for a few minutes it was impossible to touch it again without gloves. After a short wait, an R.A.F. lorry came along, and a sergeant took charge. He pulled pieces out of the car and cleaned them; he sent for tools from a camp near by; he overhauled the carburettor and the pump; a stream of perspiration, small but constant, trickled down into the machinery as he worked.

"Well, miss, I don't know what *was* wrong with it, but it's all right now."

The afternoon was past its hottest point; I thanked the sergeant in the most heartfelt manner; and began to wind steeply and pleasantly out of the trough of Jordan. I came to the high-shouldered downs, the open cornlands, and Mafraq where roads met in a dust of camps. There one picks up the pipe line as it turns to Haifa, and follows east along it, on a smooth asphalt road. The little car went humming at seventy miles an hour; the shadows lengthened; now and then a convoy came along, its trucks jumping like jack-in-the-boxes out of the unseen dips of the road; one sped through the black landscape of lava where volcanoes, dead and shallow, still rule over the desolation they have made. As the sun sank, I reached H5, the first of the stations ringed with tall wire, lit at night, that stud the pipe line along its desert length.

Mr. Herridge of the I.P.C. in Haifa had telephoned and given me a letter, and the I.P.C. everywhere opened its arms and gave me the kindest welcome, and helped me on my way. They also gave me petrol, which otherwise is a serious problem across the five hundred miles of desert. They had luxurious beds and bathrooms, and were tidying themselves after the ravage of the Iraq rebellion, which damaged some of them more than others; it had caused all the wives to be sent away, and I was the first woman to appear on this desert horizon. The rebellion had also killed hundreds of singing birds, for the water which is brought in pipes has made every one of these stations a small oasis where all the garden flowers grow, surrounded by the wilderness and separated by a hundred or a hundred and fifty miles from the next point of water: and when the pipe line was temporarily abandoned and the water stopped, the birds that had come to inhabit these gardens were found by the returning owners dead among the desiccated flowers.

As I lay that night thinking over my car, it seemed to me that its defeat in the Jordan valley had, like that of the Amorites long before, some connection with the sun. So I decided to leave early and cover as much road as possible while the morning was cool; my hosts were not yet up when I was on my way, and I breakfasted in H4, the next station, where—for want of anything else anywhere near—the frontier formalities are conducted.

I had a letter from Brigadier (then Colonel) Glubb, of the Arab Legion, and handed it with my passport to one of his men; he, with long calico sleeves peacefully unwound falling to his feet over the khaki uniform, was lounging in the sun. The name of Glubb is electric all over the desert: it had the effect of bringing out a young man quivering with eagerness, who asked after my health and enquired casually whether I wished to sign some papers.

"I will if I ought to," said I.

"It is just as you please," said he politely.

"If it is for *pleasure*," said I rather stupidly, "the less I see

153

of papers the better," and drove away, causing some trouble to the C.I.D., who only caught up with me late that night by telephone in Rutba and—with or without Colonel Glubb's letter—thought it strange for a woman to be travelling in the desert at all.

It was hot again now and the asphalt ran flat with dancing edges into lakes of mirage that retreated before me. An immense emptiness lay shining in the sun. At about eleven the little car stopped. This time I waited a long while. A truck came with a few soldiers and a corporal. He peered about under the bonnet. "There is nothing wrong," he said. I tried it and the car went on. It must be bewitched.

It soon panted and sat still again, and I began to be troubled with the thought of the real desert, two hundred miles with no road, still before me next day. I felt towards my car as the best of husbands must sometimes feel towards his wife, it seemed *so* incomprehensible and unreasonable. At this moment a taxi came with a tinny noise out of the mirage, a dilapidated vehicle driven with Arab *joie de vivre* by an elderly man with head well wrapped against the heat in his black-and-white keffiah.

Where the Army and R.A.F. had spent so much labour, he gave one careless look.

"The car is too hot," he said. "All it needs is a compress."

"How do you give it a compress?" I asked.

"I will do it," he said, rummaging under his seat. He brought out the ragged remains of a vest, tore a piece off, soaked it in water which he carried in an earthenware jug, and wrapped it carefully round the petrol pump.

"When you see that she feels the heat, you renew this compress," he explained.

I tried the starter, and the little car set off like a swallow: the heat, I was told later, had been vaporizing her petrol; after this, whenever she flagged—which was every two hours or so—I renewed the compress and all was well.

I reached H3, some hundred miles on, for a late lunch, and an Armenian chauffeur mended a puncture which appeared just as I turned into the gate: Providence could hardly be kinder. My hosts too were friendly as everywhere, and offered a room to rest in. With the help of some R.A.F., they had just found two soldiers who strayed from the station and missed their way, and were picked up half-dead after forty-eight hours, only sixteen miles from the aluminium tanks, and the lights and houses of the camp, so treacherous and so swift in their misleading are the low baffling hills that fold the desert landmarks.

The road now ended and I followed a winding track, in and out of open dips and rises that glowed in the westering light. The waste becomes cool and bearable about 7 p.m. in summer. A lovely feeling of having the world to oneself surrounded me and my car. But I lost the track; I noticed it by the leaps of the wheels over small stony wavelets; a landscape as full of points as a pin-cushion seemed to lie ahead; and, like an insincere smile, the pleasantness of the desert vanished. The sun set; the low ridges, all exactly alike, seemed to draw like a flock of sheep towards me; I thought of the two soldiers and the forty-eight hours and what a nuisance one would be. The little car had turned round and I retraced my way carefully, for the tracks scarce showed among the stones: but I had not strayed far, and, as the evening gathered, drove in to Rutba wells.

From time immemorial this must have been the half-way house between Iraq and Syria, for the water here comes to the surface from deep springs. When I first saw it in 1929 there was only the square fort with a hut or two, but now a little village with a main street has grown up, dingy but washed by the fine desert air. A charred feeling of ruin was all about it, for the war had passed here little more than a month ago; burnt-out skeletons of aeroplanes and trucks lay on the ground, and the fort where one used to find beds and meals and water to wash in, was gutted by fire, and now taken over by Sikhs. Luckily George, who used to manage the Rest House, was still there; he had often looked after our comfort, and now offered me a camp-bed and a room in the town; and I dined with Colonel Hammond and his staff, encamped outside, who were gathering what tools the rebellion had not scattered, for the continuing of the road.

They wished to give me an army escort, but I started off early in the morning, with a tribesman of the Shammar who knew the way. He was squatting in the dust, under the beginning of the dawn, girt as if for a camel journey, with a knotted staff in his hand and his head well wrapped in the red keffiah of the Sunnis. The desert lay joyous and still, brown with scrub, blue with distance, scored by innumerable pale ruts where the traffic of the army had passed. The two battalions that had relieved Baghdad had come this way, and left the surface churned into what seemed Atlantic waves to my small car. The Shammari still looked upon it in the light of a camel, and pointed to short cuts that were never meant for tyres. What he was preoccupied about was the honour of his tribe, and how insignificant were those few who sided with the rebels, and how drastically the main body had taken action against them; he spoke in what to me was a difficult Arabic of the desert, and I lost most of what he said, being anxious over the road, and interrupting him.

"Ya Shammari, is it right or left?"

"Allah is great, whichever you prefer, oh lady."

"Oh, comrade, this is no way for cars."

"Every way is good. All leads to the Euphrates." And he was back among the annals of the tribes.

A mile or two on our right we saw a camp where the materials for the road were again being gathered, and we made a détour across a flat of caked and hardened mud to report our passing there.

"My God, it's a woman!" the Captain in charge apparently said when he saw my coming.

Very few foreign women were yet back in Baghdad, and only one, Mrs. Dowson, in Iraq to the west of it. Even a year later, as I was being driven home from a visit to Habbaniyah one day, the R.A.F. chauffeur said to me: "It did us good to see you at the picture show last night, miss." (Apart from a few Sisters in uniform, I had been the only woman there and had worn an evening dress.) "You can't think what it means to us," said the driver, "just to see a lady sitting at a table pouring out tea."

Some of these men had already had five or even seven years' service away from home, in camps in the sands, often under canvas where the heat in the summer of 1942 was so great (126° in the shade) that one out of seven went sick with it. No wonder that "a lady pouring out tea," gave them a feeling of home.

The captain of the camp offered me a cool drink, and saw me off on my way, and we now descended through the hottest hours down long slopes that lead to the Euphrates. The whole landscape seems to prepare for the climax of "the great river," and sweeps towards it in one gigantic descending desert curve. I reached the asphalt of Iraq, so pitted with holes that the sand was better; and at four o'clock came to Ramadi, and the customs, and parted from my tribesman, who had relations to stay with until Allah provided some means for his return. He could scarcely be persuaded to accept a present, for, said he: "We have been companions."

I continued alone, and in a short while saw the R.A.F. cantonments among trees, and the shallow cliffs around them from where the Iraqi gunners so strangely failed to demolish all that lay below. A notice said: "R.A.F. only," and being, I suppose, demoralized by desert, I cut across a shallow ditch and an aerodrome thinking it the intended road, and soon found myself among hangars in the silence and solitude of summer afternoon. A mechanic tinkering at an aeroplane at last showed me the way, and I was told in the A.O.C.'s house, over tea, that I ought to have been challenged by all sorts of machine-guns. But it is too hot in summer to defend things in Iraq in the afternoon; and it is far too hot to attack them.

A. V. M. and Mrs. d'Albiac gave me the most charming welcome. Their house was air-conditioned, their garden full of flowers, the bath a dream; it was strange to think how nearly all this had been destroyed. They were amused at my arrival, for a colonel had just before telegraphed asking for an armoured car escort across that desert patch. My Standard Eight went to be groomed by the R.A.F., who told me that all her oil had been jerked out of the gear box, which accounted for a grinding noise, but seemed to have done no permanent injury.

Next day I set off again, thinking my difficulties over. The river, so flooded during the fighting in May, was now quiet in its banks beneath the narrow iron bridge of Fallujah, which both armies had felt too precious to destroy. The mosque beside it was intact. Beyond that little town, between Euphrates and Tigris, is the gravel peninsula where the battle of Fallujah was fought. Burnt and derelict skeletons of transport lay upon it; it was a plantless, reddish desolation. I had often crossed, thinking nothing of it in a strong swift car: but now I saw that it was a huge expanse of corrugated gravel wavelets, devastating to my coracle; and there was at that time no road across. As if it were a sea, one could watch traffic here and there upon it, sailing a different course, not within hail. When I was about half-way near the middle, a flood of hot water pouring over my feet made me open the bonnet, and there was my radiator with the fat tube that leads out of it gaping to the air.

I looked about for any sort of a sergeant or corporal, or even a private—but there was nothing in sight. So I took out a spanner and began to work by the light of nature. There seemed to be some screws that had fastened the tube: I undid them, got the two ends to meet, screwed them together: I felt immensely pleased with myself, and filled the radiator again —slowly, since the tin of water was too heavy for me and I had to do it in stages from my drinking bottle. My chief trouble was that my legs were being scorched by the sun while I did this, and no part of the metal could be touched. But it was the last obstacle. Before dark I was in Baghdad; the desert lay behind me; and the asphalt now stretches across it from end to end. It has linked Iraq into the great chain of modern communications; and that pleasant, wayward, inconvenient sort of journey belongs, on that particular itinerary, to the history of the past.

PART IV

IRAQ

CHAPTER XXII

APRIL IN BAGHDAD

" A dreadful quiet felt and worser far
Than Armes, a sullen Interval of War,"
(DRYDEN : *Astraea Redux.*)

I FIRST saw Baghdad in war-time at the end of March 1941.
The "crisis as usual" which I find marked in my diary, was
a good deal worse than usual against the background of
invasion and the African news.

Four Iraqi Generals, known as the Golden Square, long
worked upon by German whispers,[1] had seized power, with
Rashid Ali as their political colleague and spokesman. They
had taken over the post offices and radio station; every word
spoken over the telephone was listened to; and on April 1st
they had searched the palace for the Regent with—it was said
quietly—four doctors and a certificate of death by heart failure
already written out. The Regent had slipped through the
guards of the bridges, hidden under rugs beside the U.S.A.
Minister, Mr. Knabenshue, in his car, who had whisked him
away to the R.A.F. at Habbaniyah. This was a very brave
thing to do, but Mr. Knabenshue was a big man both in body
and in heart; most loyal, with a long knowledge of Iraq and
the Middle East behind him, he stood like a dreadnought among
waves, steady in his friendships.

The British at that time were not so fortunate. The outgoing
Ambassador knew nothing of the East, and of the mixture of
delicacy and firmness there required; but he went, gentle,
pleasant and optimistic, in a Buick by way of Afghanistan, and

[1] For the background to this chapter see my three articles in *The Times*
of June, 1941, and article "Iraq" from *Islam To-day*, printed in the
appendix.

Sir Kinahan Cornwallis was due to arrive by air on the 2nd of April. A scattered British and American contingent turned out to meet him: they were joined by the Mayor of Baghdad, Arshad al-Omri, small and neat under a top hat amid a conspicuous absence of other Iraqi officials. The poor effort at welcome was wasted; a message came to say the Ambassador was detained at Habbaniyah: he had met the Regent, no doubt, and was talking things over. The Mayor walked away beside us thoughtfully, saying nothing.

Sir Kinahan arrived next day and remained many days ostracized as it were in the Embassy, and scarce visited by the officials of the country who knew well enough the symptoms of a storm. The town, otherwise, took little notice; even the usurping army stood in a bored way about strategic points, holding their bayonets as if they were fans. The newspapers ignored everything. All they said was that the Police Garden Party was postponed.

Meanwhile things grew steadily worse. The Governor of Basra was arrested: the telephone wires of the palace were cut, and the Queen Mother with the six-year-old King lived intolerably, isolated and constantly watched; the devoted English nurse, Miss Borland, cooked and tasted the King's food. The Regent, said to be in a British sloop at Basra, repudiated the new government; his broadcasts were jammed in a competent way, and Reuter's fatuous message about "perfect tranquillity" was promptly scattered in leaflets by the usurping generals. The situation hung poised and explosive, while relations between Britain and the men in power were being determined.

The war threw a sombre light over this anxious landscape. Greece was finished, and we were just losing Benghazi, and were still fighting alone: there was no temptation for any small nation to join us. On the other hand, I find written in my diary on April 3rd: "We can dish the Iraq army *first*, and they know it. If 'two lines of bayonets never meet,' and we keep ours steady, theirs will wobble." The Generals were playing with Germany, but they were not eager to play until Germany was actually there. They protested that this was an internal crisis with which we had nothing to do; that the treaty with Britain continued unimpaired; and they asked for recognition.

Sir Kinahan Cornwallis now showed himself for the very fine diplomat and statesman he is. He seized on the fundamental fact that the Iraqi generals needed time, and made use of the time for the landing of British troops in Basra, under a clause of the treaty which gave "all facilities and assistance, including the use of railways, ports, aerodromes, and means of communication through the country" in time of war.

Rashid Ali and his government were outmanœuvred: if the treaty existed, the troops—badly enough needed in all the Middle East—had every right to land; and this was agreed to in the middle of April, while Sir Kinahan still kept his official recognition suspended. The effect of the landing was peculiar. The troops were received with the warmest of welcomes in Basra; I have noticed throughout the Middle East that the seaports, which saw the Navy coming in and out, believed in a British victory from the first. Basra in any case has always had a very friendly tradition towards Britain. It was more remarkable that in Baghdad the reaction on the whole was also one of pleasure. I spent these weeks almost entirely among my Iraqi friends, some of them in the opposing camp, and came to the conclusion that the country was very far from following whole-heartedly the clique in power: events showed, I think, that this summing up was correct. The Basra landing, and its effect on opinion in Baghdad, must have proved to Rashid Ali and the Generals that German bayonets alone could carry them through.

A very uneasy period followed.

The Germans were not ready; the four Generals could not afford to show their cards; their more moderate followers hoped that all could be solved by a friendly recognition: and meanwhile Sir Kinahan's friends in the country, who had known him twenty years before, seeing a firm and trusted hand in control, began to gather round.[1] One by one, a flowing desert mantle, a city robe finished off with tailored coat and *sidara*—and—gradually—the Western uniform of the effendi, began to appear in and out of the shabby arcades of Chancery. I gave a party during those days, mixing Iraqi and British and spreading the invitations in a non-political manner; few were expected to come. The editor of the worst of the news-

[1] Sir Kinahan had accompanied the Amir Faisal to Iraq in 1921, and had stayed as Advisor to the Ministry of the Interior till 1935.

papers telephoned the day before to say he was prevented by illness.

"There is a lot of this illness about just now," I said insidiously over the telephone; a dead silence at the other end. But twenty-nine Iraqis came to my party, and there seemed to be a particular touch of friendliness about it, as if men were pleased to find a little bridge still standing.

Another and more important social event had also made this clear some weeks before. Dr. Sinderson Pasha, with others, had organized a fair for the Red Cross; it was to be held in the beautifully geometric gardens of the city hall which our Mayor had built. The crisis was obviously coming, and many suggested that the fair with all its capacities for trouble be abandoned. But Dr. Sinderson has seen many troubles in Iraq; he was besieged in Hillah twenty-four years ago, and has lived in this country ever since, training young doctors, giving his services, his sensible Scotch advice, his genuine friendship to people too numerous to remember, from three generations of the royal family down to the poorest porter of the suq. Tall and good-looking, though the hair with its curly ridges has now gone grey, he is still ready to face trouble with a smile and a set of home-made rhymes, open-handed and open-hearted; it would take more than an ordinary crisis to disturb him and his doings. The Red Cross fair was opened: there were booths, there were fortune-tellers, coco-nut shies, lucky bags: the band of the royal bodyguard in dazzling uniforms blew with full cheeks their brazen notes: and everyone except the four generals and their immediate friends came to buy, pouring money in a touching way because, the ladies—Muslim, Jewish or Christian—said, staggering out under parcels: "It is good for those soldiers in the desert."

I believe that if Sir Kinahan had been sent out six months earlier, the whole catastrophe might have been averted. As it was, we were already in that smooth race of water that precedes the waterfall. A day after our Ambassador's arrival I watched the K.L.M. deposit the new Japanese Minister on the Baghdad aerodrome; his reception too was meagre enough, but there he was, and his Italian colleague beside him. And walking into the Zia Hotel on the afternoon of April 4th I found George Antonius seated amid a gowned and turbaned circle with Haj Muhammad Amin-al-Hussaini, the ex-Mufti of Jerusalem.

The Mufti sat there all in white, spotless and voluminous, a man in the early forties wearing his turban like a halo; his eyes were light, blue, and shining, with a sort of radiance, as of a just-fallen Lucifer.

Beside him sat a sad, black-bearded man with venom in his glance. A few effendis were of the party, watching my approach with discomfort. But the Mufti was an artist; he looked pleasantly excited, as at the meeting of an enemy one rather likes. He had that sort of magnetism by which a man makes a difference to a room when he enters; in his young days he had organized a dramatic society in Jerusalem and took the comic parts; and he had bewitched George Antonius as securely as ever a siren did her mariner, leading him through his slippery realms with sealed eyes so that George—whom I was fond of—would talk to me without a flicker about the Mufti's "single-hearted goodness." I looked now with deep attention: there was little good, and certainly nothing disinterested in that face—but intelligence, and a great, if bogus, charm.

"I am delighted to meet you," I said, enjoying myself. "So few of us British have a chance to do so now."

The black-bearded devotee looked as if he could have killed me. The Mufti smiled with genuine amusement. We left politics carefully alone, and talked pleasantly about modern Arabic literature, and when the whole gowned, snakelike company rose to depart, the Mufti alone turned at the door to bow—rather like a cardinal dispensing benediction. In his young days, as an officer of the Turkish infantry, in Smyrna, he had made a close and lasting friendship with Mahmud Salman, now one of the generals of our Golden Square: he was known to have pocketed large sums, both German and Italian; he was the source of perhaps more than half our trouble in Iraq. He escaped by slipping through the hands of the British in Persia across the Turkish border, disguised—they told me—as an Italian sailor: his practice as a comic actor must have stood him in good stead.

Everyone knew that our storm was going to break, but everyone thought it would hold off a few weeks longer, and on April the 25th I went up for a week to Teheran where a colony of two thousand Germans or more, all under thirty-five, were obviously getting ready for their hour. A premonition which no one shared at that moment made me start on my return three days earlier than I had intended, so missing—happily as far as I was concerned—the Ambassador's telegram asking me to stay where I was. The lovely Persian spring lay like an embroidered mantle on the hills; larks were beating their small cymbals in the sun, unseen; from the flowery pasture waves of scented air broke like invisible foam about the speeding car; and I wondered what was happening in Iraq, for as I left my kind hosts in Kermanshah early in the morning, the Oil Company there had sent a message, asking me to hear some news. I had refused to wait, as I knew that it would probably prevent my journey. So I travelled wondering what would meet me at the frontier, and was relieved to find that I could pass through the first little Iraqi post on the desert boundary, where two friendly young men signed everything and sped me on my way.

"'Every night we pray to God for a victory for you," they said. But they had no news of Baghdad.

Like Cortez when he burned his boats, I had taken the precaution of having no return visa for Persia, so that when once I was across the boundary, the Iraqis would have some difficulty in getting me back again. I have had a good deal of practice in the crossing of frontiers, and felt that I was probably better at it than an oil magnate. When we reached the little town of Khanikin, the first hint of trouble appeared with a policeman, who leaped on to the running-board of the taxi and guided it through sullen and deadened markets to where the police had their headquarters. A tall young lieutenant with wavy hair, rather long, looked up from his desk as we entered, recognized my chaufffeur, and asked if he had brought the wrist-watch from Teheran.

The chauffeur pulled three out of his pocket to choose from.

The lieutenant looked at them with dismay. "These are *men's* watches," he said. "Didn't I tell you it was for a lady?"

"For a young and pretty one, I imagine?" said I, interested in this comedy.

The lieutenant gave me a glance which adopted me into the category of human beings, and agreed with a smile.

I showed him my wrist-watch, a very plain gold one unadorned.

"You see they *are* worn very like a man's when it is with a day-dress. If you give her *that* one," I pointed to the middle one, "and tell her it is the *moda* for sport, she will be very pleased indeed."

The lieutenant held them all out in a row.

"You think she really will like that one?" he asked anxiously.

"I think so," I said. "Any woman would be pleased with it."

"*Taib*, good," said the lieutenant, and, handing back the other two, concentrated his mind on the civil war of his country.

"I am sorry you cannot be sent to Baghdad," he said. "I have interned two travellers already. A telegram came last night to say everyone was to be stopped."

There was nothing I wished less than to be imprisoned in Khanikin.

I did some very quick thinking.

"Did your telegram say that women as well as men were to be prevented from going to Baghdad?"

The lieutenant looked at me, assailed by doubt.

"No," he agreed. "It said travellers. It said nothing about women at all."

"It would be a nuisance for you to have to keep a woman here," I said, as if the matter were settled. "You would have to find a separate house; and of course you would have to find me a maid. I never stay anywhere without a maid," I said very seriously. "You would wish to do it all in a civilized way—you are not Germans after all—and it would give you a lot of trouble."

The lieutenant's face had been growing longer as I went on.

"Well," he said. "What would you like to do?" He evidently thought I was good at giving advice. "Would you like to go to Baghdad by train or car?"

"By to-night's train, I think."

"*Taib*," he said again, and called to a policeman. I tried to test whether I was a prisoner or not by asking if I could stroll through the markets: this was forbidden. My policeman took me to the station, my things were unloaded in a room of the guest-house which gave on to the platform, and my chauffeur—with a note to Teheran which was never delivered —left me. The policeman followed me in.

There is a very unpleasant feeling of helplessness in the middle of a hostile population on the verge of war. I asked for some lunch. After an hour's wait I asked the policeman to find out if anything were being done about it; he came back with an evasive reply. I realized that no one would be rude to me, but that I was already a compromising object to be avoided, and that I might soon be very hungry indeed. Somehow, human relations with the railway station of Khanikin *must* be established.

"It would be nice," I said to the policeman, "if we could have some tea. If you can bring the attendant here, I will ask him, and we will have it together."

This was a good idea. The attendant eventually came. I spoke to him for a minute or two about other journeys to Khanikin, pleasant journeys with tips and friendliness at their end, and how well he had always kept his rest-house. "It is, of course, your work and your honour to keep it well."

"By Allah, Lady, we do what we can."

"It may be difficult to get lunch to-day, as you usually do, but perhaps you could find a little tea—not only for me but for the police?"

The good man gave a glance in the direction of Power, saw that it looked benevolent, and disappeared. In a little while he came back, and there were fried eggs and potatoes on the tray. This small but substantial victory had taken me four hours.

Feeling stronger after food, I now went to work on my policeman, whom I had settled at the table beside me, with a biscuit and a tea-cup in his hand.

I asked him what was happening.

He knew nothing. The oil plant in Khanikin was being seized and there were rumours of attacks in Baghdad and Habbaniyah. "It is a pity," he said.

"It is indeed," said I. "Friends are like horses: if they are good, it is a pity to change them. How long have you been in the police?"

"Nearly twenty years," said he.

"You must have been trained by Colonel Prescott?" said I.

"Yes," he answered; his rough, rather nice and open face lit up. "He was a fine commander."

"He loved the police," I said. "And he built them an honourable name in Iraq. It is good that his work continues."

I poured out two more cups of tea. The policeman was slowly connecting the image of Colonel Prescott, whom he liked, with the abstract picture of 'The English.' We continued with reminiscences. "All this is a pity," he said again.

"It will soon pass," I remarked lightly. "Meanwhile, I am grateful to you. You are here beside me, to protect me, and I feel I need not fear anything."

The policeman had come into my room thinking he was guarding a prisoner; he now saw that he was protecting a lady of the tribe of Colonel Prescott against any possibility of trouble. His decent and chivalrous feelings leaped at this interpretation, and he was my friend for the rest of the evening. As the dusk fell, we walked together up and down the platform under a crescent moon, and taught the station-master's small daughter how to trundle a hoop with which she was having difficulties. The policeman was telling the bystanders about Colonel Prescott and Major Cones: voices here and there were saying that the English were good; the little plant of friendship was growing, in spite of a British oilman—segregated from me and also waiting for the train—who sat drinking, illuminated and solitary in the bar, fearless but, it seemed to me, tactless in a teetotal country at that moment. I think it was the fact of one English traveller (myself) and perhaps the picture I had drawn of the trouble given by prisoners, which made the young lieutenant add as many oilmen as there was room for on to the night train: the rest were all unpleasantly interned.

I was put into a sleeping carriage; my policeman stood on guard outside while the train gathered itself together; he left me with a handshake, refusing a tip, as we steamed into the night. I had a vague fear that we might be marooned on some siding along the way; but in the dawn we saw the golden domes of Kadhimain among the palm groves and the minarets of Baghdad. A small force of police were on the platform. One of them must have known me by sight. "She goes to the Sindersons' house," he said.

"No," said I.

"To the Y.M.C.A.?" said he (I had stayed there years before the war).

"No," said I. "I am going to the Embassy."

Three or four looked at me. "Don't go to the Embassy," they said rather ominously.

I was going, however, and asked them to find me a carriage —one of the small open things with a hood which jerk along behind gaunt horses through Baghdad. They loaded me and my baggage in a rather shamefaced, friendly way, and we drove through streets deserted and shuttered; when there is trouble, the East has learned through thousands of years that it is better to keep indoors. In the emptiness of the main thoroughfare there was a sudden flutter of leaflets; my man scrambled and picked one off the ground and asked me to read it. Its Arabic was too good for my driver, and I translated it into colloquial language as we went along.

The street leading to the Embassy was deserted. The iron gates of the drive were fastened; we knocked at the Chancery entrance and a small postern was opened to let me in. Our people inside looked as if they had been having sleepless nights; sandbags were about, and barbed wire. In the court, a mountain of archives smouldered, higher than a man, with flames darting about them, the same colour as the sunlight. Any person of goodwill gave the heap a poke or two with a rake in passing by; and rising from it in flocks like crows, black wraiths of cindered files and memorandums floated into the blue sky, no doubt to some official elysium.

The crisis had been precipitated by a second landing of troops in Basra; Rashid Ali and his four Generals, seeing where this was leading them, asked for the evacuation of the first armament before the second should arrive. The atmosphere grew so threatening that the Embassy and its inmates shut themselves up on April 29th, three days before my return. On April 30th, the women were sent to Habbaniyah whence in a few days, and under shell-fire, they took off for Basra. By then the Iraq army had invested Habbaniyah; the Embassy heard them crossing the jade-green bridges of Baghdad at night and sent a warning: for some reason which I never heard, Fallujah and the Euphrates crossing were not held by us; the rebels were able to deploy their artillery and superior numbers on the open ground and the low heights that surrounded the small forces of our camp. On the third of May, in the dawn, as the oilmen and I—the last people to enter Baghdad Embassy —were steaming towards the station, hostilities in the desert had already begun.

CHAPTER XXIII

IN THE EMBASSY

> "*If three brigades in seven weeks advance for half a mile,*
> '*Were it not well,' the General said, 'that they should rest awhile?'*
> '*I doubt it,' said the A.O.C., and smiled a bitter smile.*"

THE rather sad little poem to which this verse belongs was written in the Baghdad Embassy while the forces from Basra marched to relieve us, basing their calculations—we began to fear—on the gloomy fact that it had taken the last British army three years to reach Baghdad from the sea. Meanwhile General Wavell's two battalions, under the command of General Clark, and accompanied by H.H. the Regent and a good part of our fugitive Cabinet, were preparing to reach us from Transjordan in the West, by a route hitherto attempted by no invading army. Of this we knew nothing; and the B.B.C. did little to cheer us, repeating daily that the Iraq situation seemed to be stabilized—the last thing that we, in our negligible but marooned community, wished it to be. Those cultured Oxford accents seemed very remote from the emigrant-ship atmosphere our life had taken on.

The Embassy lies on the right bank of the Tigris, widespread and low, in two flat acres or so of garden where Persian gardeners, humble and gentle people, continued through the siege to potter about with hoses among the cypresses and flowering verbena, trying to keep the lawns green for the slowly circulating shadows of the palms. These gardeners were a comfort during the month of our imprisonment, for they seemed to symbolize an unassuming, indestructible strength, preoccupied with beauty and quietly building, through all the chaos of its time.

The western end of the garden, where the gravel drive came from the great gates, was fortified perhaps against the enemy, and anyway against the defenders, by all our combined motor-cars looped into a barricade with barbed wire: a few of the garrison who spoke Arabic were allowed to creep through and approach the no-man's-land of the gate to chat to the enemy policeman standing there on guard, near the little house where the visitor's book, with leaves still open at the last entry, lay smothered in dust and forgotten.

On south and north the walled garden was overlooked by houses, not high but sufficient for rebel machine-guns from the flat roofs to rake our lawns. Their cross-fire spat out against our aeroplanes, which twice dived down with messages from Habbaniyah, and we were glad that no third descent was attempted, for we felt sure the Iraqi gunners had now got the airmen's range.

Our east wing, near the house, was bounded by a paved walk and easy parapet. Here the Tigris, still flooded with Armenian snows, opaque and yellowish through the day, mauve in sunrise or sunset, filled its bed like some great animal whose scales of small triangular ripples, each with tiny crest, pressed on, one behind the other, like the armies of nations, to meet eternity. Across this expanse, which gave an illusion of freedom, lay the city surveyed by minarets, with domes now painted brown against our bombers and fine riverside houses where the rich Jewish merchants, who own three-quarters of the wealth of Baghdad, now lived in fear; and black mouths of streets ending in gnawed steps, where pointed boats were moored—a rather dilapidated Canaletto painting, whose varnish is yellowed with dust and time. Few noises came from its sullen houses; the curfew covered it with darkness, which a flare from our aeroplanes, slowly and rosily descending, would sometimes light from end to end; and now and then some sniper, shooting morosely, would send a bullet, so that we screened the passage from residence to Chancery with sacking to take the tempting sight of moving figures away from the watchers sitting there unseen.

There were about twenty foreign women collected like myself after the general evacuation and most devotedly looked after— as was the whole of the house—by Norma Pott our consul's wife, who had been allowed to remain behind. We slept in a large room turned into a dormitory, and were provided with the luxury either of a bed without a mattress or a mattress without a bed. I was given the latter and carried it to the corner of a balcony over the river, where a convenient pillar gave shelter enough against rebels shooting wildly when our bombers came over in the dawn. One of these stray but lucky shots killed the head of a German mission, Von Blomberg, as he was landing, so that the official reception committee met him dead in his seat on the aerodrome, with an over-enthusiastic Iraqi bullet through the window and his chin. Behind my pillar, and amid this spatter, I could do my hair and dress in the early sun, while the sky turned through every shade of green to daylight blue, before the heat began. As soon as the noise subsided, the doves, like incurable pacifists, took up their sleepy refrain, which lasted through the day.

From the balcony, or from the paved river-wall below, the bridges of Baghdad were easily visible, one upstream and one down, and we could watch the passage of troops in lorries camouflaged with palm fronds, and the return of Red Crescent ambulances with wounded, and judge of what was happening in the battle by the traffic on the bridge. Or we could see the crowds from the upper town, incited by speeches of the Mufti and their own wireless, advancing with banners and drums, and dancing figures silhouetted against the sky, towards our gates: they rarely came so far, and only once sent a few shots into our garden, for no rhetoric was able to stir this into a popular war.

On the riverside we could see police launches chugging up and down every twenty minutes or so to watch us. In the interval, they would lie moored by the garden wall, and I would sometimes talk to them, and reach out the crook of my parasol and a small sum for the fish they had been catching, and would guess from their words of the feeling in the town. Some of the police behaved with extreme brutality, and at the end of the siege our hearts were hot against them; but the fact is that the ethics of the Arab world—whether Muslim, Christian, Jewish or any other—are founded on a double behaviour—good to friends, bad to enemies—so that the same human being is able to show two aspects surprisingly different, with no feeling of compunction about it. "If your enemy is standing near a well, throw him in," is an Arab proverb. This important characteristic the German-paid Generals and their politicians knew, and strained every propaganda nerve to put us on the enemy side of the picture in the average Iraqi mind. Perhaps if a sufficiency of German troops could have been brought, the added prestige of force might have helped the propaganda. But the transport aeroplanes on which the Germans counted were being destroyed on the beaches of Crete: the conquest of that island was taking eighteen days instead of two: its defence was deciding the fate of Iraq, and with it that of Persia, Turkey and Syria—none of which could have held out for long. Seen in this light, Crete may rank with Stalingrad and Alamein as turning-points in the Middle Eastern war. We thought little of this at the time, and with growing gloom picked the news of our losses off the air; and listened to the increasingly savage tone of the rebel broadcasts as Messerschmitts began to appear overhead; while the thoughts of the policemen in the boat seemed to turn more and more towards rapine and loot.

"Become a Muslima, and we will take care of you when we kill the others," they said to me, in a manner shockingly reminiscent of the lady of Jericho, and (I fear) of many female conversations across the beleagured walls of history. The offer, I may say, went no further, but we kept friendly relations, so that when our bombers appeared later than usual one morning, and the men in the boat leaped to their guns, which they held between their knees as they sat and pointed at the sky—I could not help observing that it was ridiculous to think of hitting anything so far away.

"Do you think so?" said the policemen, and laid their guns down again with shattering docility.

At the other—the Chancery—end of our compound, our intercourse with the enemy was carried on with the formalities of war. The fact that we had any food at all, after the first hungry week during which we lived on our own resources, was chiefly due to our Oriental Counsellor, Captain Holt, who—at the end of a telephone—maintained friendly relations with the rebel Ministry of Foreign Affairs, and got them to send us, on a cash basis, whatever we needed every day. He knew more, probably, than any other human being about the ins and outs of Iraqi politics during the last twenty years, and wisely urged the maintaining of diplomatic relations whatever the armies of our respective countries might be doing to each other in the desert. On this typically Oriental basis things went with remarkable smoothness, and the Oriental Counsellor every day sent a letter with a list asked for by General Smith or Mr. Bourn, who struggled with supplies. It became difficult to vary this daily effort, and Adrian Bishop—most beloved of friends—once spurred him to try it in verse: the following poem was sent to the enemy minister:

"Expressions of rapt admiration
    Must flow from my suppliant pen,
Appealing each day for our ration
    To the kindest of men.

I draw the required inspiration
    From the lists you so freely fulfil,
From specifics against constipation
    To the alophan pill."

As a consequence, an astonishing variety of things was handed every morning through a little postern opened in the gate, with guards and rifles standing both inside and out. Lettuce and ice and apricots were sent in as the warm days increased. I tried successfully to ask for face powder, and then added a list from the ladies of the dormitory, so that the policemen at the gate remarked to our cawasses how strange it was that "those Englishwomen still think about cosmetics though they are going to be massacred in three days."

As an armed force we were not very formidable, and could only hope to hold our own for a few days against a mob and for no time at all against an army. We had fifty rifles or so, some of which the entertainments committee, when they came to think of a concert, found hidden in the top of the grand piano. Our only military were two or three airmen from Habbaniyah and two officers with General Waterhouse of the Mission, who became our garrison commander. Under his enthusiastic eye, sandbags and barbed wire multiplied, and it became almost impossible to lean against anything in the garden, while laundry dried on the *chevaux de frise*. Sentry watches were distributed, and no gap was left unguarded, and the decent, kindly, middle-aged men we had all known for so many years trudged up and down their hours of duty in the heat or the darkness, bored, uncomplaining, unafraid, quietly ready to make the best of it whatever it might be. In such times one comes to have a very warm feeling for the Average Man (or Woman either).

153

There were three hundred and fifty of us altogether. Many were Indians, and there were a few Jews from Baghdad, and fifty or so cawasses from Chancery and servants of the house—Iraqis who soon were threatened with reprisals by the rebels, so that they were given their choice, whether to stay or go. About half left to join their families, and were badly treated outside—but the remainder stayed, and made our lives much more tolerable through their service. I looked after them, for it was no one's business otherwise to do so, and Seton Lloyd and I discovered them, sitting about in groups, unfed and gloomy.

"Why have you not complained to Mr. Bourn? He would see at once that you have some food."

"It would be wrong to ask for it. Are you not hungry yourselves?"

This delicacy touched us, but we felt that they needed a representative. We felt it even more after Mr. Bourn had explained that he had given them their two days' ration, and they had eaten it all in one (quite an easy thing to do). So I became their representative and got them such things as cigarettes, and told them the news, which we took from the air every day and wrote in bulletins on the notice boards.

The Indians too had their representative, helpful and pleasant Mr. Souza, and a canteen of their own on a ping-pong table under the trees, where the Hindu priest with his long dark beard cooked for them, hallowing the bread with prayers as he kneaded it. He was a newspaper compositor in his usual life, and was happy now, he told me, at the chance of "offering service to his people." Sometimes they would invite a few of us from our European canteen, or some of their number would visit ours. I liked the meals there, eaten standing in the woven shadow of the palms—rice, two dates, a slice of cucumber, lentil and chupatti; when I asked a grey-haired man if he was eating well, he held out his hands with the palms upward and said: "We thank God for all the small blessings of our lives." A sensible thing to do.

I noticed how much more easily the people of the East settled into this sort of life. Nothing could look more drab than our European efforts at seclusion, whether under a tree in the garden or parked each separately round the walls of the great ballroom, with suitcases used as barricades against one's neighbour. Not so the East. From some unexpected store a samovar appeared; a kilim rug was spread on the yellowing grass; and there was a social circle—bedraggled, but with pleasant manners—and enjoying life, or so it seemed. Manners indeed are like the cypher in arithmetic—they may not be much in themselves, but they are capable of adding a great deal to the value of everything else. The Lucknow atmosphere, however, depressed these people, while it left the British imperturbable but not uncheerful. The Indians looked on and helped where they could with a wistful and touching trust; the Iraqis looked gloomy, thinking no doubt of their families outside; in different ways everyone reacted to a feeling of unpleasantness ahead.

At 6 p.m. a bar was opened under the palm trees, and there was an hour of conversation and ease over the glass to which one was rationed, and another gathering immediately after to hear Dr. Sinderson's garrison news, which he succeeded in presenting in rhyme for every day of the month. Here in the evening light, the Ambassador would stroll out for a game of clock golf on the lawn, or walk up and down with such political officers as had come in. Many of these were old friends, with years in Iraq behind them—Colonel Edmonds, Colonel Aston, Colonel Lyon, Colonel Kinch, Colonel Dowson, Major Mead; there is little they do not know of the country and its people. In the years that followed I saw much of them and was grateful for their steady help and kindness; and for that of the young men who had come into their ranks, with a tradition of service to which the re-establishment of peaceful equilibrium in Iraq was largely due. Edmonds and Aston were with us, and our Ambassador would walk with them up and down the crowded lawns while the late light probed under the palm trees. He was a skilful captain, and held the allegiance of all. His wife and daughter, protesting and much against their will, had been evacuated to Habbaniyah with all the other wives and daughters, and it was only when they returned that their good work for Iraq was really able to begin. I have never heard of anything but affection towards them from the Iraqi ladies who, in ever greater numbers, came to look upon the Embassy as a house open to them all. Indeed Lady Cornwallis demonstrated a fact so dangerous for women to forget—the fact that personal relations are at the root of every human structure, however aridly official the scaffolding that hides it.

155

Meanwhile, however, these ladies had all been flown away, and everyone was relieved when their safe arrival in Basra was told by a little pɩcket dropped on our lawn on May 8th by a diving aeroplane. The huge bedroom whence Lady Cornwallis had been able to look from her dressing-table across the Tigris, held our mattresses laid out in rows: and at meals H.E. sat lonely if not solitary at his polished table, in a small dining-room which was still kept private, eating off blue-and-gold china whose pattern was visible through the meagreness of food. All the garrison were invited to lunch or dinner in turn, and some-times to bridge afterwards in the drawing-room where fans scarce cooled the air and sleeping figures slumped on chairs looked like those pictures of tombstones at the Day of Judgement, just giving up their dead. The King and Queen, in court dress, full-sized in oils, looked down with a well-bred absence of surprise.

As the days went by and the burden of many decisions came upon him, Sir Kinahan looked tired. The threats of bombing, which at first had been very frequent, grew less; but our flag soon had to be lowered from the roof and put to flutter modestly from a black metal flagstaff by the front doorsteps, so as not to incite by its appearance a popular tumult (the rebels said.) The rebels sent to remove our wireless, or so they thought. They tried to take our cars, but were opposed. The ·unequal duel went on, with Captain Holt at the telephone. It still, through the rebel Ministry of Foreign Affairs, kept us in contact with the outside world.

With everything snapped except this thin thread and with the archives burnt, a Sleeping Beauty atmosphere descended on Chancery. The people who had offices there, Adrian Holman the Councillor, Captain Holt, John Chaplin, H. Freese-Pennefather, Leslie Pott, John Walker, Morgan Man, the ladies in the typing room, the pleasant men who lived in vaulted rooms among the files, of which there were now so beautifully few, and Pat Domvile mysteriously busy with intelligence, and Ernest Main, Seton Lloyd and myself, with our Syrian trans-lators monitoring news—all enjoyed a comparative privacy. We could sit in our own little groups, either suffocating with closed windows and the lights on, or under dim blue ghost-lamps through the evenings, open to the river and the town.

The rebels' attitude and the tone of the broadcasts, which an unctuous voice poured out unceasingly in various languages from the Baghdad station, became grimmer as the middle of the month brought the Germans to Mosul and their aircraft overhead. A little old Gladiator from Habbaniyah knocked out one of the Messerschmitts in our sight in the dawn. But the days passed and (apart from their thirty aeroplanes which Habbaniyah ꝰdealt with) the German troops still lingered: Shaikh Mahmud and the Kurds were gathering to help us from the north, delighted to have a whack at any Iraq government and indeed reluctant to draw off when friends and not enemies were again in power. The Germans began to be hated in the North, and the Shammar were against them. The army itself was not unanimous behind the Golden Square, while Basra helped the British in the South. General Clark's two scanty battalions, keeping the smallness of their numbers very quiet, took Rutba and reached Habbaniyah, and were pushing towards the Euphrates, impeded by floods.

On the 19th they had taken Fallujah, and the Euphrates bridge was intact. On the 23rd, the rebels counter-attacked and were beaten off, but the floods still held up our advance. The middle Euphrates with its tribes and towns was siding with the legal Government and the Regent. The policemen in the boat below our walls, now reinforced by soldiers, told me that evening that:

"The Germans are of the family of Satan."

"I have heard," said I, "that we have brought six of them down between Habbaniyah and Syria."

"Praise be to God," said the enemy, under cover of darkness. "But we have burnt forty of yours," they added as an afterthought.

"I take refuge with God from your untruthfulness," said I; to which they agreed with laughter.

There was now an electric quality about the news, and rumours came and went like lightning flashes, from nowhere to nowhere. They faded into something more tremendous when, early on the morning of May 28th, we heard our approaching guns. All through the morning they thudded, steadily nearer, shaking the window panes: they came unexpectedly from the north, beyond Kadhimain, where a column led by the Arab Legion was cutting towards the rebels' retreat. Their noise, so full of fate, so full of the Unknown, so different from our month's stagnation, had about it a *meaning* such as no spoken

157

word can master: it seemed to hold the very heart of Awe. In the afternoon it stopped, chilling our minds with fear, but started again at night. On the 30th, our aeroplanes flew over continuously, keeping high and going north; the police were doubled at our gates and began to build defence posts with sandbags to protect us; we watched all boats and small craft crossing to the far side of the river, preparing—we thought— a battle for the bridges in which we should be placed between two combatants. We cut our daily ration in half, in case of no supplies to-morrow, and put sandbags where we could.

The facts were different. The army inside Baghdad (two battalions) had turned against the rebels. The Germans, the Generals, Rashid Ali, the Mufti, and the Italian Minister had fled to Persia or, eventually, to Turkey. And, in the afternoon, the Mayor of Baghdad, spick and span in dove-grey suiting and with a smile all over his face, came to surrender the town. A police officer and Ghazi Daghestani of the army, a young officer very friendly to us, were with him; there was a cordiality of re-union about the whole affair. Mr. Knabenshue arrived from the American Legation across the river, looking as if he were just off a yacht, so smart and clean; he gave good news of many friends. He had been threatened with bombs if he kept the British with him, and these offered to go out to be interned. But he refused to allow it, and had carried on with his garrison of one hundred and eighty as we had with ours, and earned the gratitude and affection of all.

That night a message to ask for an armistice was sent by the Iraq army to ours, and fighting ceased next morning at 4 a.m. Colonel De Gaury, who had been made Chargé d'Affaires to the Iraq Government in exile during the Ambassador's detention, had marched with the Regent and his ministers across the desert with the battle, from Amman. Colonel De Gaury, said Mr. Bishop irreverently, was "Cornwallis' vice-regent on earth." He was a very good one, and as we drove out on the morning of June 1st to meet the returning Government, he was there standing with soft hat, exquisitely pressed suit, dark glasses, suède shoes, on a little knoll, watching the proceedings with an interested but remote air, as if they had been a dress rehearsal.

H.H. the Regent was there, looking sunburnt and happy; his smooth oval face and brown eyes, sensitive and now bright with pleasure, reminded one of some picture of the young Shelley. The whole scene might have belonged to that romantic world. For there were the Iraq police, dressed in their best, on horseback, making a lane for the triumphant meeting; there was the desert white in the morning sun, and the trenches that were to have stopped our tanks. There were the tanks themselves, and soldiers lounging in battle-dress against them, men more solid it seemed to me than the iron they handled: they smiled, pleased with the show they had provided, as well they might. There was Nuri Pasha, the Prime Minister, slight, gay, very tired, brave with a boyish enjoyment that endears him to his friends.

"I always keep a suit-case ready packed," he said. "I have had to escape across a frontier so often."

There was Ali Jaudat, who had been got away by his kinsmen of the Shammar, now in Washington, and Jamil Madfa'i, and Daud Haidari whose escape Pat Domvile had helped. There was no doubt about their feelings as they returned. While all shook hands, General Clark and his soldier group stood in the background. Our long line of cars, washed by their chauffeurs and disentangled from barbed wire, was shining in the sun. The Ambassador and Mr. Knabenshue were there together, and all the chiefs of our imprisoned family, feeling strangely in the air of freedom. (There were no women, and my presence was an irregularity, but I could not have enjoyed it more.)

Now all escorted the Regent to the King's palace, greeted, and left him, while a stream of notables came out from Baghdad to do the same. They went smiling, but there were mixed expressions, unguarded, as they came away. People who lined the streets had gloomy looks: and Herr Grobba the ex-German minister, disappointed with the country he had spent so many years in wooing, was still, they said in Mosul. That evening Pat Domvile told me that the retreating rebels had prepared a rising through their agents for the following day: it broke prematurely, with rifles snapping through the night. It was to have been directed on the Embassy, but the easy temptation of loot and the long-standing influence of Palestine together deflected it to the Jewish streets and houses. The Jews of Baghdad have every reason to deplore the Palestine question, and do so with their hearts. There was plenty of riff-raff about, and the new Cabinet was not yet formed to keep order. All through the day of June 2nd we listened to rifle-fire crackling among the houses like thorns under a pot: the little Mayor alternately struggled with the situation and threatened to resign: the British troops, encamped some miles from Baghdad, were anxious not to enter the town unless invited, and the Iraqi forces of law were equally anxious to win their own fight unaided. How many people were murdered that day will never, I suppose, be known. In the afternoon, the Iraq army were told to use ball cartridges, and killed sixty or seventy of the looters; the bridges were a strange sight, an empty-handed crowd going eastward and returning with arms overweighted with parcels of every sort. There was a curfew at five, and everyone who showed was shot; the main streets, strewn with the goods of its shops, was slowly tidied. The little King and his mother returned from the north where the rebels had held them. By June 3rd the crisis was over, and a new cabinet, under Jamil al-Madfa'i, under way.

CHAPTER XXIV

BAGHDAD EFFENDIS

"How strange a thing is man! But half a cubit of him, and a universe full of material things will not satisfy it."
(ST. PETER DAMIAN.)

FOR some weeks, no one was allowed to wander at will in the bazaars, and when I returned to Baghdad from Cairo in mid-July, I still met glowering looks in the shadows of booths beside the tattered vaulted ways, where the populace had for so many days been told by German agents to hunt us down.

It is a terrifying sight to watch such propaganda at work, first gnawing here and there like the mouse at the dam, until the time comes for the loosened structure to give way, and the destroying waters pour through in a muddy foam. This we had seen, and it was nobody's fault but our own that that insidious preparation had gone on so long unchecked. The British had come twenty-three years before, and the young men of the Arab world had received them as the bringers of their freedom: these men were middle-aged now, and in a vast majority they still believed in the decency of Britain's methods and the justice of her cause. At the bottom of her victory in Iraq lay the fact that most of the substantial, middle-aged men were on her side, and on that of democracy in general.

But Youth she had lost, or almost lost. It was caught, like many of its brothers in Europe, by the totalitarian mirage. It looked upon Britain as one and the same with the middle-aged status quo against which the German whisperers and the course of Nature impelled it. Wherever it was organized, in the schools, colleges, and most of all in the army, it had for years been growing dangerous because disregarded—and what sowing of the whirlwind is there like the disregard of youth?

Of course the British Embassy was blamed: it always is in Iraq, for everything. But the problem seems far bigger than a merely diplomatic one.

If we think of what an embassy is, we may compare it to

161

the point of a pyramid, a small specialized culmination representing the government, parliament, people, which sustain it. It is there to deal with the point of some other pyramid, the small specialized group which represents the people of whatever nation it happens to be accredited to. When each of these points really *do* represent their foundations, the diplomatic interchange deals with a reality: it did so in the Middle East in the days of dynastic rule—it does so still in countries like Saudi Arabia or Yemen, where people talked to by the diplomats are the people who represent what the government of the country really is. But in the northern Arab lands the advent of the middle class has widened the foundations of government, just as it has in Europe. This means that—to be of any use—a far greater *area of contact* must be established. To expect the diplomatic service to do this is like expecting the point of one pyramid to be equal to the base of the other: it cannot be done. A real understanding between democratic countries can only be established in two ways: either by making their governments *so representative* that foreign diplomats when dealing with them really are dealing with most of the nation; or, by widening the contacts *outside* government and diplomatic circles sufficiently to make an area of understanding below the points of the pyramids as it were, so that the masses of the nations come to know each other as well as do their diplomats. In Iraq neither of these things had happened. The Government was not representative, for the whole of a younger generation was clamouring impatiently at the door: and outside the Government, very few British took any trouble to meet Iraqis at all. The change of feeling among the young in the last three years has largely been brought about by the growing up of non-official friendships outside the diplomatic area: the *inside* efficiency of the diplomatic area will much depend on Iraq herself, and on how far she can make her own Government really representative.

At this moment of history, it was a very fortunate matter that the British Ambassador whose word was the deciding factor in immediate policy, happened to be a man who also had known and served Iraq for many years. When the Mayor with the two officers came to surrender Baghdad, they asked that the independence of the country might still be respected. Sir Kinahan, towering down on them from his great height, replied: "Many years ago I fought, together with King Faisal the lamented who was my friend, for the freeing of the Arabs, and together we built up the kingdom of Iraq. And do you think that I would willingly see destroyed what I myself have helped to build?"

This was the truth, and the Ambassador's influence was directed wisely, to moderate the feelings not only of the British —naturally furious over a great many things and not least the looting of their houses—but also of the friendly Iraqis, anxious for reprisals against the common enemy. Three of the chief friends of the Germans were executed; others, less gravely implicated, were carried off from Basra to Rhodesia; the worst succeeded in slipping away to Germany. These were local matters. What affected the whole Middle East was the treatment of Iraq herself.

From the days of the Great War and the proclamations of Lord Allenby and General Maude, Britain had declared that the freedom of the Arab nations was her intention and aim. Between the two wars she did as much as a harassed Government could to carry this out, but difficulties with French and Zionists in Syria and Palestine, and with the arms question in Iraq of which her own urgent needs prevented the promised supply, and above all, a campaign of careful enemy propaganda—all this obscured the question, so that there were many who thought that Iraq, once retaken by force of arms, might remain in the hands of its conqueror. Its restoration had an influence far beyond its own borders. It was a proof to every nation in Arabia that their integrity is in no danger as far as Britain is concerned: and the action taken in those weeks of June 1941 is, I think, at the bottom of the friendship that exists to-day.

But a great wake of trouble was left by this retreating storm, and few looked upon the Iraq victory as more than a temporary hitch in German plans. The Vichy French in Syria had refuelled all the German aircraft that flew over Baghdad, and drained our slender resources for weeks to come: we had suffered what most people considered a grievous defeat in Crete: Tobruk, besieged through the summer, was inspiring but not particularly reassuring: and when Germany surprised and delighted us by declaring war on Russia, few looked upon this as promising more than an eight-weeks' respite (a strange

163

fact to think on now). The siege of Sebastopol ended, and brought the enemy hammering at Caucasian oil wells, the back door to Iraq: and Pearl Harbour and Singapore came to sober the relief and pleasantness of having the United States in name as well as in fact beside us (for their help before they were actually at war should never be forgotten). All these things came crowding into the year that followed the German defeat in Iraq. One may say fairly that it was not the cheerfulness of the military news which turned that country towards the Allies at war.

I will now leave these high matters and come back to my small affairs, which for the next two years brought me into contact with every sort of Iraqi from one end of the country to the other. When the siege was over and I returned to Baghdad from Cairo, Pamela and I spent three happy weeks furnishing a small house in a suburb among the gardens, and here I settled and soon gathered a few courageous spirits to form a corresponding branch to our Cairo Brotherhood of Freedom.

This was no easy matter for, unlike the Egyptian students, those of Baghdad had been turned from ideas of democracy and spent much of their young lives in totalitarian processions up and down the streets, to the dismay of quiet citizens. Democracy is, however, radical in the Arabian idea of life, whether they know it or not, and the Nazi theories die of themselves when squarely looked at. A more serious difficulty was the antagonism of many of the most intelligent young men to their own Government, which was composed entirely of people who were our allies and friends. This internal difficulty lay at the root of the whole Iraqi trouble. The Brotherhood of Freedom, apart from being democratic, is a non-political society; but it took months and months of argument and struggle to make it seem possible to a young man in Iraq that anything useful *could* be non-political; and the stauncher they were, the more whole-heartedly they wished to plunge into the arena.

It was a matter of some courage to join us at all, at that time. We had a badge, a V for Victory, with two hands of friendship across it, and when it was first started, the young men came and asked if it would matter if they wore it *inside* the lapel of their coat, so that it might not provoke violence against them. When I left Iraq in 1943, we had over 7,000 members, and these troubles were of the past; but it is pleasant to remember that our numbers began and grew in the worst year of the war, in the shadows that preceded Stalingrad and Alamein.

Our success was not only our own. Many things helped it, and chief of all the work of disinterested people for education and understanding. Until recently, schoolboys in Iraq had been taught from text-books compiled by "nationalists" imported from abroad, full of Egyptian, Syrian or Palestinian war-cries, long superseded in the lands of their origin. Professor Hamley now came as Adviser to the Ministry of Education, and roused a deep and touching devotion among his teachers and his students. The British Council kept absolutely away from politics, and Tom Morray at its head, an excellent ally and first-rate fighter, was known by all the young Iraqis as their friend. So was Adrian Bishop, who lived in a fine house round a small court with trees, where the Tigris came murmuring against the railings; here he lived with Seton Lloyd who is Adviser to the Department of Antiquities, and has known and cared for Iraq and its archæologists a long while, and helped and encouraged the beginning of a school of painting there; and with Aidan Philip and Teddy Hodgkin, who are fond of economics and help everyone except people like myself to understand things like the Beveridge Report. All these and others offered what the American teachers once offered in Beirut—a hand outstretched to the young, whose foothold on the new world is not yet so sure that such a proof of friendship can be discarded.

In these houses and elsewhere, I met the men and women who built up our society. A few Westerners—Mrs. Pott, and Mrs. Beatty, Dr. Tokar, the Campbells, the Derek Andersons and the Embassy and army young men—all helped, but we did not feel ourselves the initiators of this movement so much as a means, a channel for something impelling but still inarticulate, in the heart itself of young Iraq. We were fighting an old enemy, met in Aden and in Cairo and indeed everywhere, a conviction rooted at the heart of Administrations that people *like to sit still and be looked after.* They treat one as the Victorians treated their women—ladies at the siege of Lucknow not allowed to nurse in the hospital because a shell had fallen there. The eagerness with which the ladies rush in among the bullets, the keenness with which the young men give their time, their services, their devotion, show how deeply wrong that psychology must be.

I can only mention a few of our people at random. Abdul Masih Wazir, with his mop of white hair and the heart of a boy and his excellent skill in translation. He was a Christian from the north, and his profession was that of translating documents for the Ministry of Defence; he and his friend from the army, Captain now Major Muhammad Ali Bagdadi, rather casually a Muslim, were in our first small gathering. They were inseparable; they arrived together, with a tinker's noise, in the Captain's small and decrepit sky-blue car, regularly twice a week without a miss for over two years until the dear old man died. On one day they would attend the meeting and on the next translate our bulletin into Arabic, working at it for hours with never a thought of reward for the labour. They were both almost insuppressible talkers, and the test of our chairman came to be that of seeing to it that other committee members got a chance.

There were the Haidaris Nadhim and Qadhim and Nadhimul Chelebi, and Dhia Ja'far who had married the daughter of my oldest friends in Baghdad. He was small with bright eyes, a Civil servant in the railways, often kept away by the spate of war traffic that congested us—but when he did come he had a fiery quality about him that stood out against compromise in a refreshing way. In the time of the rebels he had taken the trouble to go round to all the foreign houses in his immediate neighbourhood, to see that they were not looted. His sister, a teacher in one of the schools, also joined us; they were Shi'as, much respected in Baghdad, and she lived in a rambling decorated house of the Turkish days, in the old part of the town, with painted ceilings inlaid with mirrors, and wooden balconies, hanging over the water, while Dhia and his wife had a modern bungalow and garden.

There were the two lawyer brothers, also old friends, and very modern young men, though they would wear their own fine Kurdish dress in their own highlands. They were descended from the Babans, once chieftains of the land.

There was Hasib, who belonged to the Custom House and its club on the river where the young effendis congregated, and he took me there to meet them, and eventually came to be a

166

pillar of our committee and a most excellent chairman: and Captain Fakhry Omar, who joined us when it was most difficult for an Iraqi officer to do so and risked his career at that time.

There was our pretty secretary and her three sisters, Christian Arabs and daughters of a newspaper editor: one of them is a teacher graduated at Smith College, the other runs one of the health and baby welfare centres that have now been springing up in Baghdad; she is often too busy, but her sister comes always, neat and modern with her clothes bought in New York (though Baghdad too pores over *Vogue* with its dressmakers). The three sisters always appeared at our parties in a small and compact family phalanx, which the hostess tried in vain to disintegrate among the young men.

There was Ali Abdul Majid who taught English literature and belonged to a cultured group of friends and allies who met in the wealthy house of young Rushdi Chelebi—chiefly teachers; they are all working constructively, building the Iraq of the future and of their dreams. They belong to the new boulevards, the electric arc-lights and road-signs, the neat municipal gardens and playing grounds for children, the opera house where Lt. Chaffoo (his family also among our Brothers) teaches an orchestra to play Beethoven symphonies for the first time. They belong to the Baghdad of to-day.

We have many schoolmasters as time goes on. They are, perhaps, the van, and their students Zaid Othman and others like him come next, sons of the people who plotted for freedom in the days of Turkey and the last war. But there are many other sorts too. There is the little club of Renascence, which has got going all by itself in a back street, where they invited me to talk to them, and we found our aims so much alike that we combined and worked together. There are the charming people who own a cigarette factory and live in Muaddham above Baghdad, which is the suburb I should choose to live in, where the Tigris lies flat and broad like a mirror under palms, and the houses above it are a long mellow row of balconies, and, in the quiet streets, doors open discreetly.

In the noisiest quarter of Baghdad is the workers' committee, which Yahya Pachachi has got together—a good man and a pioneer, for there is yet an old-fashioned gap in Iraq between the effendi and the workman, and it takes a liberal mind to bridge it. I have rarely met nicer people than this committee sitting in Yahya's courtyard off the main street, down one of those quiet brick-lined alleys that lead out of the hubbub and seem to end in nowhere. There were only five or six members, master craftsmen with people under them, and they are bluff, rough men with hard hands, and eyes that look straight in your face, knowing the worth of a belief and that it matters to get it right: for the craftsmen of Baghdad at their looms and anvils have been busy for a great number of centuries, and something in the way of civilization is handed down. One has this feeling everywhere among the poorest of our groups: a feeling of old dignity, which makes hut and palace essentially the same.

One of our pleasant committees was that of the policemen who met in the wilderness of tiny courts and overhanging windows that lie off Ghazi Street. There, guided through medieval alleys, we would climb the Baghdad stair whose steepness is more than that of any other stair I know: from a court the size of sixpence to an upper storey: and in a narrow room, with Mr. Churchill's picture surprisingly on the wall, would find eight or nine of the police discussing their bulletin over little cups of tea.

"Do you know that you are the only English we have ever met to speak with?" they said. "We see them passing in the street; but no one knows them."

This is hard to avoid, seeing that there must be about thirty thousand Iraqis to every Englishman in the country—but it certainly is an argument for knowing as many as one can.

I was alone for a time for Pamela returned to Ireland, but I have been fortunate in my helpers. Peggy Drower came—whose mother has been loved in Baghdad for many years. Others, Barbara Graham and George Lawrence, stayed only a short while, but Peggy remained when I left, and no one could ask for a happier ally. We gave the whole of our time and service to our Brotherhood, and they gave us, I think, a genuine affection. Material benefits they never received, and at the end of two years had handed over £700 of their own in subscriptions and donations.

Some were poor. On one occasion we decided that we would not remind a committee that its subscription was unpaid, for it was all composed of non-commissioned officers whose salary is next to nothing. But their chairman arrived at our meeting, and pulled out of the pocket of his rather gay check coat the full amount, and ten shillings over, which he handed shyly, as a present to be sent to our fighting men in the desert.

"We are not rich," he said. "It is all we can give, but we would like it to be more."

Perhaps the young people of Iraq were glad to join us because we gave them a chance to do such things.

CHAPTER XXV

SOUTH OF BAGHDAD

And God said: "Let the waters under the heaven be gathered together unto one place, and let the dry land appear."
(GENESIS.)

NOTHING in our Brotherhood could have been done without the help of the Mighty, and this was a constant point of divergence between the more ardent of our young men and myself. Evolution, and not revolution, was to be our aim: and some thought it too tame and went from us, plunging into politics left-handed, which landed two of them in prison and strengthened the arguments for moderation. We were there to build and not to knock down, and a number of good men in office helped us. Many of these I think of as friends —the Ministers of Finance and Education and Foreign Affairs, the head of Police, the Mayor, the two Army Commanders, the head of the Chamber of Commerce, the chief of the Lawyers —people, many of them trained in Stambul, who had been at work on the practical machinery of Government for the last twenty years: not all of their ideas were of the latest, but they were our friends and stood behind us, knowing that what we were trying to prepare was an easy transition from one generation to another, an advantage to all. They helped us, and so did their wives, who were personal friends, and all more or less busy with their own evolution, the emergence from the veil. One can now ask most of these ladies to a discreet little party with a Western man or two present, and the gala nights at the City Hall or Opera are becoming constellated by a feminine Baghdad, beautifully dressed.

Outside Baghdad, in the provinces, the Government's influence became even more all-embracing, and it would have been impossible to do anything without the help of the Mutasarrifs or Governors, in every chief provincial town. In the course of two years, I visited practically every centre in Iraq, and many of them more than once, and everywhere found the greatest help and kindness from the Mutasarrifs and their wives. It is hard to compress these pictures, so many, so vivid in my mind, and so varied, into a chapter or two.

There, in the very south, is Basra, and tea on a shaven lawn by the side of the river, as it might have been the Thames except for the width of its waters and the palm groves that line its motionless creeks, where slim "bellams" dart snake-like, with curled crest and tail. Where the business part of the river begins, petrol tins from Abadan are trans-shipped on a moving belt, guarded by Indian troops ceaselessly through the hours of the day.

Baghdad has the romance of the Golden Road, of a city on the route of caravans; Mosul has memories of Assyria and a rugged enchantment of the north; but Basra is the Ocean door of Arabia, rich, buoyant, adventurous, enterprisingly-minded, easy of intercourse, speaking even to-day the language that Drake and his friends could understand. As you sail up her broad breast of waters from Fao, you can see the palaces of her merchants surrounded by flowering creepers, shaded by palms, painted and carved with wooden Gothic ornamented pillars, where the rich men spend their leisure with a fictitious coolness of water lapping in their ears.

One of them, an owner of date lands, and a friend in good luck or bad, was the head of our Brotherhood there. It was in his garden we drank tea; while a dozen or so of the Chief People, invited to hear all about it, hovered torn between a so-much-respected President and the things he expected them to do, uncertain as butterflies over a doubtful flower. The heads of the schools also invited, were genuinely keen. They would do the work: all we wanted of the Great was their benevolence; and that, in the rich and pleasant Basra garden, was ever to be found.

Basra lives on the river, but as you drive north you come to a land that lives not on, but in the very heart of waters, the Marsh Arabs' home. The dusty road, rutted by old floods of spring, flanked here and there with brick kilns like fortresses or temples, is lit by their flaming furnaces at night, and the wide river wanders unseen in the flatness of the land. It leads you through Qurna on a spit between waters, where a derelict tree shows how withered the garden of Eden must be (Qurna is said to be the site of Eden). Thence to the little town of Qalat Salih aligned on the Tigris with the marshes at its back, chief centre of the Mandeans, where they build the swan-necked boats they call tarradas: and to Amara, that has a river front of small and modern villas, an unobtrusive pleasant prosperity drawn from the rice of the Marshes (the best in the world), and the feeling of what it is, a tiny capital of an obscure and hidden land.

All this country of the south remained faithful to its Regent and friendly to the British through the troubles, and now continues its life busy with the selling of rice and the ancient tussle of Tribe and Town; for the young effendis here are particularly go-ahead and keen on a modern world, while the tribes are powerful, sedentary and rich, and settle but slowly into bourgeois life. With the wealth of their rice, the chiefs begin to build stone houses in the pasture lands that are not flooded, on the fairway of canals; but they still keep the reed guest halls, and huts that can be moved with the moving waters such as their tribesmen dwell in, in groups with great open doors and reedy columns, facing the waterways that are the only highroads of their land.

The Marshes themselves are some thirty to forty miles wide along the Persian border and over a hundred miles long from north to south—an enchanted country, unlike anything else in the world. Their reeds grow in clear deep water only, as much as forty feet high. They enclose broad ways and narrow windings, known to the amphibious Arab, and sudden lakes where the water flowers heave gently, an indolent carpet brightly woven, over the wash of the canoe. The traffic of the border goes by these waterways, and the men of the boat caravans will bend the reeds into platforms for their nightly camp, and build fires upon them, islanded in the rustling loneliness. On a day in spring when this water-land blossoms, it is a sort of Paradise untouched by man. The black tarrada, the swan-necked canoe studded with painted, black, large-headed nails to make it strong, slips with only the drip of its oars through sunlight seamed with a myriad shadows criss-crossing in the heart of the reeds, through silences that listen to a myriad noises, the dive of the white and black kingfishers, the scurry of a moorhen, the hum of small flies or mosquitoes (luckily not malarious) in the sun; and everywhere, always, the sharp-leaved rustle of the reeds, bending and singing, closing as one pushes through the yielding stems, or opening away to the clearing of a short horizon, a gentle, cruel, inexorable prison to those who have not learnt the maze of the ways. Their charm is loneliness, the opening of a door, the sharing of a secret with a world that is as it was and will be, before and after the visitings of men.

But the Arabs do live here, on islands a few yards above the water, where their huts cluster round a reed-built guest-hall shaped like a tunnel, sustained on round piers tapering and curving to the ceiling, the origin perhaps of columns, great bundles of reeds. The children live in and out of the water, and the little cows of the marshes are taken in the black boats, to and fro to their oozy pastures, which men build with their hands, out of the silt of the far mountains of Armenia, which Tigris rolls perpetually down.

Sir William Wilcox wrote a small and beguiling book in which he suggests that this building of the land out of the waters is the origin of the tale of Eden. It is the most fascinating thing to watch, for you can see here the work of geography actually being done by man, the building of a delta into dry land. It is the process by which Nature has made the lowlands of Egypt and Mesopotamia, homes for civilization to begin; and the Marsh Arabs help it on year by year, standing to the thighs in water with their shifts rolled round them to the waist, lifting armfuls of mud and slapping it down in flat and sodden stretches intersected by ditches, till a new expanse of dingy soil is added to the map of Iraq, and becomes gradually solid and grows rice, and eventually pasture, as the reclaiming of the land moves forward, out towards the still unfettered freedom of the reeds.

These marshes stretch also along the middle reaches of Euphrates, and bring you to the towns and tribes there, Nasiriyah, Samawah, Diwaniyah, where the people have a turbulent reputation owing chiefly, I think, to the fact that their lands and crops are submerged by every flood of the Euphrates, and no one seems able to do very much about it in Baghdad. They too threw in their lot with the Regent in the troubles of 1941, and it was a tribal chief of this district who came one day in 1943 to the British with a hundred gold sovereigns in his hand—a present, he said, for the men of the Eighth Army, then trouncing Rommel along the coast of Libya

—"for their deeds," said the Shaikh, "are worthy of nothing less than gold."

I like the people of the Middle Euphrates. Their towns, where there is little of historic interest to visit, lie as it were at ease in the blistering heat of the land. Before the end of May their harvests are gathered, and the long summer clamps down upon them. Their citizens collect in groups when the pleasant coolness of evening brings the day to its end, and sit talking under the stars, and sleep on the roofs of their houses; and live by the river that sinks and rises, or beside canals built by their forgotten forbears, Sumerians or Babylonians who left the heaps of Ur and Babel, and cleared with their hands the silt of these irrigation channels, which now is lifted by machines. The land is pale—jade-green or biscuit-coloured under a white sky—with a charm made all of horizontal lines, like those faint pencil tracings of background put by artists round sketches of men in abbas and flocks of sheep; the main points only are marked and the rest is left fluid in dust. And everywhere as you walk beside banked water, you hear the patient throbbing of engines pumping in an empty landscape, while some antique solitary figure in a gown pours oil into the machine.

The past and present are strangely close together. The great stone barrage of Euphrates, which rides the mass of water as a man rides a horse on a curb, is the modern world in triumph; near by is Hillah, charming and prosperous on the river's edge and, with Basra, the most thickly populated region of Iraq, a land of crops and oranges and palms, with the ruins of Babylon beside it, and many a forgotten mound and long-dried channel, to show how much was done by the hands of men, before ever they invented these machines. Not far away, beyond the Jewish village and Ezekiel's tomb, where the fiery sunsets still sink behind the palms with visions and wings of gold—are the Holy Cities, Najf, and Kerbela, wrapped in theologic veils.

Here the cinema, the banner of our day, has not yet entered. The Wise Men sit, with their disciples about them, on chairs or cushioned floors in small rooms hidden in courtyards at the end of narrow alleys, where the houses, built out and almost meeting overhead, cast a dimness even at noon. Their foundations reach down, storey below storey, built with fine brick, underground, till they touch the subterranean conduits of Euphrates water, black mazes tunnelled so long ago that men have now forgotten how they run. From these strange interiors a cold dankness comes up, even in the heat of summer. It is the atmosphere of the Holy Cities, built on caverns of the past; its fog hangs about the upper rooms where the Wise Men sit.

I have a friendly memory of the Wise Men, most of whom I know. They have not usually—in fact I do not think that apart from Gertrude Bell they have ever—received a European woman; but they have been gracious to me and allowed me to visit them several times, and have spoken with a dignified acuteness, looking as if through the mirror of Shalott at the passing shows of the time. Yet the weight of their traditions sits hardly on the younger men, and in the Holy Cities more than elsewhere in Iraq you feel a ferment, and a threat of cleavage, and the difficulty of reconciling the "ends of the ages" which have come together in so short a span.

The modernizing influence is the bureaucracy which, only twenty-six years ago, slid like a small python out of its skin from the coiled iniquity of the old Turkish administration. It is this which shuffles the human beings, transferring them from post to post. In Europe, it may be old-fashioned in its outlook—in the newness of the Arab nations, where it absorbs the educated young people as fast as they are produced, it is the spearhead of modernity.

The world, they say, is to be made safe for bureaucracy: yet how little is done for the bureaucrat himself; not for the Great Man, in his prosperous middle age, but for the little man, during all the years when he is poor and young, living in some tiny place amid drab papers, jabbing a split pen into an inkpot dried with dust, bowing perforce assiduously in the house of Rimmon, until by slow stages the time may come when others bow towards him, and he notices that he himself is Rimmon, or at any rate a lesser idol, and a part integral of Things As They Are.

Officials everywhere labour under a disadvantage in their pursuit of Good: from their beginning their eyes are fixed on other bureaucrats' promotions; stimulus and not nourishment is their daily food. When an artist looks aside to watch other people's rewards, he ceases to be an artist: the official in a country where salaries are not high, is offered no other incentive at all.

The Arab virtues anyway are warm and human and not very official virtues. To be hospitable and polite in the extreme, to give money for the good of one's soul regardless of its destination, to further the welfare of all one's family and friends: —these are excellent virtues, but if anything they are embarrassing rather than otherwise to a young bureaucrat. And now, with a modern Western education, a strange and frigid code of public duties is brought before him, an ice-rose vision to set him on his way from his last exam.

Nothing in his destiny seems to encourage the practice of these artificial virtues, so different from his background, so unrewarded and unacclaimed. Nothing but his dim, comforting thirst for abstract right. Very often, under dusty palms of Iraq, in neglected villages along the Persian border, in dingy mud-flanked streets of Kurdistan, sitting on startling velvet armchairs long neutralized by dust, drinking tea or coffee out of small cups in undistinguished offices, the stout little effendi opposite has poured out words unexpected, words of that clear and sparkling source so distant from his life of everyday. He has his dreams. He travels from post to post with those velvet armchairs for receptions with which he began in the first flush of youth: with his female household tucked out of sight discreetly in the uncomfortable rooms at the back; with his shadow of power which makes men stand up as he passes and which hangs, like Damocles' sword, by a Ministerial thread. We come back to education. When you have talked of politics and the roads, have asked each other's health and sipped your coffee, you look at the photographs askew on whitewashed walls. Family portraits sometimes, a shaikhly father white-turbaned, or children unnaturally stiffened in a row. But mostly it is the man's youth that travels with him from post to post; his class at college; himself in cap and gown; his football team; and a prize-giving with Royal presence. The yellowing unforgotten ceremonies speak their golden words to him alone. And as he looks at them, if the Celestial Vision is at one with what they taught there, even in the house of Rimmon the bureaucrat is safe.

CHAPTER XXVI

NORTH OF BAGHDAD

" *Who, that surveys this span of earth we press—*
This speck of life in time's great wilderness,
This narrow isthmus 'twixt two boundless seas,
The past, the future, two eternities!
(THOMAS MOORE: *Lalla Rookh, The Veiled Prophet*, ii. 1. 247.)

1. *Revolutions*

JUST north of Baghdad there is a country of desert interspersed with cultivation, oases sometimes touching each other, sometimes divided by stretches of hard unwatered emptiness. The river Diala flows down from Persia in the north-east and the great triangle made by it with the Tigris holds little towns hidden under their palm trees, and surrounded by open fields that gradually melt into the desert scrub. All these towns live on some canal whose sluggish waters drift beside streets of hardened mud, between mud-brick houses, with a weeping willow overhanging at the corner of some garden wall. Each of these little towns has a small and ant-like street of markets, from which the blank walls of its houses radiate before the garden walls begin. But each little town also is now building some club-house, post office, municipal centre, or school. Ba'quba, Karaghan, Shahraban, Mandali, Deltawa, Delli Abbas, and all the smaller places of Diala—and the Euphrates towns, Ramadi, Fallujah, Hit and Anah—and the Tigris towns, Samarra and Tekrit. Because of the desert that surrounds them they are less like a countryside than like an archipelago of islands, each with its history—often infinitely long—each with its character brought from who knows what far migration scarce remembered but fostered through isolation, and now gradually merging as the islands are threaded together by the ramshackle cars and ash-coloured buses that tilt and rattle through the provincial dust.

Round all these towns the tribes, once nomad, are settling on the land; and the sons of the shaikhs, and gradually the lesser tribal people also, attend Government schools. The result is a phenomenon familiar in America but less easily recognized in the slower affairs of Europe—a juxtaposition of two sharply different generations, a telescoping as it were of change. What happens when a newcomer from the Old World settles in the States and his children attend the American schools? The household comes to contain two outlooks, the products of two backgrounds, a change in direction as it were. Exactly the same thing is happening with the young effendis, sons of the tribes: and it is the problem of Arab Governments, as it is that of the U.S.A., to carry through this transformation smoothly, without the loss, if possible, of what good the older orders held.

I have often watched the contrast, with the great chiefs of the Dulaim, with my old friend Shaikh Habib of the 'Azza, with the tribesmen around Diala and Kirkuk: our Brotherhood made its way, and we would visit them, and sit with the elders in pleasant remote groups of houses that have taken the place of the tents and still have a pastoral atmosphere about them; the older men with their easy manners would offer agreement or help with the certainty (needing not even a mention) that the opinion of every tribesman could be relied on to follow in the wake of his chief; and it was only after all this was over that the young effendis, sons or nephews, would come in their modern clothes from their unobtrusive modest stations in the background (standing, usually, in the presence of their fathers), and with enquiries on committees and their reasons and on how to conduct them, would show themselves to belong to a new, more questioning world.

The young men of the towns have no such *sudden* chasm to cross; but it lies before the Arab woman, if she wishes to become Westernized, whether in Iraq or elsewhere, and whether in tribe or town. And that is why our Sisterhood went slowly, though here and there, in Ba'quba, Diwaniyah, Basra, Amara, a keenness for social welfare was awakened, and the ladies would organize themselves for the care of villagers or children, things which fitted easily into the tradition of their ways.

One is apt to forget in this female field how much ground has been covered in a very short space of time. I have a letter

178

from a friend, a Christian Arab educated in India, who became Director of girls' schools in Iraq in 1922.

"When I arrived from India," she writes, "Baghdad had just *one* Government girls' school with an enrolment of over two hundred—Moslems, Jews and Christians, but mostly the first. The teacher situation was most critical. The majority on hand were Christians from French Convents and American Mission Schools. The qualifications of this group were far superior to those of their Moslem colleagues—Turks, Arabs and a Negress. The Turks were expert at fancy needlework, and the Negress at chanting the Quran. . . . Enlarging the staff to keep up with the rapid increase in enrolment was quite a problem. Turks, left over from the old régime, applied for teaching positions. Eager young Arab women did the same. . . . Their qualifications at best consisted of reading of the Quran, needlework, incorrect Arabic, and simple addition and subtraction. I had to make them do, if only to avoid too much overcrowding, particularly in the lower standards. It was disturbing to see bright youngsters come to school and get such poor teachers.

"A tentative curriculum was in the making. Some, ambitious but impractical, wished it modelled after that of the boys' schools. Others were quite conservative. I recall one Minister of Education who said to me: 'Teach our girls to recite the blessed Quran, teach them broom-ology, cook-ology, pickle-ology. He lasted but a few weeks in the Ministry. With no dependable ministerial policy, with acute shortage of qualified teachers and with poorly disguised Moslem resentment of the better qualified Christian staff, my task was an uphill one. There was little to hope for from the then British (Irish) Advisor to the Ministry of Education; he was not interested in girls' education and did not hesitate to say so. Not so Miss Gertrude Bell, who was aware of and interested in the situation. Her attitude may be summed up in these words: 'This is pioneer work. Do what you can with it, and don't take the Ministers too seriously.' I took her advice, and we made some progress. We worked out a reading programme for the teachers, and required their attendance at a 'Methods of Teaching' class. We selected the brightest of our older girls who expressed interest in teaching and organized them into another 'Methods' class. I had to squeeze both classes between administrative work. That was the first step towards the

179

portal of Dar al-Mu'allimat (the present school for teachers). When, in the course of succeeding months, we opened several new schools in the different quarters of the city, the 'locals' were supplemented by some of our promising 'graduates.'

"Looking back on those hectic days of 1922–23, the one encouraging fact regarding girls' education was the inherent mental alertness of the Arab girls, and the lovable sociability of the rank and file of them, rich and poor alike. They impressed me as excellent material for a new order. Given an enlightened Ministry of Education, qualified teachers and sympathetic parents, these girls can go far in the new Arab world."

These requisites now exist. There was an intermediate stage in Iraq when teachers were brought in wherever they could be found, from Palestine, Egypt or Syria: this is what I saw when first I went to Baghdad in 1929. But now, there are three secondary schools, and not a town of any size that has not its intermediate school for girls, while many villages have a primary; the teachers are trained in their own college in Baghdad; doctors and nurses, teachers and even lawyers, pour out in a rapidly growing stream; and as they are produced, they are sent out, from the capital to the towns, from the towns to the villages, on a task greater than that which even the best machinery can accomplish—the compressing of generations of the experience of nations into a few short years.

It seems to me that the assimilating of strangers into the U.S.A., the transforming of the tribesmen into villagers, the Westernizing of the women of Asia, are three very similar processes, tremendous revolutions which are being carried on at a terrific speed. One watches fascinated, as one watches the swiftness of a meteor, wondering (if one is unscientific as I am) where it is coming from, where it is going to, and whether anyone is sitting there to guide it.

2. *Kurdistan*

The traveller in Iraq from south to north comes upon a great change, the change from mud to stone.

To the level of the Holy City of Samarrah all is alluvial, the very monuments of antiquity are built of the river earth.

I should like to see a picture book of brick in Iraq, from the baked Sumerian cones of Warka and the gates of Babylonian Ishtar, to Abbassid scroll work on Mustansiriyeh wharves and the slender arches and delicate lettering of the bridge that stands alone on the northern road; to the piers, stalactites, and geometric bands of the old Turkish houses and even the little villas of the twenties; down to the latest, the beautiful mausoleum designed for the Iraqi kings, the new sports club with its smooth plain lines, and some of the modern houses, for which this medium, mellow in colour and easily adaptable, seems particularly suited. You see the last of it in Samarrah; the ancient Ziggurat tower, the Abbassid walls, and the modern town, combine to show what bricks through the centuries could do. And then, as you drive northward and east of Tigris, the villages begin to cluster on rising ground; the Persian and then the Kurdish foothills push their fanlike streams into the plain; and gradually you are in the country of old Assyria, and the building is of stone.

This is a land of proud and very ancient cities, and proud and warlike people, strong races of the hills. Kirkuk, Erbil and Mosul—the stuff of history seems kneaded in their names. The wheat-bearing plains that roll between them are scattered with hundreds of grassy mounds, lost fortresses, towns and villages of Assyria. In Kirkuk, where Daniel is buried, the fiery furnace burns yet: the Royal Air Force tried to put it out, for the flames flare out of a hillside very near the oil refineries, in a patch some forty yards or more in length, a landmark for German airmen. But no means could be found to bank and smother them. They were burning when I saw them, blue and sulphurous in the starlight and shaped like a cross, as if Shadrach and Meshach and Abednego were children of yesterday.

Our Brotherhood spread in all these Northern cities with great eagerness and rapidity, beginning when I first went there in 1942. Not only the teaching people, who nearly always helped us, but, on either side of them, the leading Government officials and the artisans were keen to carry it on: and in Kirkuk we were greatly helped by Major John Chapman of the Oil Company, who was known and much thought of by all the people there; and in Mosul as in Baghdad by all the Public Relations people and the British Consul. The Mutassarifs were kind as ever, and indeed in Kirkuk most particularly kind. Among the tribes round about, in little townships like Kifri, Tauq, Tus Khurmati—received with speeches in the young men's new club-house, or fed by some landowner in the summer-houses of walled gardens—I spent many happy days; and then continued northward, by Erbil, built "on its own heap," city upon city, till now it stands risen from itself like the phœnix a thousand times and from the stepping-stones of those dead selves looks out across the plain. Here a charming, friendly Kurdish house was always open, and hence one drove to Mosul by the way that Tobit travelled, across the Zab river, with the site of Arbela on the left; and in the sunset saw Mosul lying in a fair wide saucer, neither hill nor plain, and the Tigris (with its new grey steel bridge and public gardens) flowing between it and the mounds of the ramparts of Nineveh, on which the tents of the British Tenth Army were roped in shallow lines. Here too we visited, and lunched with the priests in Christian Arab villages, and watched the women—their heads bound with circlets of gold coins, their garments many-coloured, medieval and gay—gather their harvests in; or drove to hill-townships, Dohuk, Koi-Sanjak, or Zakho where the Turkish border is in sight; or visited the high and lovely mountains of the modern Assyrians.

The Germans in 1941 had managed to make themselves disliked by the people of Mosul who took little pleasure in seeing trainloads of wheat disappear towards the north. The feeling of the town remained bitter for a time against all strangers, and, when I first went, there was a strong prejudice against letting people go alone in the bazaars. I did go, however, and seized a little lad of ten or so to carry parcels, and as I saw a group staring rather ominously at me, I asked my small guide what was the matter to cause this rudeness in the people of the town.

"They are surprised," he answered me with dignity and not a moment's hesitation, "because they see you wearing *red*. Ladies should wear white. Red is worn by grocers from Baghdad."

Overhanging all this country, with high hills on the eastern skyline under the Persian dawn, is Kurdistan. I spent a short holiday there in 1942.

There are three Kurdistans, one in Iraq, one in Turkey and one in Persia, and the Russians were in the last named, just beyond the long, gnawed, snow-striped ridge of Aoroman.

They were fighting in the far north, retreating step by step and beating the Germans back from the Volga, from the oil-fields, from the mountain barrier of which Kurdistan is the southern edge; they were preparing the defence of Stalingrad and the tidal point of Germany in the East; and the British Tenth Army in Iraq was digging tank-traps across the plain of Assyria along the Zab and below Kirkuk, in case Stalingrad could not hold.

But in our Iraqi Kurdistan there was peace—precarious, like a waiting stillness or thunder silence of summer, but not anything below the standard of Kurdish peace, which is rarely more than relative. In that tormented land, dissected by three frontiers, one dismembered portion can ever look with pleasure or distress upon the tribulations of another. Exiles flit across the dividing ridges with prices on their heads, helped and hidden by friends. Kurdistan expiates the selfishness of rulers long dead, Babans and Ardalans, who played personal politics with Persia and with Turkey, and lost their now partitioned lands to both. The Kurds themselves are a mixture of tribes, and even their language is divided; but geographical factors still hold, and keep in its mountain cradle on either side of man's artificial boundaries an enduring sense of kinship, a feudal tradition, and a healthy hardness of life and climate which makes tough, liberty-loving mountaineers.

You can see Kurds in their tobacco-coloured homespun in the streets of Kirkuk or even Baghdad, swaggering with huge tasselled turbans among the taxis and sleek cars. But their capital in Iraq is Sulaimaniyah, which is beyond the Highland Line, beyond the limestone ridge which ends Mesopotamia, over a road going due east from the feathers of smoke of the oil-fields. It was asphalted ten years or so ago, and runs with small ups and downs and innumerable corners across the shuffled petroleum landscape of the plain—tiny ridges of shale—through the lands of the Talabani and Hamavend, Kurdish tribes, to their eastern wall, which runs high and fairly even, with rocks in a row like teeth out of the turf, to the gap of Derbend that is the inner gate of Kurdistan.

Many a battle has doubtless been fought here; the last in 1919 when the British captured Shaikh Mahmud, a young man about twenty, beside a white rock just inside the hollow. They had much trouble at that time. Their military transport

183

(Burmese, I think) was ambushed, its road cut before and behind, and itself sprinkled with petrol and burnt; the Kurds at that time were described by Brigadier Longrigg in his history as "wayward and unprofitable." In the present war they have stood staunchly against all Nazi blandishments, and this is due to a scant dozen or so of British officers and officials who gained their trust and friendship—a proof, if any such were needed, of the influence of persons in the East.

Shaikh Mahmud is delightful. Since 1919, when he was condemned to death and reprieved, he has spent fifteen years in exile and six years at war. He has always been a good fighter, a good enemy, and a good friend. During the troubles of May 1941 he escaped from durance in Baghdad back to his highlands, and began to stir his tribes—this time in favour of the besieged British. Before anything could be done, a friendly Government returned to power in Iraq and the Shaikh who, undeterred by the change in the quality of his target, was all for continuing, had to be strenuously dissuaded.

The truth is that the Kurds dislike the Iraqis of the plain in the same way as eighteenth-century Scottish Highlanders disliked the English; and it will be an excellent thing if Iraq remembers this analogy, and deals with the problem on the same lines—by encouraging rather than suppressing their local nationalism. In Sulaimaniyah and the hills, they possess the essentials of freedom: their own language is taught them by teachers of their own kin in the schools; their judges, their governors, their officials, are practically all Kurds. Certainly neither Iranian nor Turk in the past has ever voluntarily given them as much liberty as is now given by the Government of Iraq. The climate of the post-war world promises to be good for small peoples, combining larger schemes of union with local freedom; if Iraq extends and develops the policy of Sulaimaniyah, there should be every chance for compromise and co-operation with a friendly Kurdistan, for a little flattering recognition should reconcile a proud people which is, after all, too small to stand alone. This is much to be desired by any power interested in Arabia, since Kurdistan is the last of the mountain ramparts that overhang the oilfields of the plains.

Shaikh Mahmud, when I went up, was living on parole in a green hollow of his own hills. It was the time when all

Kurdistan is scented with the spring. In the white mountain air, lifted above the dusts of Asia, between the piebald snow-flecked ranges, the high plains are like altars strewn with new flowers every day. They are splashed there in improbable profusion—red splashes for anemones or poppies, white sheets for daisies, yellow stretches of mustard in the grass; thin spangle-veils of pink campion in cornfields, and iris in the ditches; wild hyacinths in water-meadows and purple lilies in the rice-fields; every day a new splendour opens, a fading splendour dies. We missed the jonquils, the hollyhocks were yet to come. In grassy downland, a bowshot from the slope of the foothills, small rivers break smooth and clear; beside them a green mound may show the site of buried townships, Sassanian or medieval, or even Assyrian, for Ashurnasipal's campaign here was fought almost exactly on the ground the British later followed, pursuing Shaikh Mahmud.

The Shaikh himself was settled in a poor tent, with the hovels of a burnt-out village a little way behind him. We swished up to it in a beige Hudson car through meadows in flower and lazy streams—taken by his son, a young man who looked like a slighter and citified version of his father. The Shaikh was dressed in dark green cloth, bunched in great volume round the waist and with the braided sleeves, open to the elbow, of the Sulaimaniyah Kurds. He had a small turban, and a black moustache, and a plump face with a small round nose, and a look of a little boy, in spite of wrinkles and the comfortableness of figure. It was the eyes perhaps, lively and ready like a brook in sunlight to catch a gleam of fun, which kept the boyish look. My chauffeur, whom I thought of as rather a sophisticated young townsman, knelt down to kiss the Shaikh's hand. There was loyalty all around him. The little group of his men (all with something against them in somebody's dossier), in high sand-coloured bags tapering to the ankle, and quilted jackets and twisted sashes that looked like huswifs for knives instead of needles, would sling their rifles off to busy themselves with the ladling of the soup, or the bringing of a chair—rough outlaw comforts. Two armed sentries stood by the tent-pole; the '45 and the Highlands of Scotland seemed not so far away.

It was pleasant to lounge again on rugs and watch the green land framed in slanting poles that hold the goat-hair ceiling;

and taste the bitter coffee mixed with the scents of grass; and
listen to the Shaikh who said he was ready to fight for the Allies
whenever they asked him to do so, and spoke affectionately
of this Englishman and that, but slightingly of their policy in
general. "You make friends," he said, "and cherish them, and
make them ready to do everything for you, and then you chuck
them away."

"It is not easy for us, you know," I remarked, trying to
do my best. "Our friends are very apt to quarrel one with
another, and there we are between them."

"Well," he said. "You are wise in war. You throw small
nations to the Germans like pieces of meat to a dog, till you
can get a big one like the Russians to fight them."

It seemed too heavy a task to tackle such a point of view
on a fine afternoon; so I lay back and enjoyed it all, and
thought of the past of Kurdistan that has produced these ideas,
a past all of wars since the brief quiet Sassanian age when
the highroad from Ctesiphon to Ecbatana is said to have passed
through Khurmal in the plain of Shahr-i-Zor. At that time
it must have been a prosperous and busy country, and the
mounds of its cities are still thick on the lovely plain. From
the twelfth to the sixteenth century the Kurds of Ardalan
held the land in a feudal prosperity; but then came the
Turks, and, in 1694, Suleiman Beg Baban, whose son founded
Sulaimaniyah to perpetuate his name. A short Kurdish
renaissance was followed by a quisling policy of open doors
to Persian and Turkish interference, until in 1850 the Baban
rule came to its end in a partitioned land. Now the Persian
frontier runs beyond the high, almost level Aoroman range,
and in its villages, hidden with trees and tumbling waters
among precipices, exiles find hospitable shelter. A network of
marriages ties the tribes. Our own fair-haired young Baban
who took me travelling here, is descended from the old ruling
family; his mother, whom I love, is a Jaf, of Halabja, where
a famous woman, the Lady Adila, ruled autocratically a
generation ago.

There is an Elizabethan flavour about these Kurdish ladies.
They wear quilted coats, slim at the waist, and jewelled huge
slanting turbans, and tinsel-brocaded shawls: and enjoy their
freedom, sitting equal in the evening gatherings with their
men; and looped about their headgear and under their chins

are the coins of the civilizations their ploughs turn over among the mounds of Shahr-i-Zor.

We rode to visit them on high Arabian saddles across the flowery plains; and the men would turn out from their villages to meet us, with rifles (loot from Persia) slung behind them, their turbans aslant on their foreheads, their bridles tasselled and gay. Their present is like our past and, travelling there one has a strange familiar feeling, as of something once known and forgotten, a happy elusive feeling, as of a meeting with one's youth.

3. *The Nomads*[1]

Round all the settled, inhabited places of Iraq and Kurdistan the nomad tribes still wander, moving from winter to summer quarters and back again, in the places where the herbage is sufficient only for half a year. Such are the Harki, most powerful of all the Kurdo-Iranian nomads, a mountain people very different from the gowned riders of the desert.

On the lee-side of the hills, in a sheltered hollow, their black tents are scattered—little tents, ramshackle, fragile and lop-sided, open to weather, their privacy incompetently guarded by upright rush zaribas woven in and out with wools. The poles push the roof into many sharp points that make one speculate on the origin of Pagodas. Clamped by their spider-ropes in tiers behind each other, they lean against the slopes of the winter harbour, and in their touching precariousness awaken a strange feeling of permanence, safe and self-sufficing in a war-wracked world. For it is Peace, and not War, that can drive from these foothills the tents which have wandered there before history was written.

The grass of their winter home is already turning yellow, and in a week they will move in untidy parties, north-east across the lonely Persian boundary, on the great migration that twice divides their year. They will go to the highest pastures, taking their time with their chattels all about them, stopping four days or five, where the grazing is good. Some of the grazing on the way is rented for the occasion, some is hereditary to the tribe.

Their chief, Fattah Aga, is dressed in the wide trousers of

[1] Printed by courtesy of the *Listener*.

187

light-blue wool that looks like watered silk, and is woven by Armenian refugees in Zakho. Over the knotted cotton sash, he has strapped an English revolver. The silk fringes of his turban dangle over his eyes and serve, like a pony's forelock, to keep flies away. His brothers, young and unmarried, wear even gayer trousers, woven in reds and blues on white, gathered and slender at the waist like figures in Persian miniatures; handsome, with clear fine features, they move with an easy freedom in all their ways, and the tents are a background small in the landscape behind them.

For the sale of their sheep, they study the markets of four countries—Persia, Iraq, Turkey or Syria—and drive their flocks where the best price is found. Sometimes it is the wool only, but usually the whole sheep is sold. The flocks, yellow as the desert, the goats, black as the tents, graze over all the foot-hills; the shepherd lad stands graceful among them, like a minaret among clusters of flat houses, or a simile of priesthood, an upright figure among the prone. In a week all these browsers will be pattering northward, filling the gorges through the daylight hours; no wise motorist moves there during the migration of the tribe. And they will reach the highest ridges where snow still lies thick in May, and will look down the slopes of Persian Kurdistan and see far in the distance Urmia shining through orchards, and the lands of Armenia.

"We do not ourselves go as far as Lake Van," they say. "But we can easily hand you on to the tribe that does."

The Harki flocks, nibbling the grass round oil-wells in Iraq, are a part of that vast nomadic family whose blind movements, seeking Mongolian pastures, repeated with shock after shock across the plains of Asia, often unconsciously kindled con-vulsed or ruined the civilization of the world.

*   *   *   *   *   *

On the other, western side of the British Oil Developing Co. in Iraq, the Arabian nomads begin.

Between Tigris and Euphrates, Shammar hold the gentle undulations, green in spring, desert in summer, that cover the cities of Assyria. They guard the B.O.D.'s stores and depots, and are so to speak desert agents for this company of Oil. In the troubles of May 1941 they helped cut the railway line in their country during the British advance on Baghdad. They are finer drawn than the nomads of the hills, capricious, wiry, bitten by the sun, and less solid—in all except the figures of their gay and hospitable shaikhs, who have taken to live in houses; the desert silhouette does not survive this transfer.

The sons of Ajil live in Sinjar, his nephews in Shergat; but they still spend the spring round the flowery mounds where the old Shaikh had his great guest-tent twelve years ago.

Shergat is a modern house with a central hall running through it like a Venetian villa, and terraces front and back; it has modern sanitation; the garden below it is laid out in lawns with cypress trees and beds of verbena, modelled on what the old Shaikh saw in country houses at the time of the Coronation. One thinks of Sennacherib who stocked his park with trees and animals from foreign lands and first, as far as I can remember, brought the vine. His ruined mound of Asshur, a rhinoceros-snouted headland, is here in sight, blocking the Tigris bend. The sunset river flows in wide light round the new lawn, round the low mud walls of the village, round the runnelled heap of the forgotten capital. The garden covers at most an acre, loud with birds settling in the trees; beyond it, there is no green: the colours of the desert lie beside the flowing water, bare and strong.

Inside the garden, where darkness falls more quickly, the Shammar Shaikhs sit in a half-circle on deck chairs and watch a travelling cinema; a bony Nubian, a slave bought in Kuwait, serves cold lemonade from the ice-chest. Perhaps he was bought by my old friend the Mekka slave-trader. How lucky one is, I reflect, to combine in a single lifetime such an astonishing variety in friends and surroundings. Here one can see history as she is, the mosaic of times and places, fantastic strands visibly interweaving, ruled only by the compulsion of land and water and dust. We are watching ancient Assyria looking at the cinema and listening to the news; no merely picturesque antique can better the piquancy of this experience.

On the morning after, we chase gazelle in the desert of Hatra —a herd of fifteen beating the expensive Chrysler which the chief of the Shammar races like a horse. The beautiful creatures win and leave us, their running a sight never to be forgotten, a skyey speed. The Chrysler's "fluid drive" comes to an astonished pause at the edge of Wadi Tharthar, the longest wadi of this northern desert, filled with slow, rushy pools.

Beyond is Hatra, once a subject city of the Parthians, girt

with crumbled heaps that once were walls. Perhaps it was the Wadi, then more full of water, which produced the flies and made Trajan give up his siege in A.D. 116; one can hardly imagine a plague of flies there now; the reservoir from which Shaikh Mish'an's horse used to drink in his boyhood has shrunk, and is now barely half full; the wells are dry. The rooms stare with wide round arches and rude disfigured sculpture out over lands that know their works no longer. Here, too, they must have had the latest gadgets of their time, novelties from Antioch or Alexandria, dimly understood; the Hellenistic touch, debased by desert hands, hands that wrought its delicate traditions into stone, is recognizable however blunted. In a far corner of the ruins the little tents of the beduin are propped against walls of ancestors who left the desert ways.

The world, as it grows prosperous, will ever settle in stone, but who shall say what the Nomad is and when he dies? Prometheus' fire, Greek cornices in Parthia, the "fluid drive" Chrysler in Wadi Tharthar, London bathrooms by the ruins of Asshur—these too are Nomads, products of a spirit as old, as young, as adventurous and as eternal as the minds of men.

CHAPTER XXVII

FAREWELL TO THE MIDDLE EAST

" The great roads, whose arches are marked with Caesar's eternal name."

(SIDONIUS APOLL.)

IN July 1943 I left Baghdad for England.

My little house in its garden had become a home, and pleasantness had grown around it; the early ride, the hour stolen at midday to plunge into Tigris, strong and cold between its mud-banks in the sun; breakfasts with the young Americans on Sunday mornings; my lodgers, Hermione Ranfurly and Nigel Clive, and the time or two when we escaped and drove into the world in my small car; the constant agreeableness of friends and neighbours: Jasim who ruled all with a benevolent rod of iron, and the gardener who would drop work if one took no interest (for which there was so little time), and complain that "there is no *fun* in planting if you do not come to look."

There was the Brotherhood, now with over seven thousand members, so that we had an office next the dining-room with Mrs. Ja'far and Joan Campbell, and our clerks Victor and Mahmud and any Brother who happened to be free to help us with files, which I allowed only up to a limited number, like the Order of Merit, and maps and two typewriters, and Peggy running it with an efficiency that nothing ever ruffles and a constant gentleness of her own. All this had to be left, or rather to be folded up and carried away in one's heart.

Stewart Perowne was now in Baghdad, attached to the Embassy and doing a work as excellent as he did in Aden. He happened to be travelling in July, and offered me a lift across the desert, and we set off rather later than we meant to, and mounted to the plateau beyond Euphrates as the shadows lengthened, and ate our supper by the roadside in the long red evening light. The whole road is asphalt now. Somewhere about two in the morning, we reached the wells of Rutba, where the police have taken over the Fort.

The Officer of Police was head of one of my committees, but as his members were spread over the whole of the Syrian desert area, and as the actual meetings in Rutba were two hundred miles or more from anywhere, I had never succeeded in visiting them. I was touched now to find him ready in his uniform and waiting under the cool stars of the morning, with his young lieutenant, also a Brother, close behind him.

The square open space inside the fort was scattered with a dozen or more sleeping policemen wrapped, head and all, in blankets on the ground. Their armoured car and a horse or two were in one corner; between the bare walls, still scarred with signs of the burning two years before, the night wind of the desert blew with its strangely penetrating cold. We were taken to a small office shared between the papers and the dust, and drank hot tea in narrow-waisted glasses, and were left to sleep an hour or so on the wooden benches while the doctor of the road-makers' camp near by, who also belonged to the Brotherhood, was asked to dress and come.

It was a strange little committee meeting in the morning darkness, so far from any other habitation, lit by a lantern in the man-made office chaos under the great tidy lamps of the desert stars. The young lieutenant lifted a ledger from a shelf: in it their gatherings were all neatly recorded, as they sat, week by week, and discussed the bulletin we sent them: their ideas on Democracy, on Government, on practical things like malaria, education, tillage; their suggestions, sent to the centre for approval or advice—were all put down in casual everyday Arabic in the ledger printed somewhere in the West for the adding up of figures. The three men in their solitude turned its pages with a legitimate pride, infinitely touching as they told of their visits to the tents of the desert, and how they spoke of these things when they sat by the hearths of the coffee-makers and how their police everywhere had been joining, and how the workmen in the camps along the new road were beginning to care to hear about it all. "Soon there will not be a man in the desert who does not know what Democracy is," said the Commandant of Police.

I had to make a speech and, in that lonely setting, told them of the beginnings of democracy in England, in the days when forest and heather, solitary as this solitude, covered the land. There in clearings where the fields spread, men had begun to select a few from among their number to look after the things that interested them all: and gradually to send one to the gatherings of neighbours, separated by stretches of wilderness; until London and the Mother of Parliaments began. "This thing in England," I said, "has grown from roots in the soil and in the hearts of those who lived upon it: here in Iraq, its form has come from abroad, and it is men like yourselves who carry the seed of the little plant, and watch it take root and grow, so that it becomes a part of your land, and a living thing, and not a theory only. That is the meaning of Democracy." And as I looked at their eagerness, I thought how good this young material is, and how important that it too should know itself actively building, and not sit apart frustrated and negative until it reaches middle age. It seems to me that any widening in the scope and interest of *local* government should be encouraged, for there the enterprise is small enough for all in a small community to share, and there the little people, and the young people can practise, and eventually come to the affairs of the nation with a good knowledge of what the stuff of government really is.

The dawn was beginning to show in a lightness that could be felt rather than seen: Stewart made a good little speech of thanks, and we wrapped ourselves in all we had and started across the next two hundred miles of desert, leaving the Brothers at the door of their square fort under the lessening stars.

That was not my last touch with Iraq.

As we drove from Damascus to Beirut, we stopped at the hotel under the trees of Zahle where Nuri Pasha Sa'id, our Prime Minister, was convalescing from pneumonia. He sat on a bench, on the circular gravel constellated with geometric flower-beds which seems to belong particularly to hotels; and he was playing a quiet morning game of backgammon at one of those three-legged painted metal tables which are dotted in social places all round the coasts of the Mediterranean, nearly straight in the sunshine or the Season, or forlornly tilted in winter or in rain.

Nuri Pasha was born in Baghdad in 1888, a Sunni Muslim educated in Stambul. He speaks Arabic, Turkish, German, French and English. His first intercourse with the British was in 1914 in Basra, a year after he had joined in the founding of the secret society of Al-Ahd whose object was the attainment of Arab freedom. This object has been his lodestar ever since. In 1916 he joined the Sharifian army, led a detachment of Egyptian regular troops on the Allied side against the Turks, and had received a D.S.O. and a C.M.G. by the time that peace was signed. He returned to Baghdad in 1921, and was one of the influential Iraqis who invited Faisal to become King; and he has been in politics ever after, as Minister, Prime Minister, or in flight (during the military usurpation of Bakr Sidky).

In March 1942, when our news was bad, he was anxious to bring his country into the war beside us; the same military problem as in Egypt, the difficulty of supplying equipment and defence, caused the Allies to discourage this offer and postpone its acceptance till 1943.

His courage, his wit—impish and gay—his loyalty through good or bad fortune to friends, his genuine indifference to all the pomps of office, make him a charming companion; and long experience in many countries, and a passionate love for the future of Arabia, and a statesman's moderation, make him one of her important leaders at this time.

He represented Iraq in January 1939 in London, during the conversations on Palestine—and I have several times listened to his views on this question and on the plan that is nearest to his heart, the eventual unification of the Arab world.

On Palestine he is willing, like practically all the Arab leaders, to co-operate on the basis of what has been granted already, provided that Palestinian agreement is obtained to any increase in the Jewish home. "Your White Paper (which is based on this assumption) is, after all," he told me, "the result of twenty years' experience."

But he looks on this whole question, and on that of Syria also, as a part in the greater Arabian mosaic which is so rapidly shaping in the world. He has watched the idea of unity increasing through his lifetime.

"In Egypt, for instance," he told me, "there used to be practically no interest in the matter at all, because Egypt had so long been outside the Turkish Empire, so that she was not, as it were, in the orbit of the rest of the Arabian world. But the interest has grown now, and is continually growing. In Iraq, it is general among all the educated."

"Do you think of this unifying process which we all see

194

taking place, as something rapid or gradual?" I once asked him. "Do you look first, for instance, to an economic union which will lead to a political one in course of time?"

"That will be the process," said the Pasha. "But it should not be so very gradual, for the whole development now is rapid, and the political ought to follow swiftly on the heels of the economic—which is in sight—and of the cultural—which is practically here already. *Your* Commonwealth is the model for the Arabian world, except that it could have no single monarch, but should retain its separate sovereignties on an equality with each other. They could meet in every country in turn to decide on measures which are interesting to all. Our Arabian foreign policy," he added as an afterthought, "*has* been unified already by the force of events: we have been helping the Allies in one way or another during two wars."

In his forecast perhaps Nuri Pasha is more optimistic than most of the Arab leaders, who see the *political* unity coming more slowly, a result of the successful working of the other.

However this may be, we wished him well with the vision to which his life has been given, and left him sitting in the shade of the tall trees in the warm morning, a slight figure in a grey suit, and grey at the temples, with grey eyes light and alive in dark and tired sockets, and a certain striking, spritely youthfulness about him.

I left him, and passed through Beirut, and Palestine and Cairo, and started in the darkness of an early August morning in a military transport aeroplane for home. It was one of those Dakotas lined down each side with hard little seats scooped in aluminium, whose negligible comfort is destroyed by a whole mass of hooks and gadgets so that the very sight prepares one for all the ways in which it is possible to die. But in it we flew peacefully and smoothly across the Western Desert, where for three years the fate of the Arab world, and of a bigger world also, had been fought for and finally won.

As the daylight strengthened over Cyrenaica, the prints of the armies grew visible in the sand below—spider-web tracks of tanks and lorries, thick as the tangled gossamer that shines on gorse in the dew of an October morning. The craters of bombs and shells were pitted thickly about them, and black trenches showed like the arrows on maps, aslant towards the road. A great emptiness lay over all in the sun, so that those

195

traces, so crowded, so tumultuous, and now so solitary, acquired an intensity of drama; they needed no voice to speak. Benghazi, still white against the sea, had the blurred outline of ruins; and as we flew beyond it, the harrying among the tracks in the sand lessened, the fight had become pursuit, it ran in smooth lines by the straight coast and the burnished sea.

There, flat and deadly, lay the salt pans of Agheila, like white veils half transparent; and the neat fields of Tripoli, squared and tended, Italy's derelict colonial dream. And then more desert, and the coast fading northward, and the Mareth Line inland below us. Swamps of salt, a barren whiteness of death, lie before it; and beyond them, a great amphitheatre with giant knees, the line itself, cliffs ranked abruptly one behind the other: I thought of the Shaikh in Iraq who said of the Eighth Army that it deserved nothing less than gold.

In the last of the daylight we reached Algiers and saw Allied ships at anchor—for the campaign in Sicily was on: and I was rescued from the military bleakness of the hotel by Roger Makins and Harold Caccia, who took me kindly to their villa and that of Mr. Harold Macmillan, the British Minister, to all of whom I owe ten of the pleasantest days I can remember.

The American army was here in full harness, bull-dozers nosing their way about aerodromes whose surfaces still showed a spattered pattern of craters lately covered in. The atmosphere of a great terminus reigned, so that it was strange among the coming and going of the giant creatures to think of 1940 in Cairo when one might wait an hour to see only one machine. There were well over a hundred now on every aerodrome between Cairo and Morocco.

Even happier than this sight was the friendly spirit between the British and American armies, a comradeship that went from highest to lowest and came indeed largely from the personality of the Commander, to whom everyone was devoted.

I had the privilege of meeting General Eisenhower. He was in his office, in a hotel among bougainvillia, where the steps of the booted doughboys shook the mirrors and chandeliers. I believe most great men keep a feeling of their boyhood about them: the General gave this impression, his face was open and interested and honest, with a generosity about it like that of his own wide wheat-bearing plains. There was no trace there of any pettiness or self-seeking, and perhaps it is this simplicity of devotion, free of vanity, that has made him so universally beloved. He smiled when I said how much the general harmony had impressed me.

"I am glad you should have noticed it," he said. "We try for co-operation. But it is a thing you cannot just leave: it has to be worked for and added to every day."

It seemed to me that he expressed in a word or two the lesson which had most deeply sunk into my mind during four years in the Middle East.

IRAQ[1]

ABOUT 4,000 years ago the Babylonian king Hammurabi stamped in clay the rules and regulations of civilized life as it was then lived in the land of the two rivers, whose progress during the last forty years this essay means to trace. The colossal difference between the two figures must never be forgotten. The present of Iraq moves against an immense curtain of her past, a curtain more vast and more variegated than that of any country except Egypt. The very fact that forty years of history can be written about a land whose annals reach back into thousands shows how vital and revolutionary these last forty years have been.

Against this background of slow and gigantic evolution, the civilization of Iraq, like that of Egypt, establishes its persistent identity in dynasty after dynasty, nation after nation, age upon age. Gift of the rivers that made them, the two long ribbon-lands stretch back into a similar twilight of earliest human origins, unknown. This similarity is obvious, but as they emerge into the light of a more remembered day, a fundamental difference becomes visible between them: while Egypt lies parallel and peaceful to the routes of human traffic, Iraq is from earliest times a frontier province, right-angled and obnoxious to the pre-destined paths of man. Wave after wave, from the hills of the East, from the seas of the South, from the sands of the West, meet and break here, struggle, sink, settle and dissolve, subdued to the enduring forces of geography and climate. Sumerian, Elamite and Kassite, Assyrian and Babylonian: we are not concerned with these. But with the wave of Islam, which in its early years broke and transcended the Sassanian barrier; which overflowed the Iranian plateau to distant Khorasan and then retreated, mingled and altered for ever, so that no definite line can ever now be drawn where the Arabian and Iranian end—

[1] This article, with some changes, is reprinted by kind permission from *Islam To-day*, ed. by A. J. Arberry and Rom Landau. Faber & Faber, 1943.

198

with this we are concerned, for it provides the most interesting characteristic of Iraq to-day.

No definite border exists now between the Islam of Arabia and Iran: but the border *land* is the land of Iraq.

Here we can still see in daily process that action and reaction of races which gave its unique character to Islamic civilization as soon as it left the shelter of its deserts. The difference between Persian and Arabian, their effects upon each other, can be traced within the very suburbs of Baghdad, where the red or black headdress still differentiates those two streams whose union first built up the imperial edifice of Islam.

Like the impact of Rome on Christianity, that of the Sassanian empire on the new Muslim state was so profound as to produce something quite new and different in history. The Empire of Baghdad with its varied culture, its tradition of Government routine, its unassuaged curiosity, was a creature of a different kind from its parents in Damascus or Ctesiphon. It had absorbed a thousand years' old culture and wedded it to the new religious hardihood of Islam; an altered religion and a new system of empire emerged. The interest of these remote events to-day is that Iraq still shows the process visibly apparent: alone of all Arab countries, one may still see at work here that Persian influence which had so profound a power twelve centuries ago; one can distinguish, intertwined but never coalescing, even as they were in the beginning, and with the same latent enmity unabated, the two forces that created the Empire of Islam. This fact lies at the root of modern as it lay at the root of medieval Iraqi history: for it explains the essential disunion which has ever weakened the riverain land. On this ancient divergence two modern forces have imposed themselves, the Turkish and the British. They have formed modern Iraq. But, that ancient fissure is still and ever visible under all modern healing: it should never be forgotten: for in moments of anger or weakness it flushes duskily, like the indelible scar of a wound.

At the opening of our period Iraq "passed from the nineteenth century little less wild and ignorant, as unfitted for self-government, and not less corrupt, than it had entered the sixteenth; nor had its standards of material life outstripped its standards of mind and character."[1]

This severe judgment on the effects of three centuries of

[1] Longrigg: *Four Centuries of Iraq*, p. 321.

Turkish rule might have been even more severe but for the record left by Midhat Pasha, whose name is still remembered as one of the great rulers of Baghdad. In three years, 1869 to 1872, he laid in Iraq the foundations of the modern age, whose coming had been heralded over thirty years before by British enterprise.

The Chesney Expedition in 1836 makes a good beginning for Modern Iraq. It deposited her first two paddle steamers at the mouth of the Orontes on the Syrian coast for transhipment across roadless desert. Ibrahim Pasha, then Viceroy, refused at the very last to grant permission for the landing. Captain Chesney carried it out without consulting authority, deciding to show, by the departure of his two escort vessels, "that the enterprise would not be given up and would endeavour, by every means available, to transport our steamers across the country so as to float them on the River Euphrates."[1]

This almost incredible feat was performed. These "*disjecta membra*" of the steamers were assembled at Birijik, and floated gently down, moved every night to banks in whose low scrub the roaring of lions kept the crews awake. The lions were, no doubt, remote descendants of those whose images still live in the great hunting friezes of Assyria: their last known survivor was shot near Balad Druz fifty-six years ago. The meeting of the paddle steamers and the lions illustrates the impact, sudden and with little softening of transition, of the modern age on what had remained for so many centuries immutable, lethargic, and resigned.

When Midhat Pasha came to govern Baghdad, he found the navigation of its river already far advanced in the enterprising hands of Messrs. Lynch. He found a British-Indian post office working since 1868 in the two chief towns of the country, and a number of commercial ventures flourishing under the eyes of early British Residents, whose records make the most delightful reading. A tram horse-drawn along rails to Kadhimain, the Holy City, still bears witness to the great Pasha's now antiquated Modernity. His hospital, almshouse, orphanage, schools, were in the old tradition of Islam; but conscription, newspapers, administrative reform, and particularly the policy of settling the tribes on agricultural land (followed ever since) were signs of a new impulse from Europe. After a three years rule he passed on to other more widely active posts where, in 1876, by his demo-

[1] *Narrative of the Euphrates Expedition*: Chesney, p. 173.

cratic "Constitution" he was to continue to influence Iraq together with other provinces of the huge amorphous empire now ripe for change.

Steam navigation had been a British child in Iraq, but the early stages of the railway were admittedly German. The Berlin to Baghdad dream was slowly pursued across the Continent of Anatolia, and, in 1899, Germany obtained a concession for the last stretch—Konia to the Persian Gulf. Its progress was one of the chief causes of perturbation in pre-war years to British statesmen interested in Middle East affairs: perhaps that long thin ribbon of steel first turned the attention of Lord Kitchener to the defensive possibilities inherent in an Arabian revival. If the Baghdad railway was the spear-head of Europe in Asia, the Hejaz line, built to Medina and paid for by the voluntary subscriptions of the faithful, was a vindication of the enduring vitality of Islam. Nationalism in Arabian countries has ever gone hand in hand with religion even in the most free-thinking of its lands: this fundamental characteristic was grasped by Abdul Hamid, wily old Sultan, who hoped to turn to his own uses the missionary zeal of Jamal ad-Din al Afghani, most eloquent of Islamic teachers in the last three decades of the century, and the fervour of those ingenuous devotees who, unsuspecting, built a strategic line to the threshold of the Holy Cities. Our years of war have shown that strategic roads and railways are double-edged tools; they lead both ways; the Hejaz line united Arab regions, which had been separated for centuries, and turned Sultan Abdul Hamid involuntarily and unconsciously into a promoter of Arab freedom. By the same token he and his German builders made it inevitable that Britain would support the gradually consolidating kingdom of Arabia: a strong politically healthy block between the Mediterranean and India became increasingly obvious as a counterpoise to the continental intrigues of Germany. At the same time, British interest in Iraq was not abandoned; it advanced from the South, counteracting the German rail stations, which were springing up one by one like little fortresses in the northern steppes. Before the outbreak of the Great War, in 1913, Sir William Wilcox had completed the Hindiyah barrage: the German railway had entered the northern bounds of Mesopotamia, and was also complete between Samarra and Baghdad: Iraq was once more ready to be the battle-ground where two civilizations faced each other. She was at that time in no sense of the word, a nation: divided between Shia and Sunni, weakened by minorities whose age-old hatreds smouldered perpetually, Kurd, Assyrian, Armenian, Chaldean, Yezidi, Subba, and other minor sects, she constituted three provinces of the Turkish Empire neglected and disliked.

International policies, the German drive through Turkey and British interest in Arabia, which was its unexpected but logical consequence, were the external agents by which, out of three Turkish vilayets, the nation of Iraq was created. But these external agencies were helped by a leaven from within, already visible to accurate observers during the last decades of the nineteenth century.

"An Arab movement, newly risen, is looming in the distance," wrote Denis de Rivoyre in 1883, after extensive travels in all the Arabian lands.[1]

The first great impetus to this movement was given in 1908 by the coming to power of the young Turks. Their revolution was by no means intended to further the cause of Arab or any other non-Turkish nationalism: its effect indeed was to centralize rather than to decentralize all the functions of Government, and a wave of discontent followed the brief and illusory honeymoon between the Young Turks and the distant minorities of their empire. Their revolution, like the Wind in the "Ancient Mariner"

"did not come anear,
But with its noise it shook the sails
That were so thin and sere."

The Balkans had already fought for and obtained their freedom; the Yemen, under the veteran leader who still rules it, was endemically fighting amid its high-hung villages and rocks. With the spread of education, thoughts also spread; and the forming of secret societies, particularly in Syria, began to promise trouble for the future, like those small trickles of snow which only the mountaineer's eye detects, forerunners of the avalanche.

The only secret society in which Iraq took an active part was one called al-'Ahd, among whose members were a number of Iraqi officers serving away from their homes. In Iraq itself, there appears to have been no organized movement of any

[1] See *The Arab Awakening*, p. 90.

importance, though the feeling for Home Rule was already strong in 1913, when Iraq sent two members to the "Arab Congress," organized by young Syrians in Paris.

Al-'Ahd was founded for officers by Major Aziz Ali al-Masri in 1914. "The Iraqi element, being the most numerous in the Ottoman army, was particularly strong in the councils of Al-'Ahd, and founded branches in Baghdad and Mosul."[1] In 1915 it joined forces with Al Fatat, which was chiefly a Syrian society, and these two together actually promoted and were largely responsible for the Arab revolt when it came. Al Masri was arrested by the Turks on March 25th, 1914; the anger caused in all the Arab world showed how far the idea of nationalism had spread. The British F.O. intervened; *The Times* wrote articles; the continued pressure set Al Masri free. Arab nationalism was in the air. The future history of Iraq was being moulded, not in the musty council chambers of Stambul, but in odd corners scattered over the Arabian provinces; in quiet rooms where young men in threes and fours got together; and in the brain of Lord Kitchener and a few far-sighted like him who saw a chain of free and friendly states extending from the Mediterranean to Iran.

The Arabian desire for independence in various forms and in various regions, and British realization that the co-operation and safety of Arabia meant freedom and peace on Empire routes of trade—these two visionary streams, no longer so visionary now, together determined the resurrection of Iraq after its centuries of somnolence and ruin. The development of oil was another important factor. In 1914 both the Mosul and the Iranian oilfields were already exercising their baleful and magnetic influence in international affairs. The Mosul oilfield (Turkish Petroleum Co.) was entirely in what is now Iraq, and the capital that worked it was divided between Britain, Holland and Germany, Britain holding fifty per cent. of the shares. The A.P.O.C. (now Anglo-Iranian Oil Co.) had also quite recently come to be partly located in what is now Iraq: this was in consequence of the new frontier delimitation of 1913-14 between Turkey and Iran, by which pact of concession the area was transferred to Turkish territory, without infringing the Company's rights. The future Iraq thus came to interest two of the most important oil companies in the world.

[1] For all this period see *The Arab Awakening*, by G. Antonius.

Unfortunately, the clearsightedness which inspired our main lines of Arab dealing was not universal amongst all Government departments. British policy has always suffered in Arabia from being distributed among too many heads. In 1914 the Government of India dealt with Mesopotamia, and, far from making use of the wind of Arab freedom then blowing, looked upon it with the greatest suspicion, so that no local uprising was either fomented or encouraged between Mosul and Basrah. Iraq was the only country "where the expulsion of the Turks was entirely accomplished by British arms."[1]

The vicissitudes of the war are too well known to need much description here. On November 6th, 1914, our troops were landed at Fao where Tigris and Euphrates sweep in one great mirror out to sea. The battle of Shaibah in April, 1915, the battle of Ctesiphon in November, led up to the slow misery of Kut from December, 1915, to April of the next year. The garrison of Kut saw the relieving force across the flat river lands and in the dancing mirage of its sands; they saw it fight and retreat. It was not until nearly a year after, in March, 1917, that Baghdad fell to General Maude. He died of cholera in November, and the fighting was not yet over. British trenches still lie across the ancient mounds of Samarra, almost as clear-cut as when they were dug twenty-four years ago; their hutments still crown the Tigris ridges at Tekrit. On October 31st the Turks signed the armistice of Mudros. They had lost 45,505 prisoners. The British casualties were over 97,000. The suffering concealed by these naked figures can scarce bear thinking of. No one, says the *Eye Witness*, can be so bad as to deserve alone the blame for what happened in Mesopotamia. It is sorrowful, but possibly profitable, to think how much of this misery might have been spared if we had seriously thought to enlist and organize popular feeling on our side. The Turks were hated, the holy cities of the Shia, seething with discontents, lay on our way; innumerable minorities scattered the land with their centres of perpetual discord. Our statesmen forgot the old weakness of the borderland, the division of races marked by the division of Islam: from all these elements of conflagration we elicited no spark in our favour. We had in fact not prepared for a Mesopotamian war. We were unprovided with maps: the eastern foothills along the Persian border which alone might have

[1] *The Arab Awakening*, by G. Antonius, p. 276.

afforded cover against entrenched positions of the Turks, were hostile, unsurveyed, and unknown. One man of genius who knew the land familiarly from earlier travel, did what was possible for one man to do: this was Captain Leachman, to whom the friendliness of the western tribes, Anezah and Shammar, then and later, is chiefly owing: but except for him, it was by the blood of our troops, Indian and British, and not by policy that we paved the way to the freedom of Mesopotamia: nor were we helped by any Iraqi element of importance.

The armistice of Mudros left the three Turkish provinces of Mosul, Baghdad and Basrah under British military control and the question of what to do with them soon began to show its problematic face.

In the agreement made between Great Britain and the Sherif Husain on the general subject of Arabian independence, the eventual freedom of Iraq was clearly stipulated, though a temporary British occupation was envisaged. It was therefore out of the question to return the three provinces to Turkey. The conception of the Mandate, one of the most revolutionary measures ever invented by an Imperial power, came at this opportune moment: the King-Crane report, whose fairness no one has ever called in question, suggested that a *temporary* mandatory status be extended to both Palestine and Iraq. It may here be well to quote Article 22 of the Covenant of the League of Nations, on which the new order came to be founded.

ARTICLE 22

1. To those colonies and territories which as a consequence of the late war have ceased to be under the sovereignty of the States which formerly governed them and which are inhabited by peoples not yet able to stand by themselves under the strenuous conditions of the modern world, there should be applied the principle that the wellbeing and development of such peoples form a sacred trust of civilization and that securities for the performance of this trust should be embodied in this Covenant.

2. The best method of giving practical effect to this principle is that the tutelage of such peoples should be entrusted to advanced nations who by reason of their resources, their experience or their geographical position

can best undertake this responsibility, and who are willing to accept it, and that this tutelage should be exercised by them as Mandatories on behalf of the League.

3. The character of the mandate must differ according to the stage of the development of the people, the geographical situation of the territory, its economic conditions and other similar circumstances.

4. Certain communities formerly belonging to the Turkish Empire have reached a stage of development where their existence as independent nations can be provisionally recognized subject to the rendering of administrative advice and assistance by a Mandatory until such time as they are able to stand alone. The wishes of these communities must be a principal consideration in the selection of the Mandatory.

These utterances mark what will possibly be regarded in time to come as the chief turning point of British Imperial history. It was indeed a new voice ringing across the frontiers of the world : but, unfortunately, it was at that time a voice and not very much besides. Delays and disappointments surrounded the probationary states. The French were frankly cynical, and in 1919 ousted Faisal from his new throne in Syria. He was invited in December to London : the kingship of Iraq was in the air : but the country, tired of waiting, disillusioned by the San Remo Conference, and possibly unaccustomed to sit quietly for so long without a revolution of sorts, rose against the British in 1920.

A short and useless time of trouble followed, and some 10,000 casualties that might well have been spared. Nationalism, a vague force in Iraq, was reinforced by calls to holy war from the cities of Kerbala and Najf. Already in 1918 the latter city had murdered its assistant political officer in his bed, and stood a forty days' siege in form, an hour being left open every morning for the free passage of pilgrims from the shrine whose golden dome the British guns were told to spare. In October Sir Percy Cox arrived as British Commissioner, and began to carry out the British pledges by forming a provisional Arab government.

The rebellion had two unlucky consequences : it persuaded the younger generation in Iraq, erroneously but plausibly, that their status as a nation had been acquired by compulsion and by their own armed efforts against a reluctant conqueror : it made the

British taxpayer so tired of the very word "Mesopotamia" that *any* solution was welcome which would rid him of the burden. The truth of the matter is that the 1920 rebellion merely hastened at great expense a settlement which was already on its way. The Arab is hardly to be blamed that he could not see it coming, for the fundamental difference between British and French policy in the Arabian peninsula is hardly to-day emerging into the light of day; at that time even acute observers, like Sir Mark Sykes, were not always able to detect it.

The pledges to Iraq were recognized and maintained by no less a person than Mr. Winston Churchill, then Secretary for the Colonies.

A conference held at his instance in Cairo, in March, 1921, and a personal interview between himself and Faisal, son of King Husain, shaped out the body of the future state. The desires of the population of Iraq were as far as possible ascertained: the tradition of Islam and the influence of the Young Turk movement both inclined them towards some form of democracy, such as had been instituted in most of the territories lost to the Turkish Empire: a large majority favoured a monarchy. In June, 1921, at the British Government's suggestion, Faisal arrived in Iraq; a referendum was taken; he was proclaimed King in August. It remained to invent a satisfactory Constitution for the new government to work upon.

It is little known that from the very beginning Iraq refused to accept a Mandatory status, as being contrary to her requisites of freedom. The very fact that she lies farther from Europe, and has hitherto been less touched by European civilization, has preserved her in greater measure from the sense of inferiority, which is sadly apt to vitiate more sophisticated nations. With a conceit for which he had too slender cause, and which is the chief difficulty in his dealings, the Iraqi yet preserves a genuine love of independence; it is difficult either to discipline or coerce him. He is known throughout his history as having ever been more or less against whatever government happened to be above him. "People of plots and turbulence," said the great Wazir Ziad, eleven hundred years ago; and almost every government has said so ever since. Underneath all this turbulence, the love of freedom is however genuine; and it was allowed for in 1921, by an agreement which placed the country on a treaty basis with Great Britain, with safeguards enabling the latter to carry out her obligations under the mandatory covenant. That is to say that Iraq was never directly under the Mandate like Palestine or Syria, although Great Britain was responsible to Geneva for the carrying out of the conditions of the Covenant. This typical compromise was signed in 1922 and came into force in 1924. It was intended to last for twenty years—and full admission to the League of Nations was to come as soon as possible. Already in 1923, however, the British public, tired of Mesopotamia, its bloodshed and disorders, was agitating to abandon it altogether. It was Great Britain who suggested that the treaty should end with Iraq's entry into the League, and, in any case, not later than four years after the Turkish peace.

The next ten years of Iraq history are filled with the delicate sailing of King Faisal between the Scylla of Nationalism and the Charybdis of the British: amid these more spectacular manœuvres the real difficulties of Iraqi government, the age-long disparities of Mosul, Baghdad and Basrah that cut the country into three; the still more ancient cleft of Shia and Sunni which cut it into two; the ever-running sore of the Minorities—all passed comparatively unobserved, held in leash by the acrobatic skill of the King, whose early training well fitted him for his exacting role.

The divergence between Iraq and Britain hinged, like practically all British Imperial problems of this century, on the time factor, and on the fact that Iraq never realized how genuinely anxious we were to get rid of her. We messed up our own attitude with vague and dilatory statements instead of being content to repeat until it came to be believed the simple reality—that so long as oil production and the overland route to India were safe and peaceful, few in Great Britain much cared what happened to Iraq. Unfortunately, the safety of transit and oil presuppose a stable government, and no outside interference: and it was King Faisal's ability to persuade London that he could guarantee these two requisites which brought about the new Treaty of Alliance of 1932, with its appanage of complete internal freedom. The two British interests were safeguarded by three small R.A.F. bases at Habbaniyah, Shaibah and Basra, and by the right, in time of war, to receive from Iraq all facilities and assistance, including the use of railways, rivers, ports, aerodromes, and means of communication through the country.

It is difficult to see what could have been better both for Iraq and for Britain than this treaty, and it would be a mistake in the facile illumination of later difficulties to minimise its achievement.   Out of the chaos and languor of seven desolate centuries it created a kingdom which still, in spite of all interferences, stands compact and entire.   The national feeling has grown, and even when directed against her, is a tribute to the British fairness which honourably fostered its growth.

Severe shocks assailed the new independence and disturbed the British conscience, uneasy at having conceded it.   The Assyrian massacres, and even more so the rejoicing that acclaimed them, shocked western opinion, as yet unaccustomed to discriminating bloodshed: and the tragic death of King Faisal in the summer of that year, 1933, left the country in the hands of a young and inexperienced king,   At his death, also tragically sudden, in a motor accident in 1939, the heir was an infant, the Regent himself very young: with all their personal popularity to help them they have a rough sea to steer through.   Slowly war was again darkening over Europe.   In the Middle East its two most sombre forerunners were the Palestine troubles and the army movement, with its militarization of the young.   Both these, indirectly attributable to German persecution and to German teaching, deeply affected Iraq.   Palestine is the focus for practically all anti-British feeling in the Middle East during the last seven years; it is an incontrovertible witness to the spiritual union of Islam, and a measure by which the forces making for political union can be gauged.   In Iraq it succeeded in destroying practically all the friendly feelings towards Britain that the treaty had gained.   As for the army movement, it produced, at the very beginning of its development, the military dictatorship of Bekr Sidky, in October, 1936.

These two influences, Palestine and Army, have been paramount up to the present day.   Sensational events have scarcely interrupted them; the murder of Bekr Sidky, in 1937, was but an eddy in a current which, spreading from Germany, has captivated and carried away the minds of the young in many a land besides Iraq.   Here as elsewhere, thoughtful parents have been saddened and wearied by the sight of their schoolboys marching on all occasions, dressed out in uniforms, provided with battle-cries, excited with sham enthusiasms, their hearts and minds twisted from the gentler ways of learning to which their age belonged.   The very success of this movement, which had such potentiality for good, has made it more destructive. In Iraq as elsewhere the result of the German fever is a ruined generation—though possibly less poisoned than elsewhere: for Iraq in its fitful history has had too many military dictators to be dazzled completely.

It was inevitable that the German cry should succeed for a time. Subsidiary causes depressed the prestige of Britain: the failure to deliver armaments according to her treaty (due to her own tardy rearmament, and not her fault, but none the less unfortunate) helped to discredit her with the army: and the army, as so often before in Iraqi history, was coming to be the arbiter of politics in the land. When war was declared in 1939 Iraq stood loyally by the terms of her treaty: until April, 1941, she was not asked to implement them to the full. Psychologically it might have been better if both Iraq and Egypt had been encouraged to offer more active help to their British ally in the early stages of the war: nothing is so demoralizing as to sit by and watch while others labour, and the national pride which eventually finds an outlet in opposition might be assuaged if allowed to co-operate and employ itself in time. By 1941, when France had capitulated and the whole continent of Europe lay in German hands, it was too late: the Middle East, with few exceptions, was anxiously asking itself whether it had not backed a loser; belief in a British victory was largely a matter of faith, unsupported either by military successes or a propaganda sufficiently necromantic to achieve results without them. The triumphs over Italy counted for next to nothing East of Suez: we had also been at unnecessary pains to point out to the world that no kudos can be attached to conquering Italians. Under the circumstances it was not surprising that many years of careful German infiltration should bear their fruit at the appointed time. The Mufti and the Palestine exiles in Iraq did their share. A second military dictatorship was attempted under four generals known as "the Golden Square," with a pretence of Parliamentary government maintained by Rashid Ali al-Gailani.

One morning in April the Regent, given hasty warning, was forced to fly. British troops landed at Basra before the rebels, with no German assistance at hand, were ready to attack; and the crisis was drawn out during a few weeks by the skilful negotiations of the new British Ambassador, Sir Kinahan Cornwallis. It was due to him that, when the clash came between the Iraq Army and the R.A.F. at Habbaniyah, Basra was already peacefully in British hands.

Records of the defence of Habbaniyah, the "siege" of the British and American Embassies all through May, 1941, and the march of an absurdly small British relieving force escorting the legitimate government across 500 miles of desert from Transjordan, have not yet had time to enter the cool detached chambers of history. In the light of her millenial background they are ephemeral points enough in the life of Iraq. But other things attained during the last forty years are not ephemeral. The world is regrouping itself in larger units under the spur of new and swifter means of transport. The unification of the Arab lands in however loose a form, with however many hitches and hesitations, is becoming increasingly probable as part of this general process. Whether or not Iraq will become absorbed in a larger Islamic unity, or whether she will develop on more particular lines, remains to be seen. In the field of education, literature and general culture she is beginning to differentiate herself from the surrounding countries of Islam.

This is a slow process, and by its very nature has not yet been able to go far. Until a few years ago Mesopotamia, part of a larger whole, had nothing in the intellectual orbit that it might strictly claim. Even the remembrance of former greatness belonged to the general greatness of Islam. If I were asked what creative achievement here could be claimed by Iraq as her own, I should choose the delicate brickwork which is first recognizable in Sumerian buttresses and in the massive pillars of Warka. It flowers in full magnificence under the Abbassides; the fine arches of the Khan Mirjan, the flowery bands of Mustanseriya above the Tigris wharves, the decorations of the citadel, and bits of inscription scattered here and there about the country on bridges, or on mosques, still show the skill and delicacy of this native art. It was carried on in the old houses of Kerbala and Najf where deep wells of water, four or five stories down, and the need for summer coolness, developed an underground architecture of great interest and ingenuity. In Baghdad itself, in small streets still untouched, with overhanging windows, you may see this fine brickwork, descendant of an illustrious past. And it is comforting to see that the best of the new architects are interested in this their own particular patrimony, and that the smaller buildings, post offices, schools, private houses, as well as public monuments, begin to show what can be done with bricks in the country where they were probably first used by the children of men.

In other fields of art and learning Iraq, like most of the newly constituted Arab lands, is slowly evolving a particular culture begotten by the West. Ten years ago there were very few, if any, Iraqi teachers in the schools: the result was a strong tinge of Egypt and Palestine, or more generally Syria, in all education. The text books, poisonously inimical to Britain at that time, are still in use: but it is tardily dawning on our Ministers that a friendly nation is incompatible with education based on slander—and now that Iraq is no longer under a British mandate the anti-British text books may be superseded. New schools are turning out teachers, doctors and engineers; and soon the higher education only will remain outside Iraqi hands in the universities of Beirut and Cairo. Victoria College in Egypt, run on English public school lines, still draws Iraqi boys; an institution of the same kind, the King Faisal College, is now founded, though not yet working satisfactorily, near Baghdad. It is hampered chiefly by the great difficulty of finding enough British teachers to start it on its way. The problem, indeed, of European teachers in the East is one of the most serious imaginable: in a generation's time it will largely have ceased to matter; the good or the harm will be done; but now, while a new civilization is forming, a mixture of East and West so delicate to balance, only our best should be sent, and should be sent in profusion. Owing to the difficult conditions attached to foreign teaching, this does not happen; the institution of a proper service for teachers abroad would be one of the greatest benefits imaginable to the swiftly developing countries of the East, and one of the fairest additions to the reputation of Britain.

One parent of modern education in Iraq is European, and chiefly British, but it must not be forgotten that the other is the strong tradition of Islam. This union of East and West is no new thing in Mesopotamian annals; the scribes of Ma'mun spent their days translating Greek manuscripts a thousand years ago. When I was in Najf, the holy city of the Shia, in 1937, I found that manuscripts were still copied in this laborious and loving way, and were circulated from hand to hand among the learned: the old Mujtahids in their black turbans read them side by side with the young men who studied modern text books in the new secondary school. Amid much prejudice and doubt, two little schools for girls had been started; the teacher whom I visited, a girl in her twenties, dressed in the black abba and veil that swathes Najfi ladies, was herself a citizen of the town, and had met no little opposition before her innovations were accepted. As much as anything else, the development of motor traffic, and the habit of spending summer months in Syria has hastened the movement towards greater freedom. The Islamic influence is receding from the conscious mind of Iraq; it remains in the vast sub-conscious, the memories and atmosphere of childhood, the immense accumulated impetus of the past. To the superficial observer it may seem that the past only is the force of Islam in the East of to-day. To my mind this is not so. Islam is in spite of all schisms a unity of language and religion; not only, but it is a real unity of temperament whose peculiar fitness to the regions it covers has been proved through many difficult centuries; its action is strangely enough in harmony with the action of such modernities as the aeroplane, the wireless, the motor car: it makes for the elimination of frontiers and the lessening of the barriers that language and geography have erected between nations. It is therefore possible that the nationalism whose eager roots are spreading and strengthening through all the Middle East may graft itself on to this older plant and blossom with something less parochial than a chessboard of small states, whose discords make trouble in the world. Stranger things have happened, and the unification of the Arabian peoples will come, if it comes at all, through the material support and assistance of Britain, and through the spiritual unity of Islam. In the long process that precedes this consummation, Iraq has made her first steps. Out of a formless bulk of three Turkish provinces she has, in the last forty years, become a nation self-conscious and corporate, and is now ready to take her place in the larger destinies of that community of countries whose future is still held together by the language and the doctrine of Islam.